In This Place

Cultural and Spiritual Collisions Refine the Heart of a Young
Missionary in Liberia,
West Africa

Deanne,
May God bless &
keep you!
Kim Abernethy
Jn. 16:33

Kim Lennon Abernethy

I will open my mouth in a parable: I will utter dark sayings of old: Which we have heard and known, and our fathers have told us.

We will not hide them from their children, shewing to the generation to come the praises of the Lord, and His strength, and His wonderful works that He hath done.

Psalm 78: 2-4

DEDICATIONS

To my 3 daughters and their families (present and future): *In case you didn't know, YOU are my favorite.*

- ✧ *Michelle–may you continue to be awed by His holiness*
- ✧ *Stefanie–may He always prove to be enough in your life*
- ✧ *Lauren–may you never cease to be amazed by His glory*
- ✧ *Frank, my first son-in-love–May you continue to know His peace that endures*

To Patrick and Crystal Mitchell, when I first met you and heard your desire to make a radical difference in God's kingdom, you inspired me to make this book a reality. Throughout the writing of it, besides my own family, your faces (the representation of young Christian warriors who desire to know the fullness of His glory) were foremost in my heart. THIS IS MY GIFT TO YOU. WATCH Him do extraordinary things! And KEEP your own journals.

To Jeff, my husband of 30 years: The vows we took all those years ago still resound in my heart. "Believing I was made for you only...." That said, God certainly knew I needed adventure in my life. Following you around the world has been extremely challenging, oftentimes difficult, and more times than not, simply amazing, but never boring. I love your heart for Christ. I love your quiet, but strong spirit. You are a spiritual leader in every way though I have not always appreciated that. Thank you for loving me unconditionally.

ACKNOWLEDGEMENTS

Early in 1987 the calling to write this story began deep in my heart. God had given me a desire to keep rather detailed journals of our cultural adaptations and the emotions behind the challenging times we experienced when first arriving in Liberia! The journals were initially written out of a desire to share these experiences with our family. Although most of my journals were either handwritten or typed on an old Selectric II typewriter, I am forever grateful that I committed to document our first years as missionaries in West Africa.

I am even more grateful for my mother and father who kept those journals in a file. About ten years ago, my mother handed me a thick manila folder stuffed with various sized papers. "These are for when you write your book," she said as she handed them to me. "I know you will write one day about all that God has shown you in Africa. These should help." Stunned they really had kept all my African journals, the seed to write grew into a plant shuttering with potential.

It has been a five year journey to bring this book to reality, mostly because of the demanding yet rewarding ministry that we have with college students. Carving out time in the summers and breaks, I began to plunder through my journals and was amazed all over again at God. Though our stories are not the most compelling I have ever heard nor the most important, they are real and power-ful. Simply put, God asked me to put them down in book form for HIS GLORY! May He amaze you with His sovereign beauty as you read!

Jeff and I are deeply thankful for our parents, **BOB AND GERALDINE LENNON AND HAL AND JUNE ABERNETHY**, for how they have loved and guided us, for the vivid examples of how Christians should live through all phases of life; and for the many prayers on our behalf. We felt the power of their love and heartfelt petitions deep in the jungles of West Africa. Any spiritual fruit reaped throughout our years of ministry is placed in their accounts! We are blessed more than we could ever describe with our four amazing parents!!

***Debbie Benfield, Melissa Carrara, and Joy Almond, TR Black and Kelly Gurley-Scites*–**You blessed me with taking your valuable time to do some great editing! You were a powerful part of this project and important parts of my life.

***Janet Grams*–**for using your photography skills to provide a great head shot of Jeff & me. The pictures were taken in the botanical gardens on the campus of UNC-Charlotte where we have ministered for the past eight years with Campus Bible Fellowship International.

***Heidi Sheppard*–**an up and coming young photographer. She is the daughter of Mark and Nancy Sheppard, our former co-workers, who are still ministering in Liberia with Baptist Mid-Missions. The picture on the front cover is hers and was taken in Liberia. Thank you, Heidi, for willingly sharing.

***Nancy Freund*–**an amazing graphic designer and editor for Baptist Mid-Missions. She graciously offered to design my book cover while we were working on a CBFI project. It is evident that the cover is a work born out of her heart for God.

***April Stinson*–**you find joy in bringing the beauty out in others. Thank you for being a blessing and going the extra mile. I've seen your heart as you work and know that your love for God is real!

***Barb Stevenson*–**Over twenty years ago, I aspired to be a Bible teacher/speaker that could touch the lives of others just as you had so powerfully touched mine. You so wisely said to me, "Kim, no doubt you will, but first you must live out your own life stories. You need to see that God is exactly who He says He is." And so, I have. Just as you said. Thank you being the kind of example that I could follow.

***Debbie Johnson*–**Thank you for going above and beyond on the last edit! "Feed a sneak" is a classic! You are dear to my heart.

PRELUDE–November 1985

If I believed in omens, I would have been worried. After nineteen months of deputation and five months of planning, buying, and packing a 40-foot metal container with supplies and household items for our "maiden" years in Liberia, West Africa, our departure date had come! November 12, 1985, was the date that we had decided on even though we realized that it was very close to Thanksgiving and Christmas, making it more difficult for our families and us. Undeterred, there was just no stopping those new missionaries who had already turned eager eyes toward our country, our people whom God had given us!

Thinking back on the night before we were to leave, I do not believe that either Jeff or I slept very well. Our hearts and minds were full. We had no idea what to expect, what we should have been feeling, how we were to deal with emotions of that magnitude; a major separation from parents, family, the only culture we had ever known, everything familiar. For all that, the promised grace of God and a youthful, resilient bent for adventure were the things to which we held tightly during those early days. In the necessary letting go of precious things in our immediate lives, it had not yet become obvious to us that this letting go would be the only way to receive the reward of other precious things: souls to present to our Savior and the reality of seeing lives transformed by the teaching of His powerful Word. Often the best things come after relinquishing the good things in our lives. *For God so loved the world that He gave His only begotten Son (John 3:16).*

Early on the morning of November 12, we received a phone call from our Baptist Mid-Missions field representative. Thinking that perhaps he was just checking on us, we realized that it was way too early in the morning for that; his call turned out to be for a much different reason. During the night (but early morning in Liberia as it was 5 hours ahead of EST), there had been an attempted coup (government takeover) in the capital city of Monrovia which as a result caused the temporary suspending of all airline flights in and out of that country. It seemed there was significant chaos there, so we were told that our departure had been delayed until more news

1

about the situation could be determined. Tentatively rescheduling our departure for December 3 gave us three more precious weeks to make more memories with family and friends. This was also bittersweet because everyone involved had psyched themselves up for our November departure!

Have you ever wished you could know the future? Most of us, at one time or another, have desired to know a little about our tomorrows. That said, I am infinitely thankful that our Heavenly Father did not show us the faintest peep of what we would experience in the next few years because of the changing political climate in Liberia. We were way too young, too enamored with our call, and too ignorant of third world politics to understand the potential fallout this attempted coup could produce in that small country in West Africa.

No, I do not believe in omens, but it might have been evident to someone with more missions experience that the world dynamics were again changing. With that shift, it would become necessary to completely redefine the methods of missiology, though that kind of subtle but elaborate change often emerged slowly, progressively. This time the shift foretold of extreme political reshaping in the third world arena. No paradigm was available for what we were to experience within the next few years. Simply put, our missionary career began on the precipice of uncertain days for foreign missions.

In spite of those looming and little understood changes happening in West Africa and beyond, we did leave in early December 1985, answering a powerful and resounding call that burned within both of us. A call to carry the Gospel of Christ to the precious people of Liberia, West Africa. It had always been our honest intentions to minister in Liberia for the rest of our lives. We were young, we were excited, we were ready for all that missionary life would throw at us. Or so we thought. Having read missionary stories about those that had ministered to the same people for thirty, even forty years, we could not imagine why it would be any different for us?

Providentially, our dreams of staying in one place for our entire missionary career did not come to pass, but it has still been an amazing journey. It is a story I deeply believe is worth telling, if for no other reason than to encourage you to allow God to be God in your life no matter what is going on around you–and to dissuade you from trying to regulate His plans for your life–no matter how confused and unsettled you may feel.

This is not to say that I never questioned Him. I think the writings here are candid enough for you to see that there was enough bellyaching and complaining on my part to rival the children of Israel in the wilderness. However, in timely retrospect, God has been faithful and I am learning to trust Him with those things closest to my heart.

CHAPTER ONE

Experience is something you don't get until just after you need it. —Unknown

Long Journey to Our New Home

Traveling anywhere with a two-year old is an ordeal that any parent understands, but packing our daughter's toys into a large wooden box several months ahead for the long journey to West Africa was heart-wrenching. Michelle, our vivacious redheaded little girl, did not understand why we were being so mean as to take all her toys away from her. How do you explain to a two-year old about a call to carry the Gospel of Jesus Christ across the ocean? There is a video of Michelle right before we left the States that explicates her confusion and frustration better than anything else. Michelle was playing with a kitten outside my parents' home when someone asked her where her toys were. A scowl came across her face and in one fluid movement, she flung the poor kitten into the shrubbery and said, "APRICA!" She had not the faintest idea what "APRICA" was, but it had her toys and she didn't like it.

Michelle was not planned. We knew that we were going to be traveling to churches, doing deputation, and a baby seemed too complicated right then. Nevertheless, God KNEW what we needed: Michelle Ruth Abernethy. A beautiful, redheaded, independent spitfire of a girl with breathtaking brownish-black eyes and a smile that could bring down the hardest soul–that was our first daughter.

God had designed her perfectly for our lifestyle, and that wasn't more evident than when we boarded the airplane with her for the first time. Not once did she cower from the new adventure. She loved it! She loved the special seats that reclined back, she loved being served dinner on the trays that dropped from the back of the seats, and she loved having a window seat so that she could see the other planes on the tarmac with us. She also had no reservation in doing her "number two" business in her pants and smelling up the entire economy class section of the plane. I thought for sure we would be thrown out a window.

When we arrived at the LaGuardia airport in New York, we still needed somehow to get to the JFK International terminal. Taxi seemed the cheapest way, so we hailed one. I remember the exhilaration welling up inside me that we were finally beginning our long-awaited missions adventure. As the taxi driver helped Jeff load our luggage into the car, I tried to keep up with Michelle. It was icy that December day in New York, and for some reason, Michelle darted towards the busy street. I lunged after her and performed my very first complete split (where was that talent in high school when I tried out for cheerleading?), but I got the prize!

The dart into the street must have been too much for Michelle because she fell asleep in the taxi, and even after arriving at the JFK airport, she slept for two more hours in the terminal on a couch. It was a gift from God to these two young missionary parents who were trying to get everything together for our international flight. Before long we noticed that we were missing a piece of luggage; of course, it would be the very one that contained all of Michelle's clothes. Because it was a new suitcase, we had overlooked it. Thankfully, after a phone call to LaGuardia, the suitcase was located and put into a taxi so as to get it to us quickly.

The suitcase made it just in time. In fact, we were the last ones to board the plane, the ones that the plane was being held for–and we were also the ones that everyone already seated on the plane looked at as we tried to tiptoe down the aisle and sink into our seats. Our adventures had already started, but God was right there. We still had Michelle and we had that important suitcase. What more could we ask for?

Bad Breath in Amsterdam

Looking back on that story, I am amazed how green and inexperienced we were as travelers. A crucial first lesson is to NEVER check all of your luggage if you are planning to stay overnight en route to your final destination. It would have been wise to have had a carry-on filled with the things we would need for personal hygiene and comfort during an extra long flight. Because of a military-imposed curfew in Liberia and the timing of the flight from NYC to Amsterdam, we would have to stay one night in

Amsterdam. Not really thinking it through, we had checked all our luggage so that we would not have to keep up with those huge suitcases in Amsterdam. I repeat, we checked ALL the bags. That meant we had no cosmetics, no clean underwear, no toothbrushes, no deodorant, and no extra clothes for Michelle. Believe me, that never happened again in all of our missionary travels! Lesson learned.

Though the airline put us in a very nice hotel in downtown Amsterdam, we were feeling quite grungy with smelly underarms and breath perfumed with sulfur. But determined to make the best of it all, we headed out of the airport, impressed to find a free shuttle to and from the airport and hotel. It felt like we were living in first class that day! As we were all tired from the traveling, the time change, and the excitement of the past few days, we slept for nearly four hours, but upon waking, we were hungry, and so took the elevator down to the hotel restaurant. The airline had allotted us about $15 each for meals which was a great deal for us!

After a tasty afternoon lunch, we decided to take a walk down one of the nearby streets. It was our first chance of seeing Amsterdam other than in pictures, but after a couple of hours of dodging traffic, the rain, and the stark depravity of the city in certain area, we went back to our room. Michelle and I took a warm bath, and then we headed down to the hotel's French restaurant for dinner. Our littlest traveler was not impressed with French cuisine, and proceeded to lay down on the floor under the table for a nap. By 9:00 p.m., Amsterdam time, we were all sound asleep, but after only two and a half hours, Michelle's internal clock told her that it was morning. She came over and said, "GOOD MORNING! WAKE UP!" She did not understand jet lag and there was no point in telling her to go back to sleep. Back into the bathtub we went, and after that, we colored, cleaned up the room, and drew some pictures. Checking out early the next morning, we had a wonderful breakfast again courtesy of the hotel, and were on our way back to the airport to catch our flight to Africa finally!

From the Freezer to the Frying Pan

When we embarked in Amsterdam it was 35 degrees. The pilot on our flight to Freetown, Sierra Leone, told us that it was 95 degrees in our destination city. A sixty degree temperature change can do strange things to a body, and even though it may seem strange because we were in a climate-controlled plane, once we started crossing over the Sahara Desert, I thought I could literally feel the cabin heat up slightly. My imagination? Who knows?

We left Amsterdam one hour behind schedule which put us too late to fly into Monrovia from Sierra Leone. Because of the enforced curfew still in place in Liberia, the airline was taking no chances. No matter what we thought, there would be another overnight stop in Sierra Leone. Airlines undoubtedly did that kind of thing all the time, but for us it was just another night away from our new home. The only positive thing about the change was that we would fly into Liberia during the daylight instead of late evening as was originally planned.

Because I kept such detailed journals in the first years of our African missionary career, I can tell you the name of the hotel where we stayed in Sierra Leone that night. It was called Cape Sierra Hotel. All the passengers on that particular KLM flight were put up in three different hotels. Believe it or not, we were shuttled across a large bay separating the airport from the city in a helicopter and because our little family was so slow in disembarking the plane, we were on the last shuttle and put up in the nicest hotel in town!

There was even an air conditioner in our room, carpet on the floor, mahogany wood fixtures, dressers, tables, and chairs. The only thing really missing in that beautiful Casablanca setting was... our luggage again. Because it was an unplanned stop, KLM did not unload any baggage from the cargo area, so for the third straight day, we did without toothpaste, toothbrushes, clean underwear, or clothes. I washed out Michelle's clothes and some of our necessities, and Jeff rigged a clothesline from the a/c unit. There were only twin beds in the room, so we took turns sleeping with Michelle who was and still is a very active sleeper.

Early the next morning of December 6, 1985, we took the short flight from Sierra Leone to Monrovia, Liberia. Even though it was less than an hour flying time, it seemed long, possibly because we had been traveling for three days already. Though the Monrovia airport did not look much different from the one in Sierra Leone, the tension in the air was palpable and evident by the soldiers with guns walking purposely around the premises.

Our business manager, Brian Dickinson, was there to pick us up, and we were so grateful for a friendly American face that understood the endless maze of customs of that country. From the very beginning, Michelle's red hair attracted much attention, and so it would be for the rest of the years that we remained in West Africa. However, she was not in the mood to charm those unfamiliar people and it remained my tedious job to keep her discomfort to a minimum while going through the lines of officers ready with stamps, demanding to see our passports, inquiries about the nature of our travels, and bag searches. It was indeed a strange, fascinating, but intimidating world in which we had entered. The fast clipped orders barked out by those in charge, the employees in uniforms laughing jovially, and the smells of unfamiliar foods mixed with the body odors of those around us overwhelmed my senses. Culture shock was little by little taking hold of me; that and the enveloping tropical heat that threatened to suck the life out of us!

It was a thirty minute ride to our Baptist Mid-Missions' compound in Monrovia where we would be staying for a couple of weeks while becoming acclimated to our new country. In those thirty minutes, I reveled in the green riotous jungle that seem to wave its welcome to us as we zoomed past. Unexpectedly, we had to stop at four military checkpoints which was very unnerving for Americans who had never seen that before. Other than that, the short trip was uneventful.

As we neared the outskirts of the capital city of Monrovia, located right on the Atlantic Ocean, the scenery changed to include wooden carts being pushed by small children, roadside stands of charred meat and ripe bananas, and a perpetual bustling that surprised me for so small a city. The tropical humidity continued to grip us—like nothing I had ever experienced even though I grew up a mere twenty miles from the Atlantic Ocean near Wilmington, North Carolina. Michelle, as well as both her parents, was overwhelmed, exhausted, and succumbing quickly to the mercies of the sultry thickness. Our two year old felt no constraint in letting her feelings be known, but if the truth was told, I was echoing and amening her cries deep inside me!

A couple of hours after landing, we were able to put our hands on our precious luggage that had been elusive for three days! Surprisingly, we slept relatively well our first night in Liberia despite the heat. Who can't sleep with clean clothes and squeaky clean teeth? I remember waking up our first morning in Liberia, surprised to feel a slight coolness to the air. It took me a couple of minutes to realize that it was the unfamiliar but yet beautiful singing of the African birds that had awakened me so early. What exquisite sounds they made! They whistled and sang with a rhythm, what I would learn later—a West African rhythm. Liberia was a land of beauty, rhythm, and the unexpected; I was ready to explore and learn.

Exploration

One of the first things we found out was that our container, shipped back at the beginning of November, had arrived in port two weeks earlier! Our belongings were already there! When we told Michelle that her toys had arrived, she wanted to go to them right away. Ah! Some things are learned the hard way. She would not see those toys for two more weeks, but we thought that in telling her that they had arrived, she would be happy. It was just too much information to be processed by her two-year old mind. Thankfully, the business manager's children were generous in sharing their toys for the days we remained in Monrovia.

After four days in Liberia, we were beginning to really sense some of the bolder variations between America and Liberia and were thankful for veteran missionaries who cared enough to take the time for us, to remember what their first days in Liberia had been like, and never tired of answering our questions. To the small city, there was an organized chaos, an endless stream of people walking somewhere, small children scantily clothed playing in mud puddles as their mothers bartered their wares on the side of any given road, uncommon smells that both intrigued and perturbed me, the incessant blaring of horns and strange sounding words being spoken all around.

Our first Tuesday in the country, I went with Roxie Dickinson, the business manager's wife, on a shopping extravaganza to Monrovia's Waterside district. Waterside was the name given to the endless wooden stalls piled high with everything from plastic containers, dishes, cups, aluminum ware, cloth, food that looked strange to me, and almost anything else you could imagine. It was an open-air department store by the water. Street after street was packed with honking taxis, Liberians on foot doing their daily chores, garbage and human waste intermingled with street dirt and decay and the heat. The humid wave never retreated. However, Roxie walked bravely and confidently ahead, looking for a particular type of cloth she needed to make a dress for one of her daughters.

We had traveled to Waterside by taxi, and that had been my first experience with that mode of transportation in West Africa. I tried to keep my gasps to myself as we were whipped from side to side in the backseat. Never had I seen such driving, hollering, music blaring, and the horns! Every taxi driver prided himself in the fact that he had a horn that worked and proved that constantly! I will be forever grateful to Roxie for introducing me to the shopping side of Liberia early on, but particularly, that I did not experience my first Liberian taxi ride alone.

While in Monrovia, we stayed in a little one bedroom apartment on the second floor of the mission compound. The very first meal that I prepared in that apartment was a three bean soup with Danish ham and a fruit salad with fresh pineapple, bananas, oranges, and tangerines. Meanwhile, Michelle was having her own struggles. While stirring the bean soup, I looked out the window and noticed that she was sitting on a chair looking out in the yard at the other children playing.

There were twelve children from three other missionary families on the compound at that time. I remember feeling so sorry for Michelle knowing that her little brain and body was definitely on overload, and not having a brother or sister or anyone else with whom she was familiar, must have been hard. She had no home, no toys of her own, no friends that she knew, and no place that smelled comforting to her except her daddy and me. So she stuck pretty

11

close for a couple of days and we did our best to give her the attention we felt she needed. It was my first realization that God places children in their given families for a purpose. Despite how sad I felt for her in those days of huge transitions to a new culture, I somehow knew that she would make it. God would see to it even if I did not seem to know how.

During one of those early days in Liberia, I experienced my first really low ebb as a new missionary. Intruding into my fantasy of soon settling down in our new home in Tappeta, some 180 miles from Monrovia, was the news that there was a hole in the screen in our pantry there. All I could think of was all the snakes, bugs, and spiders that were, at that very moment, crawling into our house to give us a warm welcome when we arrived. I can remember having to fight the very strong urge to flee, to beg Jeff to let me go back to America—and he could come back and visit Michelle and me once a year or so. Be like a David Livingstone. As desperate as I might have felt at those times, I was so afraid of voicing those fears to the diehard, veteran missionaries we had met or even to my excited husband. So I pondered those things in my heart.

On the more favorable days, when I could admit an excitement and eagerness to settle down in our new home in Tappeta, I purposely noted that none of the other missionary kids had oozing sores from insect or snake bites from living in the deep, dark African jungle. Even so, there were those moments when it was very hard to fight down the *what ifs*. Probably one of the most defeating and damaging things that we can allow our minds to do is dwell on the *what ifs* in life. No matter what my mind was conjuring up, the reality was that in three short days we would load our container of belongings, board a one-engine Cessna, and head into the lush rain forest of Liberia! Ready or not, we were coming, and I went from excited to anxious and back again!

Groceries Enough For Six Weeks?

There was much to do on those last three days before we headed towards our new home in Tappeta. We had to check on our visas, exchange money into Liberian currency, buy appliances, and buy groceries to take with us since Tappi had no grocery stores beyond what an American gas station may offer. The day before we were to leave, Brian, Jeff, Michelle and I went into town for some last minute shopping. As Brian drove up in front of a grocery store that looked more like a very large general store in the States, Jeff smiled as he handed me a pouch ladened with Liberian money (which were coins at the time). He said, "Babe, now you need to buy groceries for us to carry up country. And, oh yeah, because of the conditions of the roads to Tappi and uncertainty of when we might have another flight down, JUST BUY ENOUGH FOR SIX WEEKS."

He and Brian drove off, leaving me with the heavy bag of coins in one hand and a curious, but rather agitated two year old holding my other hand. This is NOT a good combination any time. It was the *buy enough for six weeks* that kept ringing in my ear as I stood there on the sidewalk feeling the thick breeze of humidity around me. When had I *ever* bought enough groceries for six weeks? I wracked my brain to remember if I had missed a class in Bible school about a scenario like this. I could not imagine trying to come up with a plan that would include enough meat, cheese, canned products, seasonings, spices, and staples for six weeks. I had a bare-boned list, but now knew that I would be compelled to put some meat on that list in more ways than one!

Michelle began to whimper as we stood on the sidewalk, but after carefully mulling over the situation, I would declare that it was probably me that started the uncouth sniveling and she had just picked it up from me. Bravely picking Michelle up in one arm, I held tightly to the heavy money pouch in the other as we went inside and got a shopping buggy. After Michelle was situated in the buggy, I started hesitantly down the aisles of groceries, walking with a confidence that I was not feeling inside.

Gazing at the unfamiliar packaging of food items, my eyes felt like they wanted to glaze over! But I kept going. After the first buggy was full, I parked it near the front checkout counter under the approving eye of one of the owners, then started down another aisle with a second buggy. By the time the second cart was halfway filled, I was, no doubt, in full-fledge hyperventilation, my heart pounding, I was sweaty and feeling weak. The strange sounds and smells of the store rushed over me and I wasn't sure that I could walk another step. Michelle had opened a bag of chips and one of the owners had given her a bag juice (much like a Capri Sun). She was good to go, and for that I was thankful.

After a few minutes of mentally giving myself a pep talk, my survival instincts set in and I calmed down, becoming intrigued by the strange smells around me. Most of the grocery stores were owned by Lebanese business men and the smells tickling my senses were the spices, coffee, and other items indigenous to their part of the world. It was a smell that I learned to love and appreciate quickly! No Africans were in the store while I was there; only foreigners like myself. Most of them were friendly and openly admired Michelle's Celtic beauty, as one Lebanese man described her.

Filling up both buggies, I could not, for the life of me, calculate how much money was represented in those two carts; so I just decided to check out and see if there was any money left! I do not even remember the total that day, but it was a good thing I was only twenty-seven years old with a strong heart. Never, ever would I have imagined spending so much on groceries at one time. There was some money left, but I was beginning to not feel well again, so I decided not to spend it. The verse in Proverbs that says, "*The heart of her husband doth safely trust in her,*" kept ringing in my ear as my stomach churned in too many directions.

I knew that Jeff had so many things on him, so I guiltily fought down the anger welling up inside me for being put in such an overwhelming situation. I gratefully took a cup of strong espresso that the kind owner's wife gave me. Surely she must have seen the panic welling up inside me? The espresso-like coffee, though rich and ambrosial, only served to jolt me with more agitation because of its high caffeine content. Thanking her, I walked outside with Michelle and a much lighter money pouch. Two employees parked the two carts brimming over with groceries beside me on the sidewalk.

By the time Jeff and Brian returned for us and our horde of groceries, I was not in good form. They tried to soothe and assure me that I had done fine, though Jeff's face paled when I gave him back the small amount of money that was not spent. He touched my face tenderly, smiled at me, took Michelle from my arms, and in the midst of my anxieties, I felt totally safe and loved. He was forgiven.

CHAPTER TWO

God hears no sweeter music than the cracked chimes of the courageous human spirit ringing in imperfect acknowledgement of His perfect love.
—Joshua L. Liebman

Perspectives

Perspectives are respectful insights though not solid foundations on which we should try to stand. They are, after all, personal interpretations. Frames of reference, points of view. As we loaded up the small Cessna aircraft for the hour flight to our new home in the jungle, I realized that I had absolutely no perspective on which to base the next phase of my life. Everything in front of me had no referral point. No magical number of class credits or talking to someone who had done it could fully prepare me for the cultural impediment of being a middle-class white American woman going to live in West Africa for the first time. In 1985, there was not the wide spread awareness of international affairs as there is now. The African world is almost now fully available to us by video, books, music, the internet, or even by having met African nationals who now live in the states. Not so much in 1985. Africa was still somewhat perceived as the "DARK CONTINENT."

Heading into the jungles of West Africa was something that I would just have to experience. Pure irony since I had in my rather recent past told God that I absolutely would not be caught dead in Africa. Well, I was alive and I was in Africa. As we took off into the bright West African sky, I pondered the goodness of God and how His amazing grace had brought me to that place.

Flashback of a Jonah Kind of Run

Missionaries are fallen, depraved humans saved by the amazing grace of Jesus Christ—just like a Christian architect, a Christian banker, or a Christian childcare worker. We all must bow in awe and gratitude to the exclusive salvation provided on the cross of Christ through God the Father as a penalty for our sin. Look all you want. Look where ever you want. The Truth has been, is, and always will be in Jesus Christ alone. That being said, perhaps this book would be more meaningful if I elaborated on my own journey in becoming a career missionary.

Saved at the age of seven, I grew up in the rural town of Delco, located near Wilmington, North Carolina. Livingston Baptist Church, the church where my family attended was small but friendly, and I always felt well nourished there in spiritual and physical love. Unfortunately, as I went into my teen years, rebellion permeated my heart and I turned to the whims of my own flesh. Despite that, when I was home in Delco, I was expected to attend church. And so I did. Between my freshman and sophomore year of college, I attended a missions conference at my home church and was intrigued by the desires and emotions that welled up in me when I heard a missionary speak of God's work in other countries. Overwhelmed by God's wooing, on July 3, 1977, I walked the aisle of the country church and told the pastor that I felt God tugging at my heart about becoming a missionary.

Later that night, the flesh almost immediately washed over me, prompting regret that I had made such a public commitment. A few days later, I was faced with one of the greatest spiritual dilemmas that I had ever experienced in my young life. Previously, at the end of my freshman year in college, I had been chosen to be the next editor of my college's newspaper, and since Journalism was my major and my passion, I was struggling about giving that up and having to enroll in a Bible College to begin my training for missionary service.

As I had so often done, I succumbed to the flesh and its cry for immediate gratification. I determined to return and gain the experience of being a college newspaper editor, and later consider what I needed to do for a possible missionary career. Satan is, in some cases, subtle, knowing our desires and with what to tempt us. In my case, it was a royal flush! During that next year, I continued dating a young man who I knew was instrumental in leading me astray as a young Christian woman. In essence, he was not good for me. He was not right for me. Despite that, I felt that I loved him and in my own stubborn way, continued to incorporate him into my plans. I was selfishly using him, stringing him on. Giving him false hopes.

One year after the call on my life to be a missionary, I found myself farther from God than ever before. Having graduated from junior college, I looked at my future with confusion. Always tugging at my heart was the reality that I was to be somewhere else. Haunting me constantly was the deep-seated knowledge that I was missing something, that I was to become a woman whom God would use for His glory. My thoughts pursued me: *To Africa, if I say yes to You, God; you will send me to Africa ALONE—living in the jungle where it is dark, remote, and certainly dangerous. I CAN'T DO IT.* So, I ran. Just as Jonah ran. Only there was no large whale to swallow my miserable self up. But my bitter, fearful flesh was swallowed up with the ugliness of what my life had become.

Ironically enough, I moved to Charlotte, to the hometown of my future husband, though I knew none of that at the time. Jeff had surrendered to be a missionary just twenty days after my own calling to missions. Just in a different city and church. Thankfully, he had chosen to obey God and was already at Piedmont Baptist College preparing for that call. Me? Deciding that I would go into Broadcast Journalism, I enrolled in Carolina School of Broadcasting, and lived in an apartment alone during my training.

Those were dark days and I do not choose, nor is it necessary to summon back the things that so easily ensnared me. I lived in a false light with forced happiness as my companion. During that time, my longtime boyfriend proposed to me and I snatched at the opportunity to bring something exciting and happy into my life. It seemed that surely it was the right thing for us to be married. So I accepted his ring and we set our date for April 8, 1979.

During Christmas, my mother attempted to talk about wedding plans but I diverted her questions. Something was not right, but I could not speak of it. I know that deep in her mother's heart, she understood there was a battle going on. Some days I barely ate or slept. I felt irritable, hemmed in, threatened by the powerful way God was stirring my heart. Though my spirit was malnourished, it was not dead. It is impossible for a Christian's spirit to die within him. Quenched, oppressed, overwhelmed with sin—yes, but never dead.

After graduating from broadcasting school, I snagged a job at a local television station in Charlotte. I met some very interesting people. During one assignment, I traveled with a crew (I was a camera grip for a few months before coming a script editor) to Raleigh where Madalyn Murray O'Hair was speaking at a forum. Being only the lowly grip, I was not given entrance to the conference room, so had to settle with waiting in the foyer outside.

Soon, Ms. O'Hair's son, William, came out to take a smoke break. He usually traveled with her, he told me, as we introduced ourselves to each other. Though not a strong Christian, I did relate to William how I had felt back in fourth grade when we were told that we could no longer pray. Again, speaking more out of my limited knowledge of the Bible than where I was spiritually at that time, we discussed Christianity for more than thirty minutes, and he seemed drawn to the conversation. When it was time for him to return to the room, he allowed me to enter with him.

Though I was never able to talk with William again, before leaving the conference room at the end of the program, our eyes met and he gave me a slight salute. Within a year, the news came out that William Murray, son of Madalyn Murray O'Hair–renowned atheist—had become a believer of Jesus Christ and not surprising, his mother hastened to denounce him as a shame and disgrace to her family. I have always wondered if anything I said that day had prompted him to turn towards the Truth. God does not need us to do His work, but He certainly delights in using us.

It had felt good to share my faith—what little bit there was of it. *"But God hath chosen the foolish things of the world to confound the wise; and God hath chosen the weak things of the world to confound the things which are mighty." (I Corinthians 1:27)* As the cold of winter blew through the city of Charlotte, my spirit was chilled by the reality of my life. I became disgruntled with all of it, dreading even to see my fiance. My starkly decorated apartment became a prison, and of course, it became difficult to sleep at night. The only deterrent was music. LOUD music. Music that appealed to my flesh, keeping it fed and strong.

One night I was getting ready for a soiree with some friends and was shaving my legs. I had cranked up the music and was working on my "party" attitude. While holding the razor in my right hand, I sensed that the music had stopped. Later, I was to realize that there was nothing wrong with the radio. It was God calling me out to listen to Him. One more time. It was the still small voice of God–not audible except in my spirit–but a distinct and definite conversation between my spirit and His. "KIM, I HAVE STRIVED WITH YOU FOR A LONG TIME. I HAVE CALLED YOU OUT. YOU KNOW THAT AND YOU CONTINUE TO RUN. YOU ARE DEFAMING MY NAME INSTEAD OF PROCLAIMING IT. THIS IS YOUR LAST CHANCE, CHILD. I HAVE SUCH GREAT PLANS FOR YOUR LIFE. TRUST ME."

With the reality of what I heard, the razor cut deeply into my leg. My heart pounding, I jumped out of the bathtub, ran to my bedroom, and dove into my bed pulling the covers over my head. I had been found wanting and there was no excuse. For three days, I stayed in my bedroom, not answering my phone, not answering my door, not eating. I found my Bible which had been packed away in the back of my closet. I fumbled with the unfamiliar pages and tried to read.

More than anything, I teetered between anger and fear. Angry that God would invade my privacy and rock my world in such a way that I had no recourse but to listen. Fearful because I believed that I might not live to see the end of the week. My mind flashed back to the last time I had taken communion while at my home church and how emotionally and spiritually sick I had felt to do so. I knew God was not a vengeful God, striking us down and threatening us to make us fear Him. Deep inside me, I knew that I had long since crossed the threshold of what the Scriptures clearly taught in I Corinthians 11:27-31. God had been merciful and very long-suffering with me and my wicked choices.

In my flesh's last stand, late on the third evening, I pointed my finger to heaven and cried, "Leave me alone, God! Please leave me alone a little longer! I will go and be a missionary in the future. I am just not ready! I CANNOT AND WILL NOT GO TO AFRICA! Don't make me!" Feeling like I had gone too far, I buried my head under my pillow and waited to die. At that point, I was so exhausted, I really did not care. Any change would be welcomed. A solid, impenetrable wall was in front of me and I felt as if I would suffocate in my sin.

"Then when lust hath conceived, it bringeth forth sin: and sin, when it is finished, bringeth forth death." (James 1:15) Finally and mercifully, I slept for more than fourteen hours, resting my tired, battered flesh as the spirit within me was renewed.

Waking up the next day, the only thing I could think to do was to call my parents and ask them to come for a visit. In the couple of days that I had to wait for them to work out their schedules, I numbly began to pack my things, choosing to try and ignore God's presence—though it was palpable.

The next evening my parents arrived and after seeing that my pantry consisted of only rice and bologna, we headed for Red Lobster. That evening I told them I was going to Bible college to prepare to be a missionary. My mother dropped her fork and there was silence among us for some time. The prayers of those two had been answered and they were overwhelmed at God's working. I apologized for the money that I had wasted over those past couple of years and asked if I could move home while I explored my options about missionary training. It seemed surreal to me. My parents were spiritual and physical bulwarks to their floundering prodigal. I could never thank them enough for their unconditional love throughout my life—through the good and the bad.

Starting out slowly in my reacquaintance with God, I began reading my Bible, but because it revealed so much of my depravity and shortcomings, I could not stay in it very long. In spite of that, I applied to three Bible colleges and naively told God that I was going to the first one that accepted me. Though that may sound shallow, it was a reflection of the kind of Christian I was then. But God knew me and used that pitiful prayer to show me His will. Piedmont Bible College (now renamed Piedmont Baptist College) in Winston-Salem, NC, sent the first acceptance letter, so Piedmont it was. Before I even arrived on campus, I had decided that if I dated at all (I had broken up with my fiance in a heart-rendering, all-night drama, just a few days before I moved back home), I would only date missionary pilots. Though I deviated from that a couple of times, that did remain my focus.

I met Jeff at some point my first year at Piedmont and felt extremely drawn to his quiet and calming presence. But it was not time for that. After the first year, I remained in Winston-Salem during the summer because I had a great part-time job at Wachovia Bank. It was during that same summer that God called me out again. "AM I ENOUGH, KIM? WILL YOU COMMIT TO GO ANYWHERE WITH ME—EVEN IF THAT MEANS YOU GO ALONE?" I physically trembled at the thought of it, but I also could not ignore it. Struggling with that question several more weeks, finally one evening in the quietness of my room, I bowed to God and His will for me. Sobbing through my prayer of surrender, I said, "YES, FATHER, I WILL GO ANYWHERE WITH YOU, EVEN AFRICA...ALONE, IF YOU CHOOSE."

Three years of running, trying to hide. But His grace and beauty captured me! The floodgates of my soul released into the soothing balm of tears, sorrow, fear, expectation, and a joy that ignited deep within. It was a menagerie of emotions—and very hard to describe. But He stayed right there with me. His unconditional love over-whelmed me! At that point of surrender, I began to live like I had never lived in my Christian life. Choosing purposely to please Him. My flesh roared with disdain!

A few weeks later, Jeff returned from a six-weeks mission trip to Haiti, finally asking me out. Our first date was on October 17, 1980, and we were married some ten months later. Both 23 at the time, we just knew that it was right. His major? Theology and Missionary Aviation. Imagine that!

Giving up my plans for my life was the most beautiful but dif-ficult thing I had ever done. As the vibration of the Cessna 180 brought me out of my spiritual flashback, I smiled as I found myself right where I had, for so long, feared to go—to the jungles of Africa. But somehow, though I still felt some trepidation about that new experience, it seemed right. Very right.

Welcome Home

Armed with a fresh head cold and a two year old daughter tired of being displaced, I entered a world that was starkly unfamiliar. I tried to focus on the present, to become aware of the drone of the one-engine, four-seater plane, attempting to center myself into that new world with adventurous perception. Looking down into the dense green jungle below, I tried to pray. Thankfully, Michelle was sleeping in my lap as trickles of sweat slowly dripped down the sides of her beautiful cheeks. That reminded me of my own trails of sweat, forming one huge waterfall on my back. Where was the climate control in the plane?

Looking down, I noticed that the tops of the trees looked like lush bunches of ripe green broccoli ready for picking. Peeping through the green was the faint outline of brown woven huts and dark, murky rivers intertwining with unending, thick foliage. How a pilot could know where he was going without instrumentation was beyond my aviator-challenged mind. Jeff, however, was in his element, being trained for that very thing. Hearing the excitement in his voice, I could not help but smile as I watched him.

After an hour's flight, the plane suddenly took a sharp turn to the left and then cut veeringly to the right. It was the first real civilization that I had seen since leaving the capital city of Monrovia. Six houses, an airplane hangar, a Bible school building, a medical clinic and an OB clinic, along with a few other buildings spaced alongside the airstrip. The airstrip? As I looked, I only saw a long open strip of grass. Looking carefully at the faces of my husband and the other pilot, neither seemed disturbed by the lack of tarmac, so I just held on tightly to Michelle and watched us descend into that new world shrouded by a welcoming lush green canopy.

After an impressive landing, I looked straight ahead to see a massive crowd of people standing by the hangar, but it was the sprays of colorful, exotic flowers that took my breath away! Pinks, blues, yellows, and purples woven exquisitely around the poles celebrated our arrival. Half of my heart beat gratuitously for the warm welcome, but the other half felt like I was falling into a black pit from which I would never again ascend.

As the plane came to a complete stop and the engines were cut off, I heard the singing and was involuntarily initiated into the rhythm that is uniquely African. The women were dancing and swaying perfectly to the music. It was beautiful and I liked it immensely. Even in his height of excitement, Jeff remembered and turned to take my hand. With his beautiful brown eyes beaming, he squeezed my hand and said, "WELCOME HOME, MISSY ABERNETHY."

CHAPTER THREE

Though I speak with the tongues of men and of angels, and have not charity,
I am become as sounding brass, or a tinkling cymbal.   I Corinthians 13:1

Fat and Sassy

We stepped out of the plane smack dab into the middle of a strange, but intriguing world; the place to which God had asked us to move, to live, to raise our children, while sharing the Gospel of Jesus Christ to those around us. After respectfully giving us time to greet the waiting missionaries, the African Christians moved in to take a closer look at the new arrivals. Soon I was surrounded by at least a dozen African women pressing in, trying to touch Michelle's hair. She would have none of that and held on to my neck tightly.

At the same time, I heard some of the Africans praising Jeff, pumping his hand enthusiastically as they kept looking back at me. It was an effort to understand what they were saying even though it was in English. The Liberian English accent was a uniquely rounded, musical sound that took time to pick up. Nevertheless, I thought I heard them rhythmically chanting, "TANK YOU, TEACHA, FOR YOUR FAT WIFE! SHE'S TOO FINE, SHE'S TOO FAT! OH, TANK YA TEACHA FOR YOUR FAT WIFE!" (Thank you, teacher, for your fat wife.) It was at that moment I was glad that I had a head cold to blame for my watery eyes.

Our belongings were cursorily loaded into several well-used wheelbarrows as we were invited to walk the fifty yards to our new home. After we had been shown to our mud block house with concrete floors and only screens in the windows, I succumbed to the despair of realizing how far away I was from my mother and that I was stuck in the African jungle ministering to people that enjoyed calling me fat! Jeff had forgotten to warn me about that unusual "perspective" on body size.

To an African, if you had any meat (and fat) on your bones, you must surely be blessed by God. For you see, that would mean you had the means to buy and eat all the food you wanted. Once I heard the explanation, I felt humbled and somewhat thankful. It still stung my pride a little about the "fat" part, but I tried to submit to the cultural contradictions that were certain to happen frequently.

As much as I loved our house, the layout of the rooms, and the simple quaintness of it, my mind was still on overload with the reality of how far away we were from America. I started fantasizing about how I could get in the one engine plane, return to Monrovia, hop a larger plane headed to Europe, take another plane to NYC, and from there board a plane that would take me to Charlotte. A plane where it would be climate-controlled, where they would speak English in an accent that I could understand, and where they would serve peanuts and Cokes. However, that conjecture did nothing but make the helplessness and despair mount up in my soul even more! I was a panic attack in the making if I didn't stop.

For weeks, I battled the fantasy of leaving that intriguing, but strange place and never coming back. Though I did not write down the verses God used to assure me that I was in the right place, He reminded me of how I was created...to be an adventurer for this very time! God tenderly revealed to my hurting heart that He knew my frame and exactly what I was supposed to be doing. I was reminded of that repeatedly as I learned the idiosyncrasies of living on a mission compound in the African jungle and little by little acknowledged that He would be sufficient for me and that He would use me in spite of myself.

Pampered American

A couple of days after getting used to our house, I wrote in my journal:

> *After we started unpacking our container, we realized how much we had as Americans in comparison to the Liberians. Some items that we brought out now seemed silly and frivolous, but yet, there they were, a reflection of the person I had been just a few weeks before. It was an ethereal feeling but yet freeing to think that we could really live without so many things. The American mindset can so often trap us into thinking that we simply cannot do without our things.*

Jeff paid some of the Bible school students to help unload our belongings into the house, and I remember feeling a little shiny and pampered. The men were so kind and never made any comments around us about what they were unloading, but their silence did make me wonder what they went back and told their wives about the American missionaries and their things. I have learned over the years of living in West Africa that most Africans expect that we would live differently than them, so perhaps they were not thinking anything negative at all.

Another notion to be accepted was that we were fundamentally, in most every way, somewhat distanced from them because of who we were and where we came from. There was no way that we could understand them on their basic cultural level. The most comforting thing was that we had come to share Christ and when that was accepted, the bond we had in our Savior would cross over many of those physical and cultural barriers. All of that took time. One basic truth that spanned the years that we spent ministering to and with Africans is that even in that tight Christian bond, there was also a fragile liberty of mutual acceptance of each other's culture and perspective. That acknowledged, anything was possible.

Food, Food, Food of the Jungle

So many Liberians came to our house the first week to welcome us, it almost seemed overwhelming! Many of them remembered Jeff from the year before when he had come out on a survey trip, but it seemed that all the people we met were thrilled that we were there. I was personally thankful that there was no more discussion about my fatness. It was heartwarming to see how much they cared that we had come to live among them. One of the most endearing things about an African is that they never visited without bringing something meaningful. Our pantry floor was quickly scattered with bowls and bags of exceptional West African country rice, fresh vegetables and fruits, and some cooked dishes that took a little courage to sniff and taste. It meant so much because they, who had so little, wanted to share with us.

This is a good place to describe some of the rice dishes that the Liberians cherished as their "bread of life". They call their dishes "rice and soup" even though the soup is much more like a thick stew that is put on top of the rice. Liberian soup is prepared by first cooking meat and onion in a good amount of oil (mostly palm oil) until very tender. They would then add whatever vegetable they had on hand: eggplant, okra, bitterball (a small round eggplant-like food that was indeed very bitter tasting), potato greens (much like the tops of a sweet potato here in the States), cassava greens (which was much like collard greens in texture but had a much more pungent flavor). Cassava green soup or potato green soup became one of my family's favorites; however, after all the years of living in West Africa, I just could not acquire a taste for either of those green soups though I did eat them when they were offered.

African cooks would add the vegetable of choice and then some bouillon cubes usually as the only seasoning, unless they were a Liberian tribe that cooked all their soups with hot peppers. After simmering the soup for a while, they would serve this flavorful concoction over their delectable country rice. My two particular favorites were peanut soup (chicken and ground peanuts in a tomato-based broth) and okra soup. When available, which wasn't very often, we would also enjoy green bean or collard green soup.

One of their poor man's meals when they didn't have rice would be something that the Gio people in our area called "dumboy." They would prepare the cassava root into a starchy eatable dish that was served with any kind of very slippery type soup such as okra. They would boil the cassava, pound it in a mortar until it became sticky and then would be shaped into a ball. Pinching off small amounts of the dumboy, they would roll it into a ball and then dip it into the "slippery" soup. Because the dumboy was of a chewy substance, the key would be to dip the ball into the soup and then swallow the ball without chewing. I, for one, enjoyed chewing my food too much, so I never really got into making an entire meal of that dish. It was a true favorite of most missionary kids there in Liberia.

Palm butter soup is perhaps the icon of Liberian food, though it is the hardest to describe. It deserves its own paragraph and its own place in the annals of unique and exotically delicious international dishes. Indigenous to the West African region (as far as I know), palm butter is a taste that rivals any of the foods I have ever

26

experienced. There's nothing, however, in our American fare that compares to it, and we've been told that describing how it tastes is no where near like actually taking a bite of its fibrous golden texture. In a nutshell, palm butter soup is made entirely from the red, ripe palm nuts. They are boiled until the hard, outer shell and the fibrous covering disintegrate. Using a strainer, they remove everything except the butter. Boiling the butter until thickened–much like broccoli cheese soup–they then added chicken and onion. Though it is one of the most popular meals among the Liberians, the cooking process was also very tedious.

Little Help From My Friends

Friends are special, holding important places in our lives no matter who they are, where we meet them, and how often we see them. I had learned back in high school that friends did not have to be the same color as me or even have the same cultural background to bring depth and joy to my life. It was no different in Liberia. From the very beginning of our Liberian ministry, Mary Kwiah was such a friend.

From the beginning, there was a special connection even though she lived in a dirt floor hut and had delivered ten children with only seven having survived. There were some things that I could not understand about her life and vice versa, but we knew that we both loved God, both loved our husbands and children, and we both loved to laugh. Laughter protrudes delightfully beyond cultural and language barriers, and it was definitely so for Mary and me. Seeming to understand some of my struggles of adapting to her culture, she would show up at just the right time, teaching me so much about living in Liberia. And though she laughed at some of my perceptions of her birthplace, she gently explained some of the unfamiliar nuances as best she could. Months later, she was instrumental in encouraging me to learn her tribal dialect that I studied for the first two years while we lived in Liberia.

Liberian "Chocolates"

From day one in our new home in the West African jungle, Jeff, Michelle and I were initiated into the world of Liberian

"CHOCOLATES." It is not a pleasant thing to talk about, but was so much a part of the new missionary experience that it must be told. Bodies that have been pampered with consistently clean drinking water do not passively accept having to ingest water teeming with hoards of deadly microscopic parasites. Have you guessed what "Liberian chocolates" are? Foreign bacteria in water, oily and unfamiliar foods and meats: all those things are very hard on a virgin American digestive system. My journal reads:

> Let me go back to our bathroom episodes. Whether it was the water or something we ate, Michelle and I both got the Liberian "chocolates" as Jeff affectionately called this. Shell didn't know what was happening to her. I found the "chocolates" everywhere. Bless her heart, she would try to go to the potty, but it never came like that. Today Jeff has the problem. Michelle is better but has a bad rash and I think I'm pretty cleaned out for now. It was the total detox program, but one that you would not want to experience very often!

We had only been in Tappi for about three days when I was forced to acquaint myself with one of the ways clothes would have to be dealt with if they became soiled between wash days (mainly on Saturdays). We inherited large metal washing tubs from a previous missionary, so I carried them outside and attempted to wash clothes much like my great-grandmothers must have. I put the soiled "chocolate" clothes in a tub with mild Clorox water, letting them soak for an hour or so, and later rinsed them in the large sink located in our wash kitchen. What an initiation! The only thing that seemed to be missing was a scrub board. Probably just as well as my knuckles would not have appreciated the work out!

Inspired By a White Gio Man

For years, our mission compound had been host to one of the largest Christian conferences held in northern Liberia. The annual Mano/Gio Conference attendees were people from the surrounding region consisting of two cousin tribes (in that many of the words translated close enough so that a Gio could understand a Mano and vice versa). The conference was always held around the first of the year and brought a bustling to our compound that I never imagined could happen in our remote area. In perspective, Tappeta was a rather large town compared to many of the small villages where some of the attendees lived

We had only been in Tappeta for one month when the 1986 conference began, and so it was with great excitement that we planned to attend much of the festivities. The highlight for me during that conference was when Missionary Tom Jackson, an American man, who had felt led to translate the entire Bible into Gio, stood up to speak. A man short in stature and closing in on his 70th year, he bellowed out his greetings in both Mano and Gio— and then continued to preach for almost an hour totally in the Gio language! I was mesmerized. It was so obvious that those attending had the upmost respect for Tom and his wife June. When I asked a Gio woman later about how well she thought Teacher Tom did with her language, she said, "Huh! The man wrote our language! He know it too fine!"

Tom was esteemed as a true white African Gio man. I heard that from several pastors during the conference and it touched the linguistic side of me like nothing else. Always having a love and natural affinity with language, it evoked in me the realization that I, too, could possibly speak to those precious people in their native tongue. Tom was a great encouragement to me over the next couple of years, and even visited on several occasions (they lived in a village about 30 miles from us), passing on his burden for translating the Old Testament in Gio. He was concerned that he would perhaps not live long enough to finish the task and saw in me, the continuance of his dream. I was both honored and petrified! Taking it as a challenge, I offered God my willingness to do that kind of work down the road if it was what He would want me to do.

My first practice site became the weekly market there in Tappi. Each town of any significant size hosted a weekly market day where those living in the area could bring their food or wares to sell. It was a little bit carnival, little bit farmer's market, and a little bit family reunion kind of thing. When I first visited the Wednesday market in Tappi, I realized that the majority of women who were selling at their individual booths only spoke one of the two local dialects. They did not understand English at all. That was a frustration for me who loved nothing more than to be able to communicate with everyone around me. That realization aroused the need in me to learn the local dialect even more.

The reality was that without me learning Gio, I would never be able to communicate with some of the market ladies, so with a little convincing from my friend Mary and others like Tom Jackson, my attempt to learn the Gio dialect was launched. Loving a challenge and having a great desire to communicate effectively with the town women, I stuck with it.

After about six months of studying and practicing short, simple phrases, I went into the Wednesday market. A little timidly, I meandered around and started greeting the women in their own language, carrying on limited conversations with some of them. The fervor grew when the news that the white woman was speaking their language, and within minutes, some of the market women had put the "fat" white missionary lady on their shoulders and began to dance around the market. The celebratory dance was their way of showing gratitude for my efforts in learning to talk with them in their own dialect. That day remains a highlight of my entire African ministry!

At the following annual Mano/Gio conference in January 1987, I was slated to teach a Bible class to the older women. The first day I surprised the ladies by reading all my scriptures from my very own Gio New Testament, giving all my scripture references in Gio. So thankful was I that God had allowed me to learn some of the language of those around us! I prayed, too, for the ability to love them just as He loved them. Speaking their language without loving them deeply in my heart....well, surely that would be way too brassy!

CHAPTER FOUR

Life is a grindstone. Whether it grinds you down or polishes you up depends on you. —L. Thomas Holdcroft

Full House

No matter how long we ministered in West Africa, I never really became totally accustomed with the constant presence of someone other than family in our house. Granted, they were helping me with the never-ending household duties that seemed so much more arduous than what I ever had in the States. As I've mentioned before, there was no glass in the windows, only screen and "rogue bars" (metal crisscross bars to keep thieves from cutting the screen and climbing into the windows). So you can only imagine that dust was a minute by minute accumulation. Despite my discomfort with house help, it was necessary if I was going to be effective in ministry; however, it was still very difficult for me to share my private domain. My journal, after only a couple of days with house help reiterated that:

> *I am still having a hard time getting use to people in my house working. But I am so thankful we have two good young African men that we can trust. I have to remember that they appreciate their jobs as much as we appreciate their work. Our youngest worker asked us to keep his pay for a couple of months and buy him some new athletic shoes in Monrovia.*

Two things compelled me to keep using house help throughout our African missionary career: I knew that it provided much-needed income to Bible school families, plus I recognized that I could not possibly scrub concrete floors, dust and mop a house where the screen windows seem to beckon the dust, haul water from an outside well, build a fire and boil water, and wash clothes in tubs if I was going to keep up with the care of my family and do any ministry at all. No matter what my American upbringing may have been telling me, I had to learn to live with the phenomenon of house help. The cultural collisions had begun.

Today we have a college ministry at the University of North Carolina @ Charlotte, and I do not have house help. Believe me, there are now times when I pine away for those days when I would come in from the African market or from teaching English at the Bible Institute, and the floors would be freshly mopped, savory food set on the stove, and the bathrooms cleaned to the max. Ministry with college students is extremely demanding and time-consuming, but the domestic conveniences in our American homes make it easier to keep up. Still after all those years in Africa with someone doing it for me, cleaning is not one of my favorite things to do. I admit it–I simply got spoiled. Again, cultural collisions pursue me!

It also dawned on me that having these African young people in our homes gave us the awesome opportunity and responsibility to teach them by our example. You know how it is: we can often live like we want to be perceived while out in public, waiting until we are in the privacy of our own homes to be who we truly are. Not so out there since our home was accessed by some of the very people to whom we came to minister. That reality brought all that to light! In many ways, it was a good exercise in living out our faith–off the cuff–not rehearsed–and in front of a perpetual audience!

Molly Maid, Jungle Style

About ten days after we arrived in Tappi and after indulging in the generous meals offered by fellow missionaries, I began cooking on a charcoal grill outside the back of our house. It was also the day that one of the Bible school guys started working with us. Paul, a well-trained Liberian, who had worked with another missionary family for several years, washed clothes in a tub outside for almost the entire day! I kept watching him through the window and thanking God that it was not me doing it, though there was also a part of me that felt guilty to realize someone else was doing the work I should be doing. I could never get over the fact that another person was waiting on me in the domestic realm that had previously been solely my responsibility. My *Americanness* never quite knew what to do with that reality!

Then there was the communication gap. One of the first lessons in relating verbally with someone from another culture is to never assume you are completely understood and to be very specific with instructions, using phrases from their cultural vernacular if possible. Paul, who I have already noted was helping us that first year we lived in Tappi, was a life saver. He taught me so much, he laughed with me about my ignorance of the West African ways, and was patient in showing me how to cook African chop (food) and how to use ingredients easily procured in that region. I felt like a wealthy woman who could afford to have a full-time chef in her kitchen, freeing me up to spend more time with Michelle, as she, too, adjusted to our new world.

One day it was my turn to laugh at Paul, although the laughter was initially hard to come by. If you remember, I said earlier that we always tried to buy enough food and staples to last at least six weeks. For that reason, we bought white and brown sugar and flour each in twenty-five pound bags. Before leaving the States, I had been given some extra large Tupperware containers that were perfect for storing the sugars and flour, since we had been told ahead of time that the ants and bugs would find their way into our food items that were not canned or well sealed.

Our mission plane had just arrived with a large quantity of food for all the missionaries. As became a tradition, either Jeff or I would roll our wheelbarrow to the airplane hangar where the men were divvying up the groceries for each family. It was an easy way to haul a large amount of groceries to the house, and also was not unusual to see Michelle riding on top of the mound of groceries down the hill from the hangar. Yes, it was indeed an exciting time for us when groceries arrived! Seriously, it was. Just imagine being cocooned 180 miles from civilization and then someone would bring you the food you needed. It was as good as a food drop!

As Paul and I were putting the groceries in the pantry, I was called away for some reason, so I quickly instructed him to put the large bags of white sugar, the brown sugar, and flour into the three containers that I had set on the kitchen counter. Simple instructions? I thought so, too. A couple of hours later, I came into the kitchen to begin supper preparations. Paul had already left for the day, so thankfully he was not there for my reaction to his detailed artwork with the sugars and flour.

Setting on the counter were the three plastic containers filled with the sugars and flour. Nice, right? Well, the one small detail that floored me was how he had painstakingly layered all three into each container: white flour, brown sugar, white sugar, brown sugar, white flour, and so on. ALL THREE CONTAINERS WERE PERFECTLY MELDED INTO THAT PARTICULAR FORMULA. I snapped. I cried. I called for Jeff. (What was he going to do about it, I didn't know, but it made me feel better to know I could call him) As I recall, it had been a rather demanding day for that young missionary woman, so that incident was the point used to break me. Me, who has one of the biggest sense of humors that I know, did not laugh. Could not laugh. Not that day. Putting on hold my intention to make biscuits for supper, I went ahead with preparing a slightly altered meal for the family—sans the biscuits.

The next morning I remember trying so hard to make light of the layered containers of mixed flour and sugars when Paul came to work. I apologized for not being clearer in my instructions, and together we separated–as best we could–the flour and sugars. Weeks later, as I opened one of the containers to bake a cake, I started laughing out loud, alone in the kitchen as I pinched pieces of brown sugar from the flour I had poured into a bowl. Little by little, I was either going mad—or perhaps learning to let go of my American expectations. Either way, I conceded I would be happier.

Pillsbury Dough Boy

Those first few weeks of living in Tappi found me without a working oven. The gas stove (inherited from the last missionary that lived in our house) worked fine—the top elements anyway. The oven had some issues that could not be resolved easily, so I did without. Probably after hearing me whine enough about it and considering that I surely tempted him with chocolate cakes if I had an oven that worked, Jeff came up with a brilliant idea! He says that the inspiration came from his family camping days in the Carolina Hemlocks. His father, Hal, and his Uncle Warren, used a large metal flour container and constructed it into a makeshift "oven"

34

that set right on the coals of the campfire. Though the concept was primitive, it did seem like a wonderful plan.

Somewhere out in our storage building, he found a very large, antiquated Pillsbury Flour can. Ingeniously, he welded, melded, and shaped a small portable, metal oven that I could set on top of the fire which was usually burning outside our back door on a brick grate. I was so excited about using that unique "oven" to bake cakes and cookies, that I failed to initially take into account that there was no way to regulate the temperature. The first several attempts, especially with the cookies, were a bust. With practice, though, I finally was able to bake a decent cake and some casseroles in that camp style oven.

Even when another missionary helped us temporarily repair our oven, using it for baking was still a rarity because we were not used to the cost of a tank of stove gas. As much as I can remember, a tank of stove gas would cost us nearly $50, and it was our desire to get at least six weeks out of one tank. A few months later, after Stefanie was born, my parents came to visit, and while there, my dad was able to properly fix the stove and oven so that it worked so much more efficiently. Way to go, daddy!

Fire and Ice

This is probably a good place to explain how we were able to have a refrigerator and freezer that worked twenty-four hours a day, even when we only had electricity for three hours in the evening and four additional hours on Saturday morning. Our fridge and freezer were both powered by kerosene. Honestly, I didn't even know there was such a thing before we lived in Liberia, but appreciated them in spite of the atrocious smell that constantly permeated my house.

The process worked by initiating fire in the bottom of the appliance with kerosene, and then eventually, ice would form in the top compartment. By the heat going into an exchanger and cooling down rapidly, we were able to have a cool refrigerator. Never did I even somewhat understand the principle of that system but was just thankful that it worked. The five-gallon kerosene tank and burner sat on a shelf at the very bottom of the refrigerator. The room temperature and how often someone opened its door determined the efficiency of the cooling process. To secure the door, Jeff installed a hook which made it a little harder for certain small people to open and close the door all day long.

It was an amazing thing that we were in the middle of the West African jungle with limited electricity, popping ice cubes into tea glasses or pulling out frozen chicken to thaw. Though my kitchen perpetually smelled of kerosene, I complained very little. Funny, the things I would have not tolerated for very long in America, I embraced and was thankful for in Liberia. It was Jeff's job to keep the flame burning constantly by adding kerosene as necessary. We looked at it as his contribution to the food process. Never really having learned to cook, he knew he was at my mercy for meal preparations. In those early days, it was a heady feeling to know that my ministry of taking care of my husband, who was busy learning so much about the Liberian ministry, was very important. As I am a front line kind of gal, I did struggle with being in the shadows at times, but with the privilege of feeding and caring for that incredible new missionary, I perceived that his crowns were my crowns.

Inflatable Christmas Tree

After nearly two weeks in Tappi, my journal of December 20, 1985, reads:

> *Liberia is feeling more like home, even though at times I pine away for America. I'm sure this is normal. The house is coming along fine. It thrills me to know that it's mine! I can't wait to get settled. No one will ever know what I felt those last few weeks in America before we left. No real place to call my own. A woman has got to have her nest, right?*
>
> *Christmas is in five days! I would love to be able to decorate more, but it's just not feasible. I found a ceramic nativity scene in a barrel (left by a missionary who lived here previously), so I put it up and hung a red bow by the door. And thank you, MawMaw (my mother) for the inflatable Christmas tree because that's what we are using! But just wait until next year! I'll go all out.*

I desire to start a ministry, but I know I must get settled first. I am so excited about serving the Lord here. Jeff really enjoys working on the helicopter and airplane, and being able to fly again. Many of the Liberian men come to visit and talk to him. He's going to be a continued blessing to these men, I just know it. God has given us a great peace and joy about being here.

Sometimes I am amazed how my mother anticipated my needs as a woman heading to West Africa before I even did. Now that I am a mother of grown daughters, I understand it more. I am so thankful for the support and beyond that, the practical ways my mother and mother-in-law found to touch my life, even when they were certainly struggling with the separation from their children and grandchild. The inflatable Christmas tree was a perfect example of that. It was exactly right for that first, quickly put together Christmas in our African home. The pictures of Michelle sitting beside that tree are some of my favorites! In retrospect, and now, because I have lived a little life, I know that Christmas is not in the size of the tree nor in how many decorations in your house. If the spirit of Christmas is not lived out in our lives 365 days of the year, none of the rest of it really matters.

Little Things That Get You

Taken from my December 21, 1985, journal:

Perhaps the most aggravating thing today is that I don't have a stopper for my kitchen sink and I have to put a cloth under another smaller drain stopper to keep the water in. Sometimes I pull it out by mistake and lose all the hot water that has been heated on our wood stove outside. It's very frustrating!

There was no hot water available in our house, so I would have to step outside my back door and pour water from a container into a metal bucket already setting on top of the wood fire. After the water was heated, I lugged the steamy container into my kitchen. Bringing in hot water in a slopping metal bucket was a dangerous thing, and I had many burns on my arms and legs to prove it.

It took me a little while, but I discovered by carrying only a half bucket at a time, that this proved to be safer and easier. It was quite an ordeal just to get the hot water in the house without losing it down the drain before I was finished washing the dishes. That was a BIG deal! Sometimes it would take me almost an hour to wash a few dishes from lunch and breakfast because of that problem. Granted, our Bible school students who worked for us did it ALL the time, but it was something they had always known to do. For me, it was foreign, frustrating, and tedious. Occasionally, I would find myself looking around for a hidden dishwasher, but it never appeared. I have to admit that, for the first few months, I cried quite a bit over those small things in my new life that seemed so BIG.

Feet First

After our first week in Tappi during a weekly station meeting, I was asked if we could host the station Christmas party. Our house, we came to find out, had always been used for these kind of gatherings because of how the front rooms were long, spacious, giving ample space for tables and guests. Our zinc-covered porch would accommodate tables for the children. My disposition towards hospitality was already being put to the test. So, I agreed. I mean, why change tradition just because I had only been in that strange country for a couple of weeks?

Jumping to the challenge, it took three days to get the boxes out of the family room, rugs laid, and pictures hung. I wanted everything to be as homey and lived in as possible. I do have to remember that I was only 27 years old then and nothing seemed impossible. Today, I would probably most likely still host the Christmas dinner, but the boxes would be stashed in another room or at least a tablecloth thrown over them. I now know that endless mounds of boxes were just an integral part of a missionary home more often than not.

As Christmas approached, we settled into a strange, nostalgic funk. Everything seemed a little surreal and looking back, I realize now that our bodies and emotions were in "survival" mode. We were completely out of our element, had never faced a Christmas without our families before, and found ourselves in an environment that in no way felt like the Yuletide merriment to which we were accustomed. Our emotions changed like the tide, and so tempted was I to lie down and sleep until the day after New Year's Day. At first, we eluded the real issues which were no doubt causing us to react so strangely by staying busy unpacking, learning, organizing. Jeff and I became snappy at each other over the smallest things as we succumbed to pressures that we had never known and feelings we chose to suppress out of fear of sounding weak. Ever been there?

Looming closely in my mind was the reality that, come Christmas Day, sixteen people, most whom we barely knew, were coming to my disorganized, albeit spacious home for holiday cheer. I grumpily quipped that they had better be bringing that cheer with them! Granted, I was cooking very little of the meal, but the thought of having missionaries that were familiar with jungle living, those houses, the African people, the smells, and the confounded inconveniences at times seemed too much. I peaked high as one more picture was hung and then I would crash hard when I looked at the sparse Christmas items with which I had to decorate. I began to see the seemingly mile-long stretch of spider webs, the dust that multiplied hourly on everything wood, and the concrete floors that glared ominously from alongside my braided living room rug.

It was one of my first, but certainly not my last disillusioned moment at where God had placed me. I was both disappointed with myself for what I was thinking and perplexed with God for "allowing" me to think in such a defeating way. I had not yet embraced that biblical principle of taking hold of my thoughts and not allowing them to consume me.

> It's 6:00 p.m. in the States now, and they are probably eating Christmas Eve supper at Grandma Horrell's. Oh, how we long to be there! This is the most homesick I have been yet. But I know they are missing us, too, and that also hurts. Michelle had a rough day (or maybe it was just me projecting on her). She cried and whined most of the day. We also found out that some missionary kids were giving Michelle something for Christmas and a missionary couple was giving us something. I feel terrible because I did not anticipate that.

39

I was very hard on myself for even the little things that I did not think to pack in our container. As a lesson to pass on to someone heading to a foreign country, I wish I would have brought out little gifts from America for the other missionary children on the field for Christmas, and perhaps some small treats for the adults, too. We were unversed missionaries with so many large and small things to learn. No one was harder judges on us than ourselves.

The Day After Christmas

My journal of December 26, 1985, reads: *Christmas Day was a very emotional day. It was the hardest day we had so far. It wasn't just us, all the missionaries were like that. I never really realized how hard it is for missionaries, and most of the time we never even take the time to pray for them during holidays.*

I could find nothing in my journals or letters where I accurately described how overwhelmingly hard that first Christmas in Africa was. When I asked Jeff what he remembered, he simply said, "WEIRD." As for me, I do remember being painfully cognizant of the time difference and what would be going on in the States at a particular hour.

However, having the entire missionary population of Tappi at our house that Christmas Day helped to keep me from despair. It was only when everyone was seated around the table that I realized my struggles with Christmas were not unique to me nor would they necessarily go away in the years to come. All the missionaries seemed to be a little more open and sentimental, speaking nostalgically about family and holidays in the States. Oddly enough, knowing that I was not struggling alone with missing loved ones and family traditions helped me make it through that day.

I do believe that I started to feel like "one of them" that day, clasping my heart around the knowledge that we all shared a bond that knitted our hearts together as family. In time, they did become our "African" family and remain as such to this day. Twenty-five years later, we stay in contact with almost every one of them who sat around our table that Christmas of 1985. If, by chance, we are able to personally see them, our time together is sweet and we simply pick up where we left off. Family does that. Or should.

CHAPTER FIVE

We teach what we know, but we reproduce what we are. —John Maxwell

The First Reality Show

The African kids (and sometimes the adults) had no problem nor felt any shame in sitting on our porch and watching us inside our house. It was the best television program ever—a reality show, for sure! Jeff was constantly, but gently running people off our porch. Because we were new, they liked to come and watch us unpack our boxes, mesmerized at the different items we had brought with us from America. Jeff was really good about explaining that his wife was American (as if HE wasn't) and was not used to the public display of curiosity.

To add to that, during our first few days in Tappi, we saw several young guys walk behind our house, and after some questioning, we found out that they had shot with a slingshot a chicken hawk who had been perched in one of our trees. Unfortunately, as the rock hit its mark, the hawk had spread its wings as it involuntarily descended and was caught in a branch. One of the African boys started climbing the tree, hoping to shake the hawk loose. Now, I always loved to climb tress when I was young, but that little boy had made a profession of it! He slid up that tree trunk in a way that I had never seen! The chicken hawk fell, but still was not completely dead. I felt sorry for it and could not watch as they finished it off. However, my very inquisitive two year old Michelle was fascinated by the whole process, even after one of the young fellows had slung the limp, bloody bird over his shoulders and headed down the path dreaming of a meaty supper.

I knew that I needed to get used to people working in our yard as well as in our house. It was nothing like America where people had distinct boundaries and sacred personal space which others usually did not invade. That incident with the chicken hawk helped me to understand that sometimes, especially for the young African boys, the only food they might eat in a day's time was what they killed themselves. Even if we caught them early in the morning, during our afternoon rest hour, or late in the evening climbing and shaking our mango or avocado trees, I tried to remember that I had plenty to eat, but they probably did not. On the other side of that was the desire to teach them to at least ask permission since the trees were in our yard. That is where the line of intersecting culture and biblical beliefs must always be carefully considered in a sensitive manner. We lived off the cuff with those kinds of situations, attempting to pad authority with love and humor as much as possible.

Perpetual Balancing Acts

In January of 1986, I wrote in my journal:

> *Yesterday a little boy came to our house wanting a Bible. Jeff talked to him for quite a while about his salvation. He even brought money to pay for the Bible, but Jeff gave it to him for free. Today another boy came and asked for a Bible. I talked to him and found out that he did not bring any money, but was also expecting us to give him one for free. I did finally give it to him–how can you refuse to give anyone a Bible? However, it started something. Later that day fifteen boys came and asked for Bibles. I had to send them away because we did not have that many Bibles. It was a sad time for me.*

Little did I know that the constant asking for things, money, food and more would become the norm for so much of our African ministry. During our many years in West Africa, hundreds of people came to our door wanting something. Unfortunately, the majority of the time it was not for a Bible or even spiritual help; it was for monetary substance.

We never became accustomed to dealing with the constant begging for money though we learned to always weigh each request individually. There were times when we also knew that we were not hearing the entire truth from the person asking. In our later years while in West Africa, there were days and sometimes weeks that we just refused to go to our gate because we had grown so weary of the begging. We were too overwhelmed and tired to constantly discern whether a person truly deserved help or not. As an alternative to shutting down from the daunting needs of those around us, I prepared sacks of food essentials for anyone that came to us begging. We had long since stopped giving out money except on those rare occasions when we felt distinctly that we were to do so. Measuring out rice, onion, canned meat, oil, and bouillon cubes and putting it all in a bag, I would give it to the person who said they were in need. Often they would be extremely grateful, but too many times, I had the bag of food refused or thrown on the ground. That did help me to divide the sheep from the goat, so to speak. If a woman with a little child in her arms could throw down my gift of food along with my promise to give more the next day, then I knew the woman was not speaking truthfully about her need to feed her child.

Different Points of View

Even in the middle of the myriad of cultural collisions, there protruded into my unrealistic fantasy the hope that all missionaries were created equal: meaning that we would always think the same way, feel the same way, minister the same way, and live the same way. In case you don't already know the fallacy of that thinking, learn it now. Missionaries are all different. We think differently, minister differently, and run our homes differently.

I am sure that it may have seemed extreme to some that I packed so many "niceties" in our first container from America. More than anything, it was simply a matter of preference and priority. In my journal I wrote this:

> *Yesterday one of the missionary wives was talking about how she could just walk away from her house tomorrow and not worry about leaving a lot of things behind. My philosophy is that the Lord called us here to live and minister. If I do not try to make this "home" and live totally in this place, I feel I am only halfway serving God. Sure, if we were forced to leave tomorrow, I would probably cry to have to leave some things, but I refuse to live in that attitude. I will trust God with those matters and put my whole self into these people and the work–and at the same time–I will strive to*

*have the best home for my family right here, not saving all
that for a one-year furlough time in America.*

In the following fifteen years of ministry in West Africa, my
philosophy concerning my homes in Africa changed very little.
Though after our first evacuation and the loss of our household
goods, I did become a little more selective on the things that I
brought from the States; it was still in my heart to make my home
as comfortable and colorful for my family. As I stated earlier, I
learned that a missionary should not only be willing to adapt to
another country, culture, and people, but also be willing to embrace
the challenge to learn and accept the philosophical differences of
each missionary with whom we had the privilege to minister.

Missionaries come from different parts of the United States,
so there were those obvious "subcultural" variations. Accepting
the unique characteristics found in Minnesota, Iowa, Michigan,
New York, and other states far from the southern state of North
Carolina, was necessary for both ministry harmony and establish-
ing solid friendships. Over time, we learned to understand and
embrace many of the others' peculiarities.

My convictions of how I managed my household stayed with
me, but that never hindered me from finding common ground with
the other women on the compound. It was, more than anything, a
difference in philosophy. It held no great hindrance in our relationships that I recall, and deep inside me, I wanted to learn what the
"veteran" missionaries could teach me without losing the unique
spark that made me who I was. That is not to say that it is wrong
if a woman preparing to be a missionary feels that she should only
carry a backpack and a sleeping bag to the place God has called her
to minister. Of course not! As I said before; it is a matter of priori-
ties. God gave me (eventually) three daughters to whom I desired
to instill the color and creativity that can be placed in a home no
matter where that home was. Live out your personality and dreams
no matter where God puts you!

African Pioneers

During the first January in Tappi, we had the privilege of meeting the pioneer missionary wife and her daughter when they came

out for a visit. Mrs. Mellish and her husband were the ones that started the mission station in Tappi almost fifty years before we arrived. In 1939, the only way for them to reach the interior parts of Liberia was to walk. Mrs. Mellish told us of how she and her husband would set out from Monrovia and walk the 180 miles to the small town of Tappeta! Taking them several weeks to accomplish that incredible feat, her stories made me vow right then to never complain about the one-hour plane ride to Monrovia.

As we missionaries of the 1980s sat around and enjoyed the stories told by Mrs. Mellish, it was clear that we had much for which to be thankful. Baptist Mid-Missions had sent the Mellishes out to Liberia because of a hunger in their hearts to see the Liberians reached with the Gospel of Christ. The mission station where we lived was a result of their desire to see missions remain a vital part of that country—even when their active ministry was completed. To this day, I am so thankful that Jeff and I could begin our missionary career in Liberia by meeting one of our missionary foremothers. She was an inspiration to me and helped put many things in perspective!

Faraway Food

Getting used to some of the foods that were available to us and having to do without some of the ones that were not available was certainly a challenge those first few years. Sometimes just finding the most basic food was a chore. There were countless days when we did without eggs, fresh vegetables, and such.

My journal of January 3, 1986, says:

> *This has been a rather good day–I seemed to enjoy it. We didn't have much to eat for breakfast except cereal. We were out of bread and eggs. Jeff bought bread later, but still looking for eggs. The bread is really good, but you wouldn't believe it seeing where it is baked. Jeff took me down there to see it the other day. It's an outdoor kitchen with big black pots and a "baking hole" under a shed but they do keep it clean. The bread was soft, round, and very tasty, much like a round Italian loaf found in a bakery. Only the crust was soft like the inside of the bread. We called it Ghanaian bread*

because it was baked by a pair of sisters from the country of Ghana who had married men from Liberia.

When I first rode with Jeff on his motorcycle to buy bread, I could not help but hone in on the seemingly unsanitary conditions where the bread was made. The crude oven and pans that the bread was baked in were always suspicious in my book. Looking back, I laugh to think how afraid I was to eat the bread though I wanted it so badly. I recall that I would take a cloth and wipe the loaf off before cutting it. What did I think that would do, I wonder?

As time went by, we started missing foods from the states. In my journal dated January 7, 1986, I reflected: *The two things that I miss the most right now is my mama's sweet iced tea and some real, homogenized milk! This powdered milk is for the birds. Jeff says he misses ice cream, candy bars, chocolate milkshakes, and his mom's chocolate cake with white icing.* I never got used to the powdered milk that we had to buy in West Africa, especially in those early years. It was much like Carnation powdered milk, only the brands imported into Africa were whole milk powder and had a much stronger taste. All three of our daughters grew to love it; so much that they would just eat the powdered milk out of the can with a spoon. I substituted my lack of milk by really chowing down on the amazing European cheeses that were available in the grocery stores in Monrovia. We would buy an entire ball of cheese which was probably the equivalent of 15-20 pounds, grate it, bag it, and freeze it to keep it for as long as possible.

Someone gave me a copy of a West African inspired cookbook written by and for missionary wives. It was an indispensable guide for any American food preparer trying to find her way in a kitchen surrounded by strange foods and ingredients. In that cookbook were several recipes for making milkshakes using a blender, powdered milk, ice cubes, sugar, vanilla, and cocoa powder. Within six months, we had refined one of the recipes to our liking and it became an almost nightly treat. Minutes before the electricity was set to turn off, I would run the blender and we would all enjoy a cool, refreshing milkshake in the middle of the steamy jungle. Now that's adapting!

Espresso and the Gospel

While ministering in Tappi, I would at times fight the sensation of being claustrophobic. The first few months were the worst until I became more aware of the freedom and beauty of the jungle around me. Jeff stayed so busy at the airplane hangar or riding into town or flying with one of the other pilots that I do not think he understood when I would tell him how I felt. There were just times that I found myself missing the opportunity to travel somewhere. Though Jeff might not have understood, he still was sensitive to my restlessness and would take me into the little town of Tappi once a week for a little outing. One of the highlights was visiting the Lebanese women in the small downtown mercantile area of Tappi. We're talking four or five stores on a dirt road–almost like a town in the wild, wild west—without the horses and hitching posts, of course.

My journal of December 31, 1985, reads:

> *Yesterday Jeff took me to visit one of the Lebanese stores. The wife was there and she asked me to have some coffee with her. She fixed a cup for Jeff, but he knew what kind it was and graciously refused it. It was the real thick espresso coffee that is almost the texture of mud or syrup. That's definitely not Jeff's kind of coffee. But, of course, being the gourmet that I am, I loved it! Michelle said she wanted to try it, but I had finished most of it and there was only the real thick stuff in the bottom of the cup. She took a swallow and oh, you ought to have seen that face! She opened her mouth with a grimace and it looked like she had been dipping snuff!*

One cup of that strong espresso, as it is now called, was always enough to get the heart rate up and spike the body's energy level to a peak. One time, a few months later, I was enjoying the coffee so much that I accepted a second cup. By the time I arrived home, I was wired to the max and our house got an electric cleaning like I hadn't done since we had been in Africa! Anytime, after that, when I was particularly sluggish, Jeff would joke about getting me a cup of that electric magic.

I became very fond of my two Lebanese friends. At first, admittedly, visiting them in town was mainly a diversion from my house and the compound, but after a few weeks, we became friends; sharing, laughing, learning from each other, and celebrating the differences. Early in our emerging friendship, God gave me a distinct burden for them spiritually. Later, I was asked by one of those Lebanese friends to prove my belief in Christ and my faith in His salvation in a very unusual and unexpected way!

CHAPTER SIX

Courage does not always roar. Sometimes it is a quiet voice at the end of the day saying, 'I will try again tomorrow.' —Unknown

Let There Be Light

Our electricity schedule in Tappi was the one constant that everything else revolved around. Because there was no local source for electricity, our compound provided its own. We had a 20 kilowatt generator that ran six houses, the Bible school building, the clinic buildings, airplane hangar, and carpenter shop. Each missionary men took his turn turning on and switching off the generator at the set times. Each evening we had electricity from 6 p.m. to 9 p.m. In addition to the evening hours, on Saturday mornings, the generator would be turned on from 9 a.m. to 12 noon. It was mainly for work in the carpenter shop, welding, and laundry.

At night when the generator was running, one of my main jobs during those crucial three hours was to boil our drinking water for the next day. White porcelain-coated three gallon buckets were used for the task. Electric heating coils were inserted into an almost full bucket of water, and after about thirty minutes, the water would begin to boil. I then turned the timer to twenty minutes. Boiling water for twenty minutes, we had been told, would kill most bacteria and parasites, so you can be assured that I never shortchanged the boiling process. There were already enough microbes and parasites to go around!

In those early days, we had a gallon-size Catadyne filter mounted on the wall in the kitchen which was an important part of the filtering process that took out the mud and dirt sediments from the water. After the water cooled, we would run one bucket of water at a time through the Catadyne filter. It usually took two to three hours for a gallon of water to run through the filter, so we had to plan ahead to make sure we had extra drinking water on hand. The other two buckets of boiled water were usually stored in the kitchen with a lid on top of them to keep out any nocturnal creatures.

Because of the amount of people using the same generator, there were certain combinations of things that could be performed using electricity and there were combinations that would blow the generator's circuit in an instant! Two heating coils at a time would max out our house circuit breakers if used with the microwave or the iron. That would sometimes cause the station generator to overload. It was a delicate dance of watts and amperage, and I didn't understand it one bit!

Home Alone

One night, after we had been in Tappi for about six weeks, Jeff had to go back to Monrovia to buy more groceries which precipitated me being home alone for the first time in our African home. Our house jutted up against the thick bush on the south side of the compound, and during that first night of Jeff not being there, I heard creatures that I had never been aware of before. Not enjoying the complete darkness with only the distant stars to light my surroundings nor the coolness of the shadowy night, I really missed my strong brave human protector. So began one of the many lessons that God would have to teach me about not putting more confidence in my husband than I did in Him, my Heavenly Father. I argued frequently about that lesson—expounding eloquently that I was very human and needed the comfort of another "very" human being.

However, in God's persistent but loving way, He never gave up teaching me that He desired to be my total Sufficiency even in the dark, looming jungle. He reminded me that He had created the jungle and everything in it. Honestly, though, I must admit to you that it was a constant battle of my will and submission to that truth. Thinking about Michelle and me all alone in that house on the edge of the unpredictable African bush was enough to almost send my body into a sort of panic attack.

My first night in charge of balancing all the amps and watts was exhausting. I heated water for baths, boiled water for drinking and cooking, typed on my Selectric II, and used the microwave all in three tightly packed hours of electrical bliss. Michelle was in the tub and I was typing at the table when I remembered that there were a couple of things that needed to be ironed. Absentmindedly, I set up the ironing board, plugging in the iron while rounding up the few clothes that were just too wrinkled to wear as they were.

Before I could get back to the ironing board with the clothes, the entire mission compound went suddenly and ominously DARK! All I heard in the black, African night were loud gasps and the words, "OH NO!" coming from someone's mouth that sounded very much like mine. I knew deep inside that I had drastically stumbled in the amperage and wattage dance and had put the whole compound into premature darkness. To make my musings even worse, I heard yells and screams all over the compound since any sound made in the jungle blackness carried easily through our screened windows. Little kids shrieked for their mothers—as did Michelle from the bathroom, a glass broke in another house, and then the inauspicious sound of a motorcycle starting up and most assuredly heading towards our house.

Well, that put me in a huff as I recall. (*Why is it when we know we are guilty that we usually react with the most defensiveness?*) "That's right," I said as I placed a flashlight in the bathroom so Michelle would stop screaming about roaches being in the bathtub with her. "Come over to the newest missionary on the compound first! What if it wasn't me who maxed out the generator?" I muttered as I scuffled back to quickly unplug the evidence. Chick Watkins was one of the finest missionaries that I have ever known. His passion, his humor, his adventuresome spirit, and his kindness just stayed with him day after day, and I was so hoping that he was bringing his sense of humor with him that night. James Wittenberger and Chick drove up to our dining room window, staying seated on their motorcycles. Through the screen, I could have declared that I heard a chuckle. James, always the diplomat, said, "You all right in there?" "Yeah," I hesitantly said, and then foolishly asked, "What happened?"

"Well, I don't know. Probably somewhere the generator was maxed out. Can you tell us what electrical things you had going when the lights went out?" Taking a deep breath, I ran down the list of things that I knew would find me guilty. Two heating coils, the microwave (*did I forget to tell you about the piece of bread I was warming to eat with some honey*), and, oh yea, the iron, but it had only been on a few seconds, I reiterated. More chuckling as they both started up their cycles and said, "Okay, we'll talk about all this tomorrow. Just get your flashlight and be careful. We'll have it running again in a few minutes."

I can remember being totally humiliated by that encounter and was already dreading to face the other missionaries the next day. If the truth be known, most of the women (and yes, occasionally, even the men) had taken their turns at blowing fuses and putting the station into darkness. I saw it happen several times within those next three years, and I'm pretty sure I smiled in the darkness when it did. *Not me this time, folks!*

Working It All Out

Our two young workers, Paul and Mr. T, who had been with us since we arrived in Tappita, would be starting back at their respective schools in the middle of January, so deciding that there was still a need for someone to help me in the house during the day, we hired a young girl to do light housecleaning, watch Michelle outside as she played, and even cook a lunch meal every now and again.

My journal of January 10th says:

> *I have a new girl coming in the morning. She'll only be working on weekends right now. When Paul and Mr. T go back to school, if I like her, I will hire her full time. She is about 15 years old and already has a baby. That is mainly because it is customary in this country to try to show you can have children as soon as it is possible to become pregnant. I will talk to her about her salvation and see if she is willing to forfeit this way of life. I cannot hire her if she continues to sleep with men before she is married. Maybe I will be able to lead her to Christ if she is not a Christian.*

Femmeto was a sweet quiet girl who was referred to us by another missionary's worker. It was our first time hiring someone from the area that did not have a background in one of our churches. It was a big risk, we knew, and if anything, opened our eyes to the way things really were in the Liberian culture. Fornication was as common as breathing in Liberia. When a

Liberian girl or boy was old enough, the proclivity of the culture pointed to teaching that sex must be pursued as a normal part of life from that point on.

Coming to us as a young mother of only fifteen years old, it was evident that there was a long line of young men who were vying for the opportunity to prove Femmeto's childbearing abilities once again. Another reason for a young girl in the Liberian culture to give herself to a man would be so that she could acquire school supplies, uniforms, and even be established in an "elitist" position in the school itself if she could sleep with one of the male teachers. To us, as missionaries, it seemed to be a clear cut example of prostitution with a twist. Getting the unsaved Liberian young people to understand that was another story. The sexual cultural in Liberia had been that way *ever since*. Traditions were hard to fight, we were told by the Liberian Christian leaders who, too, were also burdened to see that destructive part of their culture changed.

Though I cannot remember exactly how long Femmeto worked for me, we never connected like I did with some others. I tried teaching her Biblical principles and to be a godly example, but somehow she seemed to keep her distance, my American whiteness perhaps intimidating her. I would never allow her to bring her baby to work except once when her mother could not keep the little boy for some reason. In retrospect, I do not know whether that was the right decision or not. Again, cultural collisions confused me at every turn.

One of my most vivid memories of Femmeto was the time that she showed up at work after having been sick for a couple of days. In she walked sheepishly, holding a jar containing some undefined, unpleasant gummy looking thing. Bringing the suspicious jar to show me was somewhat like showing a doctor's note to prove someone had a valid reason for missing work. In the jar was her excuse for not being at work. Worms were a fact of life in Liberia because of the food, water, and living conditions, producing a climate conducive to breeding all kinds of worms: tapeworms, whipworms, pinworms, etc... She told me her own gruesome story of the woes of worms. While she was asleep one night, she woke up suddenly coughing and gagging, feeling like she could not breath. Something was tickling the back of her throat and causing her to regurgitate severely. After an agonizing ten minutes, she finally pulled a 2 ½ FOOT tape worm from her throat. Being still a somewhat new and conscientious employee, she had saved the worm in a jar to prove why she was sick.

I know. I know. I'm sorry. That section should have begun with a warning, but I didn't have a warning! I do not recall being duly impressed by that note of an "excused absence," but it made such an impression on me–the visual in the jar–that every time I would think about the contents of that jar, I would heave and gag. For months, if I felt a slight tickle in my throat, it was a battle to fight down the panic that would overwhelm me just thinking of the possibility of a fat, bloated tape worm crawling slowly out of my throat while I slept.

Sunday Morning Blues

If you change churches in the States, it may seem strange for a while, but getting used to a church in a totally different culture was quite the challenge! On January 13, I wrote this:

> *Sunday morning Jeff preached at the Gio church. It's a big church of about 200 people and has been established for many years. Six people came forward but we don't know why because they were talking in Gio. Right in the middle of the service, a woman came into the church and walked down the aisle shaking her finger at people. She sat down in front by the altar for about five minutes and just smiled. Evidently she has done this before because no one seemed to be upset. Jeff did good to keep on concentrating. And there was an old man sitting in front of Michelle and me that kept turning around and trying to take her Bible. He would shake his finger at her and make faces. So much for teaching my daughters to act respectful in church!*

The Africans had long accepted the reality of "crazy" (the Liberian term) people and allowed for most of their erratic behavior as long as it was not harmful to others. Most "crazy" people became that way because of an extreme case of malaria or other jungle illnesses. Some others were, most likely, just born that way.

Aside from the human distractions, we saw chickens, dogs, cats, and goats meander up the aisle to get things right with their Creator as well as mother hens with their chicks, cats rubbing the pastor's leg during the sermon, or pigs rooting out the morning's offering of rice, corn, and other produce. All of that was what made going to church in West Africa an adventure. When the unusual disturbances threatened to deter us from the service, we tried to take our cues from our African Christians—and just keep worshipping!

We resigned ourselves to such things as animals visiting the altar, the mentally challenged worshipping among us in their own unconventional ways, as well as getting used to nursing mothers in church services. One of Jeff's (and any other western-oriented male visiting in West Africa) biggest challenges, while preaching in African churches, was the mothers nursing their babies while sitting on a bench in the front. There seemed to be no inclination or need to put the "spigot" away when the baby was finished. A woman's breast in the African culture was pure and simply a tool of nature. There was no sensual attraction to it by the African men. That was saved for a woman's thighs or legs, and thus one of the main reasons why the dress code in West Africa for all missionary woman (and girls) were modest skirts, no pants or shorts. It soon became evident why it was in place. We could have easily offended Liberian brothers and sisters if we had dressed as what might had been acceptable in our American culture. For the sake of the Gospel anything could be done!

Not only were the visual challenges to our American missionary preachers prevalent, but also the need to adapt to using interpreters while preaching. It was quite a balancing act to be able to concentrate, sentence by sentence, thought by thought, and then remember to stop so to give the interpreter his turn at putting the thoughts into a dialect we could not speak. Deciding how much to say before stopping for the interpretation was always an issue. Often in the back of Jeff's mind was the fear that the interpreter might not understand some of the words that he was using or that he would decide to say something completely different. However, it was evident that the churches knew who their gifted and biblically astute men were and trusted that they would interpret as closely to the missionary's meaning as possible. With twenty-six different dialects (and people groups) just in Liberia, it would have been next to impossible to learn even a few of them in order to preach without an interpreter. So, the faithful preaching interpreter became crucial to the missionary's ministries.

Always in the Back of Your Head

Malaria. It was an unfamiliar creature to those coming from the western world, something we read about, but never imagining that we would have to look deeply into its face. It stalked us quietly in the night when all the lights were out and a mosquito would zing past our ears. Holding our breath, we would pull up covers around our necks and pray that the insect which had gotten into the confines of our mosquito net would not be carrying "the fever." The odds of that was slim to none!

Malaria was so prevalent in West Africa that there were many prophylactics available. However, many Liberians could not afford to take preventive medicine, and so, when we would meet a Liberian and notice that his friendly eyes were yellowed and weak, we assumed that he had probably not escaped the snare of the probing insect. Malaria has always been a killer, and in the jungle, much more feared and respected than even AIDS.

Other life threatening diseases melded into the corners of West Africa, but the predominant disease looming throughout the towns and rain forests was malaria. At the end of our African missionary career, only Jeff and Lauren, out of our family of five, had escaped the snares of malaria. In my journal of December 27, 1985, I voiced the first of many concerns about malaria:

> *Yesterday and Thursday night I was down with a headache like I never had before! It started Thursday night right before I went to sleep and pounded all night long. I was so scared it was malaria. Whatever it was, it had me down until late Friday evening.*

Most likely, early in our missionary career, it was the prophylactic side effects that were bothering me. Or it could have been just a change in barometric pressure, food, water, or overwhelming stress taking the form of that awful headache. It was not malaria. I know that now because since that time I have truly had malaria—twice. There is a specific "feel" to malaria when it attacks the body. It is like a seizure of the bloodstream, a screaming of the joints and muscles, and nothing will remedy it for a long, long while. It zaps your energy and your coherence. It captures the very essence of life and dangles it tauntingly in front of you.

Jungle Jargon

Our very first bed in Tappita was a king-sized waterbed that Jeff worked hard in making himself. Laboring methodically and masterfully for three months, he designed a bed frame out of rich mahogany wood. Delicately draping from the ceiling above our wonderful bed was a white netting, sewn together around the edges with solid white cloth that we kept tucked into the sides of the mattress. Using a mosquito net took some getting used to, but we knew that it was the least we could do for our little family in the middle of the jungle.

We wanted to avoid interacting up close with nocturnal and not-so-nocturnal creatures that might want to share our beds. Spiders, snakes, roaches, and mice ran freely, particularly at night. We had heard the old missionary stories about waking up with snakes slithering across them! Just the thought of that was enough to send me into a tizzy, but after time, it became less rampant in my thoughts. At night, when getting up to go to the bathroom and before putting on bedroom slippers, it was always best to shine a flashlight on the shoes while giving them a good shake; sometimes the creatures of the night could hide away in the small crevices of shoes. Or so we had been told. Who was I to question that!

The night brought on a different aura and it was then that I remembered that we, as humans, were definitely in the minority in the thick, lively jungle. Sounds of tree bears, frogs, fruit bats, night birds, flying squirrels, and other unidentified creatures would taunt my imagination with their jungle jargon. I began to enjoy the sounds of the night and the cool breeze that rustled the tall trees, soaking in the fresh, clean smell of rainforest life. It mesmerized me, and after a few months, it was the sedative that gave me some of the best sleep of my life. OH, TO BOTTLE THAT!

CHAPTER SEVEN

If ye then, being evil, know how to give good gifts unto your children; how much more shall your Heavenly Father give the Holy Spirit to them that ask Him? Luke 11:13

Crossing the Ocean

In 1986, one of the only ways that we could still "cross the ocean" and visit with our families was to call them on the telephone. A few years before computers were mainstream and cell phones were available in West Africa, telephone or ham radio, and of course, snail mail were really the only ways to stay in touch. However, in Tappita, there was only one phone located in the entire town, and even then, it only worked maybe two weeks out of the whole year. Fortunate for us, there were a couple of missionaries on our compound who were ham radio operators, so it was by far the best way to communicate with our stateside family while living in Tappita.

Any time we were in Monrovia, there usually was a working telephone right at our mission compound in the business office, and it was a delight to be able to make clear contact with our parents. Limited because of the exorbitant cost, the times of communication with them, whether by radio, telephone or the written letter, were precious; and it seemed that I just never got enough of it. We grabbed hold of any possible way to shrink the distance by way of telephone, bathing ourselves in the love of our families! Talking to them was always a treat and never ceased to lift our spirits. Hearing the girls' voices must have been extra special to them, too. We had so much to tell them and wanted to hear everything that was happening with them. The thrill of getting news from home was as primitively fascinating as drinking fresh clear water from a mountain stream. Proverbs speaks of the joy of receiving news from afar and what it does to our spirits in chapter 25:25: *As cold water to a thirsty soul, so is good news from a far country.*

Food Challenge

My journal of January 25, 1986, reads:

> *Jeff told me that Randy Dodson (son of missionaries Richard and Millie Dodson) was bringing some meat he wanted us to try, but Jeff would not tell me what it was. Then as Randy brought it into the house, Jeff slipped and said that it was rabbit. Now if you're smart, you would know that there are no rabbits in the jungle of Liberia. But I wasn't that smart—not that time. So, I was happy to show them that I could certainly eat rabbit.*

I remember being so proud of myself as I ate the meat along with the two guys. Randy had done a great job preparing it into a tasty stew with vegetables. However, there was something a little funny about the way Jeff and Randy were acting as we were all eating the "rabbit." Soon, Randy could not contain himself and blurted out, "So, Kim, how do you like PORCUPINE?" He and Jeff were grinning from ear to ear by that time and eagerly watching my face. As the realization of what he had just asked me sunk in, my stomach began to do flip flops. I did not feel well at all and promptly spit out the bite that was in my mouth.

While Jeff and Randy laughed at the trick they had played on me, I just sat there and did my best to keep the already-eaten stew down in my very angry stomach. They knew that I had been adamant about not eating any strange African meats for a while, and that was their way of making me eat my words. Really, all I learned that day was to never trust Randy nor Jeff again when it came to food. Later, as my stomach was attempting to digest the little piece of porcupine stew that I had ingested, it seemed that hundreds of quills were pricking my insides. A little frustrated with myself, I remembered that I had really enjoyed the taste, and not until I knew what it was, did it start tasting funny! It was so true that our minds could definitely rule over what we were tasting.

A few months later, after I had started teaching an English class in one of the Bible school divisions, the missionary nurse, Rachel Schildroth, and I decided to have a feast for our students. They had challenged us about not wanting to eat their African

60

foods on a daily basis just as we challenged them that they did not even want to try "Kwi" (American) food. Deciding to have a feast of both African and American foods, we all determined to be open and try whatever was put before us. Trying to think of the strangest American foods possible, we put together our menu. We offered spaghetti noodles with marinara sauce, homemade pizza, fried chicken, mashed potatoes, and pickled carrots. The Africans were as excited as we were to have a party. They did love to gather, share food, stories, and have sweet fellowship. It was an art that, no doubt, had its place in an earlier America, but has fast become extinct in the pursuit of the mighty dollar and more things.

In the middle of the mission compound was an opened, screened building with only a large picnic table inside. It had been called the "croquet court" for many years, and it was there that we gathered for our food challenge with our Liberian students. That challenge, I knew, was to be a battle of my stubborn will against my unwilling stomach. Rachel and I had made a pact that we would eat any of the African foods put in front of us in order to win the challenge. Even though I cannot recall all the details about that meal, I do remember gagging through a couple of bites of anteater and cassava greens...but I did it.

The most memorable part was a student named Joe and spaghetti with marinara sauce. We had mixed the noodles and sauce together before serving it. Many Liberians up country used very little canned tomato sauce and long spaghetti noodles. Joe, an older Liberian Bible school student gasped as we served the long white noodles covered with tomato sauce. He declared that he absolutely could not eat tapeworms, especially when they had been cooked in blood. He was dead serious. We were hooting with hilarity over the look on his face and what he thought it was we were challenging them to eat. So, Rachel and I played on that and started slurping down the noodles as some of the students watched in awe.

Please Litter or Be Fined!

Because we were new missionaries and had not yet mastered the science of buying enough groceries for six weeks or more, Jeff had to make several unplanned trips to Monrovia those first few months. One particular week we were getting low on groceries when there came the need for a medical flight to the town of Phoebe. Jeff hopped on that flight as a passenger and then from Phoebe, which was located halfway between Tappeta and Monrovia, took a taxi for the three hour drive to the capital city. There were no fast food restaurants along the road, so I had packed him a lunch that morning before he left. On that trip, an African couple rode with him in the back seat of the chartered taxi, so Jeff seized the moment to witness to them as they traveled through the Liberian countryside.

During one of the few stops, the Liberian man bought a beer and was drinking it, laughing and talking to Jeff, obviously enjoying the challenging discourse about good and evil. Jeff told the man that the devil was happy that he was drinking the beer. The man got suddenly agitated and slung the bottle out the window yelling, "GET OUT OF THE CAR, DEVIL! THIS IS GOD'S MAN TALKING TO ME AND I AM GOING TO LISTEN." We always had to remember how much influence the word "devil" had on our Liberian people. It worked many times in favor of sharing the Gospel; sometimes not.

A little while later, Jeff pulled out his lunch and was eating his sandwich, cookies, and a banana. He carefully put the trash, including the banana peel, back into his brown paper bag. The whole car exploded with laughter! They mocked him for several minutes about not throwing his banana peel out the window along with the entire bag. Jeff tried to explain that in America it was called littering to throw trash out the window and that sometimes the police would force you to pay a fine if they caught you littering. With that explanation, the Africans in the car with him laughed even harder. Finally, the man in the backseat said, "Missionary, you are in Liberia, and we will fine you if you do NOT throw your bag out the window!" Jeff resisted, but eventually did throw out the banana peel. You can't imagine the clapping and revelry that went on in that car when he finally slung that peel out the window.

The best remedy for dealing with culture shock? Hit it head on by riding public transportation with the very people you are there to win for Christ. In doing that, it won't take long to become spellbound in their culture and learn that giving them an American explanation is absolutely a waste of time! We were in their country now, so we best learn to do things their way.

The Plane Truth

Our mission compound had the only airstrip with an on site airplane and helicopter in the northern part of Liberia. While the aviation capabilities on our mission station were primarily and most importantly for the expansion of the Gospel into hard-to-access bush towns, there was always the residual ministry that included medical flights and transporting expatriates such as Lebanese or missionaries with other missions. Regardless of the patient or passenger, the missionary pilots always found time to share the Gospel before or during those flights. Having the capability of flying a very sick patient to a hospital in thirty minutes or less always opened the door of evangelism in ways that would have otherwise remained closed. The pilots sometimes made cargo flights for expats who lived in the area and needed transportation of goods for their business. Making the airplane accessible to the local expat community also helped to build up the aviation fund for continuing the expansion of the Gospel to that region of Liberia.

In 1986, the standard price for our mission planes to fly from Tappeta to Monrovia was $90 (one way) and $180 (round trip). Before any trip, someone had to agree to be responsible for the cost of the flight whether that be a missionary family, an expat business man, or someone needing a medical flight. If a missionary family needed the plane, they would often check to see if a Lebanese merchant wanted to share a flight; if not, the entire $180 would be the responsibility of the person who initially asked for the flight.

During our first year of living in Tappita, the only two aircrafts in running order were the Cessna 180 tail dragger and a Hughes 300 helicopter. The airstrip was a grass strip, as I described to you earlier, measuring approximately thirteen hundred feet long. When I asked Jeff what his first impression of that strip was, he said, "Wide." I just remember thinking how very short and grassy it was. It was not a completely level strip and because of that, the planes always landed uphill (towards the hangar) and took off downhill. The Cessna had a total cargo takeoff weight (which did include the weight of the plane) of 1000 pounds. While the missionary pilots were extremely cautious and mindful of safety, there were times when the weight could not help but be slightly exceeded and during those times, the plane would almost kiss the rubber trees at the end of the runway before being lifted into the beautiful African sky! Any open sky would be beautiful when a grove of foreboding rubber trees were not giving way.

Dear Mr. Soldier: Playing With Guns Can Be Dangerous

There is story after story about the interesting people that came to our mission station seeking medical help. One sunny afternoon the pilots were working at the airplane hangar when a government-issued truck rushed quickly up to the hangar. With much commotion, two of President Doe's bodyguards jumped out of the back seat dragging a bleeding man and deposited him soundly on the concrete floor of the hangar. The driver also sailed out of the car and dashed toward the missionaries explaining that the man needed to be flown to Monrovia immediately. They had just come from President Doe's rice farm that was located about twenty miles from our mission compound.

Doe had flown back on his government-owned plane earlier that day with his other bodyguards while the rest were driving back in a truck. The roads in our area were all dirt, rutted and washed out in most places, until about ninety miles from Monrovia. For some unexplained reason, the soldiers traveled with their guns cocked, barrels up, setting between their legs. At one point, the truck hit a very pronounced bump and as the guard tried to get control of his bouncing rifle, he touched the trigger and shot himself in the chest (right below the heart). The bullet exited out his left shoulder, but he had lost a good amount of blood by the time he reached our compound.

Jeff flew with another missionary on that flight, and most likely no money was ever collected even though promises of President Doe reimbursing us for the flight were made. After the men returned, and it was obvious that the bodyguard was going to live, the laughter among the missionaries ignited. Why would anyone travel on bumpy dirt roads with a cocked and loaded rifle, barrel up? No matter, the pilots were able to give the man the Gospel. Everything we did, even outside the normal realm of evangelism, was influenced by the passion and desire to spread the Gospel; no matter how God would bring the opportunities. And if those opportunities came because of humorous situations, then we just enjoyed them!

Gladys the Chicken

If you really wanted to measure what the majority of African Christians possessed, it would be by what they gave in tithes and offerings and would generally far exceed the ten percent we are taught to give. Though hard to compare, it would be somewhat like us Americans giving ten percent of our weekly earnings, and then adding an extra twenty percent to that.

In our early days of ministry in Liberia, Jeff preached in bush villages a fair amount of the time. None of those towns had a population typically larger than five hundred people, and those villages far off the main roads were accessible only by walking paths or small two-track roads. The people in those remote villages made their living by farming, fishing, and hunting without the exchange of much currency.

The very first offerings Jeff received after preaching in the small village of Dahnpa was a white hen. Now, Jeff is a city boy from Charlotte and had not had much exposure to handling live chickens. The church people had carefully chosen the whitest hen from the village poultry population to give to the visiting preacher. Thanking the people, Jeff tried to take the chicken in his arms somewhat like you would hold a puppy, but she only started flapping her white wings in his face. The Africans laughed and showed him the way to hold her by the feet which were tied with string to keep her from making the great escape from the white man!

That would have indeed been a classic Kodak moment. White missionary walking out of a remote village with his Bible under one arm and a chicken dangling upside down in his other hand waiting to catch his ride home. How endearing is that!

Flying back to Tappita, Jeff deposited the chicken by his feet as he clocked in more air time flying the helicopter. Usually a new missionary pilot would need to fly about a year with the veteran missionary pilots as they learned the ways of the aircraft, the landmarks, and the airstrips. There were no navigational aids flying in the jungles of Liberia, so intimate knowledge of landmarks was essential. Jeff had momentarily forgotten about the chicken on the floor, so wrapped up was he in the wonders of bush flying, until the hen decided to remind him that she was there. She pecked at his feet and ankles most of the way back to Tappi.

In the quietness of our jungle home, I could always hear the drone of the incoming airplane or helicopter when it was still a couple of miles away. Unless I was teaching Bible school, was sick, or involved in some other task, I always stopped and went to the airplane hangar to watch the landing. I never tired of thanking God each and every time the aircraft landed safely.

Flying in the jungle was treacherous, dangerous, and took great skill and a sharpness of mind, so I constantly prayed for Jeff when he was flying. While I believed that Jeff was probably one of the most capable pilots that I had ever known, there were still times when the realization of what he was up against threatened to weaken my resolve in the worst kind of way.

That afternoon, Michelle and I were waiting for him at the hangar as he disembarked the helicopter. He reached back inside and tediously took out the white hen. Michelle was instantly smitten with the creature, and, as Jeff was telling me about how he had procured her, Michelle said purposefully, "HER NAME IS GLADYS." To this day, we do not know where she came up with the name Gladys, but it did seem to suit the hen. We learned quite quickly that you should never name an animal you intend to eventually eat. Jeff and I did not expect that we would keep Gladys and watch her raise baby chicks and provide us with eggs. After embracing the name that Michelle gave her, there was really nothing else to do.

Gladys was a daily reminder to our family that the Liberian Christians might be poor in material wealth, but their hearts were ample enough for them to be willing to give of what little they did possess. They gave out of hearts full of gratitude to their heavenly Father and the minister who brought them His Word. What possible excuses do we have as Americans?

Lessons From the Life of a Hen

Gladys had not been on the mission compound two days when the kingpin rooster visited our yard early one morning. As proof of that visit, within six weeks, there were twelve baby chicks trailing close behind Gladys. When the eggs hatched, we knew about it. I had never in my life heard such clucking and squawking! Michelle, having always had a nose for the out-of-the-ordinary, found the two eggs that did not hatch. Before I could explain that it was probably not a good idea to mess with them, she decided that Gladys needed her help. She pounded one of them on the ground until a disgusting black ooze started seeping out of it. The smell ejecting from the cracked egg was enough to bring me to my knees. I was about eight weeks pregnant with Stefanie, and for the rest of the day nothing could make me forget that smell and the sight of the deformed, rotting chick. I found myself holding my stomach as if an omen would affect my human baby "chick." Surely I was not becoming superstitious, was I?

I knew we were in trouble when Michelle did not even flinch, but wanted to crack open the other egg to see what she could find. She has always had a stomach of steel and a huge interest in biology at its most bizarre. If someone was killing a chicken or goat nearby, there you would find my beautiful, elegant looking brown-eyed little girl watching with keen analysis and interest. She was always so generous with her descriptions of what she had just seen even when I had not asked for details! How could a three year explain the violent wringing of a chicken's neck in such exhilarated details?

In the ensuing days, we enjoyed watching Gladys teach her chicks how to peck the ground for food, also training them to become accustomed to the wiles of the infamous chicken hawk. We learned many things from just watching and observing how Gladys handled the challenges of her life. I wrote:

She's one smart hen. If she senses a chicken hawk in the area, she hides her chicks in the shrubbery. If I come outside while she's hollering, she'll take me straight to her biddies. She has learned to trust us.

Lesson in that? Sometimes things are just too big for us to handle on our own. We need God's wisdom and His strength. Gladys knew that she was probably not a match for the speed and size of the chicken hawk, especially when her chicks were extremely small and vulnerable. So, she cried out for help. How often do we try to do things on our own until we have exhausted all our resources, all our energies?

Another lesson? I don't know how it happened, but Gladys started bringing her chicks to our back door in the mornings and in the late afternoon. She was begging for rice to help feed her growing brood, and if we didn't come as quickly as she thought was fair, she would peck the door and even parts of the screen until we did. Sometimes Michelle would be the one to feed Gladys and her little ones, and so it happened that one afternoon, she left the door opened as she was throwing uncooked rice to the hungry little family. Gladys and a couple of her braver chicks decided they would come in for a "look-see." It took a few frantic minutes to get her and the chicks out of the house and then even longer to sweep up the white feathers that had been dismantled in the chase.

That story of Gladys pecking at the back door reminded me of Luke 11 where the friend had a guest show up unexpectedly at his house one night, and he did not have the provisions to take care of them. Perhaps Gladys had heard that story while she was living in Dahnpa because she sure didn't have a problem asking for help. God wants us to be the same with Him. He desires that we remember that we can go to Him for whatever is needed in our lives.

CHAPTER EIGHT

Faith is believing in things when common sense tells you not to.—G. Seaton

Musings From a Young Missionary

Struggling against the cozy American axiom that presumed women needed to stay home, "barefoot and pregnant," having her husband a warm dinner on the table by 5:00 p.m., I found it hard to separate my desire to make a difference in my little family with the growing discontentment of my role in the home being my sole contribution to the world. Jeff's missionary career already seemed so romantic, so exciting, dynamic and stirring. It was hard not to compare my seemingly smaller role at home with his exciting odysseys into the mysterious African jungle to preach the Gospel and his piloting responsibilities that saw him flying a sick person to receive medical help.

I seemed to have forgotten one thing. God knew me then as He knows me now. He created me, so it remains undisputed that He was not surprised with the things with which I struggled. Motherhood was an extremely important part of the woman that I had become. Don't misunderstand me: I loved being Michelle's mother, being the person she looked up to, and being the one she depended on for her daily nurturing. When you really put it in perspective, there is an undeniable power in motherhood. Those little lives that are released from the gestational care of our bodies are moldable, teachable, trainable, and most importantly, precious souls in need of Christ. Their immortal souls are as equally as important to God as were the thousands of Africans living in the remote bush towns.

It took God a little while to get that through my thick skull, but when it stuck, it really stuck. Today I am so thankful that God helped me place epic importance to motherhood while still giving me the opportunity to be a missionary woman in other ways, too!

Missionaries could be perceived as an elite group, eccentric and maybe a bit singular in our thinking by those who do not understand us. When I was a little girl, my parents would invite missionaries to stay with us or have a meal. I remember how intrigued I was by their stories, by their smiles, by their sheer presence. There was almost something magical about the word *missionary.* Their commitment to do something unusual and out of the ordinary, for me, put them on a much higher plane than others. Then God called me to be one and I'll admit that I was a little bummed to think how I was going to weaken the strain. I knew who I was and who I was not. Surely God had made a mistake by thinking that I belonged in that seemingly unparalleled group? I struggled with that presupposition for quite some time.

One of the most important things that I learned was that most missionaries do not arrive on the mission field spiritually mature and certain of every step they should take. Just as with any Christian, God grows us–DAILY–as we allow Him more control over our lives. One day at a time. When we first came to Liberia, I was excited to rub shoulders and learn from the "true" missionaries, yet a little anxious that they might be offended when they found out I was not yet one of them in spiritual depth.

Surprisingly, what I discovered after working elbow-to-elbow with them for a couple of months was that they were just like me! Though extremely brave and passionate servants of Christ, they, too, had their spiritual struggles. I think when that truth is amply embraced by missionary partners in American churches, it could make a difference in how they react to and relate to missionaries visiting their churches. We get tired, we get grumpy, we get hungry, we get overwhelmed, we get excited, we love deeply. Treat us like you do your closest friends. Accept us as one of your own. Get to know our hearts. You'll find many similarities.

True, the veteran missionaries knew more about the Liberian culture, but relieving my spirit tremendously was the realization that they were human beings who were in love with Jesus and His call—just as I was! There were times that we fought to have our own way in a matter, but when all was said and done, there was a definite desire to bow to the will of the One who called us all to minister there in Liberia. I was thankful that they accepted me, embraced me, and respected me as one of their own as quickly as they did.

The Unexpected

All that was to preface how incredible it was when God handed me a totally unexpected ministry within the first two months of being on the mission field. On our station were two buildings reserved for medical outreach: an OB delivery clinic and one used as the medical dispensary. If the aviation ministry was our most effective tool in taking the Gospel into the most remote areas of northern Liberia, our medical ministry was by far the most potent way to expedite the Gospel by drawing people onto our mission compound.

On Tuesdays alone, between fifty and a hundred pregnant women would walk out of the African bush to receive, appreciably, the best medical care available in those parts. A large majority of the women were of the Mandingo tribe–predominately Muslim. In a missions outreach, would it not seem like the perfect opportunity to preach the Gospel to those who would be very unlikely to darken the door of a Baptist church? That is exactly what our missionary nurse organized for those Tuesday morning "pregnant women" clinics. It was a sight to see! The terrace area in front of the dispensary would be teeming with pregnant women and their children as the Gospel was proclaimed in English and then in the Mandingo dialect. Any woman and child who came, even if it was only one time, heard the Gospel and heard it plainly.

Our missionary nurse, Rachel Schildroth, and I became instant friends. She, like me, was outspoken and strong-willed, and taught me so much about the Liberian culture while laughing with me, never at me. I always knew where I stood with Rachel and I loved that. She was patient with me, but not accommodating, seeming to understand that particular part of my nature that wanted to be in the middle of whatever exciting was happening. Out of that knowledge, I believe, came her unexpected request to me just eight weeks into our missionary tenure.

There was a young lady in labor at our OB clinic. She was becoming increasingly hysterical, refusing help to get through a difficult part of her labor. Rachel, being a single woman, and never having had a baby, had already picked my brain about why women in labor acted like they did. She was professional and sympathetic,

71

but there were some things that eluded her—the unpredictable and passionate ways a woman births a child being one of them. That particular Tuesday, the number of pregnant women who had come for treatment was staggering, and on top of that, she had a frenzied woman in labor which was taking her time and energy away from seeing all the women who had come for prenatal care. So, she broke away from the bedlam long enough to come to my house and ask if I would please come and do something with that poor laboring girl. Though I was excited to be asked to help her, I was also nervous about doing what was expected of me. Rachel shooed me into the labor room, introduced me to the woman in labor, and then just as quickly she exited, giving me brief instructions to send word when I thought the woman was close to delivery.

Those instructions completely baffled me. Having had a baby did not necessarily qualify one to know when another woman is ready to have her baby. But, I went to work, swimming through the uncertainties and learning to live by the instincts that God had placed in me. The woman was beside herself thrashing, hollering, rolling from side to side, and practically hyperventilating through each contraction.

While I was pregnant with Michelle, I had taken a Lamaze class which seemed to me, a wonderful and helpful way to breathe your body into submission during those hard contractions. Holding the laboring woman's face firmly as I saw a contraction building in her belly and breathing with a staccato rhythm, I attempted to find the pulse of the woman's labor and do what I could to help her rise above the contractions. I spoke loudly, almost climbing on the bed with her to keep her from thrashing about. After what seemed like a very long time, she began focusing on what I was saying— more out of a desire to survive the ordeal than anything else, and so I continued to breathe with her through every contraction. I would keep my hand on her belly so that I could feel when the next contraction was beginning and then attempt to gain her full attention before the contraction heightened to its peak intensity. I was a Doula in the making and loving it!

Even though I had the woman's response to her labor somewhat under control, there was still an edge of chaotic tension that clung to her tired body and though I doubted if I would know when it was the actual time for the baby to be born, God did help me perceive it. I sent someone to call Rachel as I tried preparing the young woman for the next phase of labor. A few minutes later, I felt so proud and relieved as that tired mama delivered a four pound baby boy. Incubators? None! Even though I knew that out there many preemies died soon after being born, that particular little boy lived. He was extremely small and fragile, but if that baby boy had as much passion as his mother did in birthing him, he would survive, I had no doubt.

After that day, I was hooked. I begged Rachel to call on me anytime that I could help with a delivery. Just watching the African women deliver new life in a simple, no frills room in the OB clinic helped me gain a new appreciation for God and His amazing design called Life. As Americans, we only know babies being born in sterile, medically-infused rooms with high-tech machines at our fingertips. But, as I was reminded that day, for thousands of years, babies had been brought into this world in quiet, simple rooms with no bleeping machines, or perhaps on grassy areas under trees, or in raw leather tents in remote areas of the world....or yes, even on a bed of hay while the animals watched reverently. At least in my mind, I would like to think that the cows didn't moo, the goats didn't baa, and the chickens didn't cluck while Mary was going through her birthing period.

My perception of God's integral role in life had changed forever. It was not the machines, the tubes, the medicines, nor was it the highly trained doctors that really made the difference in this thing called *Life*. God centrally, fundamentally, and singularly holds the breath of every life. In America, in Liberia, in every place.

Burping in the Commode

Soon after my new found passion for assisting laboring mothers, my own struggles began with the little one that was growing inside my belly. (In Liberia, when you were known to be pregnant, it was referred to as "having belly.") As we left for Liberia in December of 1985, we had already decided that we were ready to have another child. It wasn't enough that we were leaving for the mission field right before Christmas, that we would experience full-blown culture shock, and would also need to acclimatize our bodies into a new way of life; we just knew that we were ready to have another baby. We had been in Liberia a mere two months when I *got belly*.

Thinking back now, I wonder what kind of crazy woman I was to pile all that emotional and physical stress on my body while we were still assimilating all the different things in that unfamiliar country. Living in the middle of the jungle of West Africa was not similar to anything either of us had ever done before, and then I wanted to add pregnancy to that mix? The leading of the Holy Spirit or insanity? There were times when I would have assumed the latter.

By the middle of February, the effects of my second pregnancy hit me with a vengeance. There was no ignoring the reality of it. I was, as they say, "sick as a dog," and nothing to do about it. If I lay completely still on the couch during the day, I could somewhat pretend that I felt normal, but if I had to get up to tend to my two-year old or help out with the many other things that needed to be done on a daily basis, what I had eaten would expel itself from my body quickly and certainly.

Jeff was and is the best husband any woman could ever have. He was a great pilot, a wonderful teacher, my favorite preacher, and a loving, hilariously fun person to live with. Lest you think he was perfect, I will reveal to you one of his biggest flaws back then. His cooking knowledge was limited. That had never been an issue in the five years we had been married, but in the middle of the dense African jungle with our mothers' cooking and fast food restaurants thousands of miles away, it was quite a hurdle for our family.

When I was so green around the gills with morning sickness, my Liberian friend Mary would bring me nourishing food that she said helped her when she was pregnant. Some of them did not set as well on my finicky and pregnant American stomach, but her thought and care for me was priceless! On the home front, omelets became my best friend for those few weeks, and Jeff became quite adept in preparing them. Out of his great love for me and an innate sense of responsibility, he did his very best. He and Michelle became very handy in the kitchen as they boiled hotdogs, opened cans of green beans and corn, and even attempted to bake a microwave chocolate cake. He was a trooper as I lay on the couch with a metal bucket beside me. Michelle became completely clinical and professional even at her young age. I dropped twenty-six pounds within about a six week time span. I tried Phenergan and any other medicines that promised to help the nausea. We even discussed sending me back to the States for a few weeks, thinking that might help since Rachel our nurse and some of the other missionaries were concerned about the baby and how it was developing. I grew weaker and weaker, and was aware that I was sucking much of Jeff's energy on a daily basis. True, he was living out his vows to me in an amazing way, but I felt so guilty and helpless.

Here's the rub. It is so hard to know what to do when missionaries on a foreign field face medical dilemmas. I want to be quick to tell you that every case is personalized and should be dealt with as such. God does not work in our hearts and lives and bodies in exactly the same way as He does in someone else's. My journal during that time reads:

> When we mentioned that I might fly home to the States for a few weeks, we got all kinds of advice. "YES, IT'S BEST YOU GO." "NO, YOU WOULD BE DEFEATING EVERYTHING." "MAYBE YOU ARE JUST HOMESICK AND LETTING YOUR EMOTIONS RUN AWAY WITH YOU." "THAT WOULD BE VERY EXPENSIVE AND YOU NEED TO THINK ABOUT WHAT YOUR CHURCHES WOULD THINK."

We learned posthaste as new missionaries that though there is always wisdom in the counsel of many, when it came right down to it, we had to personally seek wisdom from the Lord. As badly as I wanted my mom's chicken soup or her sweet mother hugs, we felt that it was not those things that God wanted for me then. He wanted me to know Him to be enough. Sufficient for the day... though I was trying to allow Him to be my All in All, don't be fooled into thinking that I learned all the heavy spiritual lessons that easily. It was very confusing and emotionally draining, but it was also a time that God was drawing both Jeff and me to Himself, willing us to see Him clearly and soundly as the *Wonderful*

Counselor, Bread of Life, and *Great Physician.* That He is who He says He is and a Keeper of His promises.

So, instead of buying a ticket back to the States, we decided to take a few days and fly down to Monrovia for a change of scenery and an expanded food menu for me. As we ate at a restaurant that first evening, I was able to keep the food down for the first time in a long time. Per the suggestion of missionary friends in Monrovia, we made an appointment to see a doctor at a local hospital. The doctor took blood and urine samples, prodded and probed, and asked many questions. We revisited the doctor at the hospital that next day for the results from all the tests. He walked into the conference room with a "NOW, NOW, NOW" look on his face and a paper sack of medicines in his hand.

Nothing could have ever prepared us for the next words he spoke. He told me that I did have a type of tropical fungus which could be treated easily enough; however, the other disease that he said he found was a little more complicated to treat since I was pregnant. As our eyebrows lifted with suspense, he told us that I had gonorrhea. Before we could utter any sound at all, he began explaining that it was really nothing to be ashamed of, that he sees it all the time, and that it was as treatable in the man (looking at Jeff) as it was in the woman (looking at me).

I could not ignore the fact that the whole time the doctor was talking, Jeff was not looking at him, but at me. Those beautiful brown eyes that I love were looking at me in a perplexed and soulful way. I swallowed hard, held my hand up to quiet the doctor's medical spiel and spoke emphatically, "THAT IS IMPOSSIBLE, SIR." To be brief, we walked out of the hospital without the paper bag of meds with the doctor yelling his displeasure at our backs. I cried like a baby as the shame of the event hit me.

Timidly, we told other missionary friends about what the doctor had told us. They laughed and were not surprised that the doctor at that government clinic would tell us that. Wisely, they recommended we visit the hospital at the ELWA compound and see one of the missionary doctors. We did that and were quickly told that I did have a tropical fungus, but definitely did not have gonorrhea. Thankful and relieved, we enjoyed the rest of our stay in Monrovia though I continued to fight severe nausea for a couple more weeks.

One afternoon Jeff had gone into town to pick up some supplies and I was left in the capable hands of nurse Michelle. After a great lunch, I regrettably could not hold it down, so I ran to the bathroom. Michelle got a wash cloth, wet it, and wiped my face (as she had seen her daddy do many times). When Jeff walked in the door a few minutes later, I heard Michelle running and saying, "Aw, daddy! Mommy burped in the commode again!" There's no better way to explain those first few weeks of my pregnancy with Stefanie than that!

Swimming the Ocean Blue For You

Looking back, I know that we really had no clue as to what our commitment to be missionaries in an African country really did to our parents. While both sets of parents are Christians and while they were supportive of our call to missionary service, it certainly could not have dispelled all the fears and uncertainties that they experienced. I have been a parent for twenty-seven years and now know that parenthood brings great joys along with a longing to do whatever we can for our children at any age.

While living in Liberia, I was never one to hold things back in my letters that we sent to our parents, but in retrospect, I am wondering if I should have been more sensitive. When I was pregnant with Stefanie and so sick for those first few months, I remember my parents writing me a letter expressing their feelings about not being able to be near me to help. They wrote, "*We would swim the ocean to get to you and help you if we thought that's what we needed to do.*" How profound and loving were those words of my parents. Written at a time when I was sick, lonely, overwhelmed, and in need of that assurance; it was just good to know that is how they felt.

CHAPTER NINE

Call unto me, and I will answer thee, and show thee great and mighty things, which thou knowest not. Jeremiah 33:3

Sweet Revenge of a Mother Hen

Today Gladys got her revenge on the chicken hawk. He must have bravely swooped down in an attempt to snatch a baby chick. But Gladys was waiting for him! She jumped right on top of him! For at least three or four minutes, she held him down pecking. She drew blood–we saw that–but then he got away. Despite his strength and because of Gladys' fearless protection of her little ones, he flew away without a baby chick. She was clearly an amazing hen as she dauntlessly protected her brood even at possible peril to her-self. I learned so much by watching her as she nurtured, nudged, and taught her proteges. No matter what age our children are, it is extremely important that we be vigilant in prayer for them, so much so that our prayers will draw "BLOOD" from the enemy as he attempts to attack the ones so dear to us! Being vigilant and bold in our prayer life is the key! Thanks, again, Gladys, for another lesson to ponder.

To the Uttermost Parts of the Jungle

We hired a teenage boy whom I will call Mr. T, and from the start, he helped so much with keeping the yard up, building the fire that was used to constantly heat water on our outdoor stove, and hanging our mounds of clothes out to dry. He came from a small town of Ziah which was located about twelve miles from Tappeta and was always an invaluable resource for explaining culture anomalies. I am certain that we amused him many times with our questions and obvious ignorance on so many things Liberian.

Most missionary families on the compound owned at least one motorcycle because of the convenience of driving on the small, busy dirt roads and for getting around the mission compound quickly. For the first few months, Jeff's Suzuki 185 was our only means of transportation. One day, Mr. T's father, who was a pastor in Ziah, called for some of the missionaries to come for an evangelism meeting. Because the trip to Ziah was Jeff's first trip deep into the African bush on his motorcycle, he and three other men decided to travel together on two motorcycles. When they came to a bridge, which simply meant that there were a few wooden slats laid over a small body of water, they tediously pushed their cycles across the slats. They drove past driver ants and saw a nine-inch scorpion waving to them with his ominous pinchers. Traveling in Liberia was never your typical "Sunday afternoon drive."

Upon arriving in Ziah, the pastor introduced them to a young man who had walked from a village about five miles away. The town chief in that smaller village, having heard there were going to be missionaries in the area, desired that one of them would come and preach to his people, citing that it had been several years since someone had taught any Bible in his village. Jeff was very willing to leave the other three missionaries in Ziah and go; so climbing back on the motorcycle, he and the young man hurtled through the jungle to the waiting village.

When they reached the small remote settlement, the town chief and some of the other officials of the town welcomed him warmly and thanked him for coming. Before long, they had gathered the townspeople and Jeff stood in an open area in the middle of the town because there was no building large enough to hold everyone. Preaching for almost an hour in the blazing sun to spiritually hungry people, four souls came forward to receive Christ at the invitation. Was that the plan those four missionary men had when they left Tappita earlier that morning? No, but it was God's plan from the beginning of time. Someone in that remote village accessible only by a small two-track road had a desire to know Him—and He is always faithful to make Himself known! How do we react to changes that come to our daily agendas? Could God be giving us the opportunity to make a difference in His kingdom in a way in which we had not planned?

The Brown-eyed Princess and the Driver Ants

Once upon a time there was a very cute, but stubborn and curious little girl who had to learn about driver ants the hard way. Difficult to explain was the fierce and deadly power that a drove of driver ants held as they relentlessly moved from place to place. If you've watched the workings of ants at all, you know that they are always on a mission, always busy going somewhere, hauling something, doing something.

Driver ants are no different; they are only larger and somewhat more aggressive in their plans. There was a queen who was vehemently protected by the guards; there were scouts which were in charge of hunting prey, and there were the doctor ants who administered anesthesia to the prey: some poor unfortunate animal like a snake, frog, turtle, ground hog, or anything that could not break free from their corporate grip.

While in Liberia, we heard horror stories of sleeping babies left alone in huts who were killed by hoards of driver ants during the night. There was also the story about the missionary who had a monkey in a cage who came out one morning to discover that his monkey had been completely eaten by the ants. They had left only the skeleton.

After we had been in Liberia for about four months, Michelle had her first experience with driver ants. She was playing with some of the other missionary kids one day when they spotted a huge column of driver ants passing through the edge of the yard. Her young friends extolled the woes of the ants to Michelle, telling her to stay away from them. To most children, that would have been enough, but not for my Michelle. Against all advice, she had to see for herself if the bite was really that bad.

My missionary friend Beth saw Michelle from her kitchen window as she purposefully stepped into the path of the ants. As Beth hurried outside to stop Michelle, she knew that it was too late. My little girl turned into a banshee, shrieking and thrashing about as the ants took vengeance on her stubborn little body. Beth brought my traumatized girl to me wrapped only in a towel, having stripped all her clothes off to help remove the ants from her body, but when we put Michelle in a bath of cool water, ants galore floated out of her ears and hair to rest on the top of the water. I poured baking soda into the water and tried to calm her down. After that very dramatic run in with driver ants, I do not recall having to worry about her purposefully going near them again. Experience, one of the best teachers!

Walking Barometer and Rainy Days

It did not take long while living in the jungle of West Africa to realize that the weather was very different from what we experienced in America. Rainy and dry were the two distinct seasons, so from October to April, we would experience very little rain, while April to October would see the rains crank up drastically. By July and August, we experienced more rain than dry. It didn't take long for it to dawn on me that Liberian's heaviest rainy time corresponded perfectly with North American hurricane season. Off the West African coast form the beginning of many of the hurricanes that visit North American territory. Because we had no access to radar or local television where we lived, those violent rainy season storms literally seemed to come out of nowhere. We have watched as trees were twisted from their roots and were amazed to see that just one storm could dump as much as three inches of rain in a matter of moments.

After a few weeks of experiencing the beginning of our first rainy season, Jeff and I made an observation about my sinuses. They were an accurate weather barometer. Approximately forty-eight hours before a big low pressure would dump its havoc in our area, I would be hit with extreme sinus pain until we heard the rain moving towards us through the thick foliage of the jungle. I became known to some as the "walking barometer." Even today here in the States, if there is an extreme drop in barometric pressure, my sinuses will tell me.

Those rainy days brought a refreshing, cool scent to the air that is hard to describe. After months of dusty, dry, hot days, we learned to relish in the rains–until we had experienced them daily for a month or two. Then it got a little old because even when it was not raining, the humidity in the air could be cut with a knife. Clothes could take up to three or four days to dry; and even then, that was only "rainy season" dry (which meant *wet to the touch*). In those early years, with no dryer in which to place the slightly damp, pungent smelling clothes, we had to learn to wear them as they were.

Our clothes were not the only thing that took a "rainy season" beating there in Liberia. Salt inside our shakers became wet mounds of white and no amount of rice or anything else helped. We learned to put away the shakers and start putting a small dish of salt on the table from which we could pinch out the amount needed. Because we only had screens in our windows, everything, literally everything, would become soggy and perpetually damp during the rainy seasons. The couch cushions, our bath towels, our bed sheets, and paper (of any kind) would sop up the humidity. In a cruel play of opposites, we dealt with the covering of wet on everything during rainy season just as we dealt with the constant film of dust that found entrance into our house through our screen windows during dry season.

A Cup of Cold Water and a Loaf of Bread

The first three years of living in Liberia stretched our commitment to love people as Christ loved them. The demands that never ceased, the demands that made no sense, the demands that were not truthful, the demands that were bigger than our coffers. There were times when it all became too much. About four months into our first term, a man came and asked for "Teacher Jeff." When Jeff stepped out on the piazza, the man said, "Teacher, I was told to come to you and you will give me bread to eat." Jeff asked who had told him that, and the man replied, "GOD DID."

In our early ministry years, those kind of meetings were encouraging, entertaining, and challenging. Even though it is not recorded in my journal, I do believe that we gave the man bread and a cup of cold water while Jeff did his best to introduce him to the Bread of Life. In my memory, we distributed many loaves of bread to those who came by our house asking questions and seeking monetary relief.

One day, about a week after that first man came to our door asking for bread, we found out that someone was selling clean kerosene from Ivory Coast. If you remember, we used kerosene not only for lanterns, but also for both our small freezer and refrigerator. Most of the kerosene we would buy locally was dirty which meant it was not processed well, and if that was the case, it would burn rough—lots of smoke and smell in the house! So, the possibility of clean kerosene made us happy. The man who brought the kerosene was of the Mandingo tribe (generally out of Guinea and Mali and predominantly Muslim). Jeff began witnessing to him as he was unloading the barrels of kerosene. The man suddenly stopped and turned to Jeff saying, "I only came to deliver kerosene to make money. I do not want to talk Bible," to which Jeff replied, "You may think that you are mainly here for the money, but I believe you are here because God said it is your chance to hear about His Son, Jesus Christ, and to know the only true Savior who rose from the dead." The man listened, but did not say anything else.

Clothes, food, water, fruit from our trees: whoever came, young and old, and no matter for what they asked, we tried to give them the Gospel. Every opportunity. Every person. It might have been the only chance that they would have to hear about God's salvation. It was not our responsibility to worry about how they felt or acted or what they did when we presented the Gospel. It was just required of us to tell them in a way that would meet them where they were in life and always done with love, of course!

Something Doesn't Smell Right

One day I drank a glass of cool water from the refrigerator and thought, *Something doesn't taste right*, as I clicked my tongue to the roof of my mouth. A far fetched taste of **rotten** is what my brain told me. Later that night, while pouring water into metal buckets for the boiling process, I got a faint, but distinct whiff of **rotten**. I asked Jeff to come and smell. Nothing. The next day the pungent smell was becoming more prevalent. I handed Jeff another cup of water, insisting that he concentrate on really tasting the water. He gave me a look that said, I WILL APPEASE YOU, MY DEAR, BUT WATER DOESN'T HAVE A TASTE.

Still, I was relentless for three days as the taste and odor became fetid. Jeff remained emphatic that nothing was rotten in the water. By the fifth day, when I had resorted to drinking only Coke or

Sprite because I could no longer endure the taste of the water, two other people brought complaints about the water tasting a little funny.

You know the look a wife can give a husband when she is vindicated or proven right about something? That is exactly the look that Jeff got from me. Determined to solve the mystery of the water phantom, he and two of the other men headed towards our well. I did not go with them, because I knew they were going to find something and certainly did not want to see what we had been drinking.

Sure enough, when the cap from the well was removed, the smell hit them between their nostrils! As if that was not enough evidence, floating on top of the water was a decaying possum. Obvious that it had been dead for a while, they worked to drag the bloated body from the water and then poured an insane amount of Clorox into the well. Whether that did any good or not, it certainly made us all feel better. Mollified that they found something meant that my imagination was not "gone wild," but the fact that an actual decomposing possum had been floating in the midst of our drinking water caused digestive issues of epic proportion!

Chickens Can Talk?

Mr. T once told us that chickens could talk. That is exactly what he said as he pointed towards the piazza of our house where Gladys our white hen was clucking vehemently and loudly about something. Taking a long stick and moving stealthily towards the bushes in front of our house, Mr. T seemed to know exactly what he was looking for. Sure enough, there was a small black snake hidden deeply in the shrubs, and without a warning, it immediately took a brusque whack on the head from Mr. T's stick. Gladys looked at the African young man with her beady eyes as he smiled at her. It was obvious that they were communicating, but I had the feeling I was missing it.

Without hesitation, Gladys calmly led her chicks back into the shrubbery to stay cool during the heat of the day. Mr. T walked away saying something to the effect that chickens know how to tell you when there is danger if we would listen. I stood there looking

85

at the chicken and then back at Mr. T as he rounded the corner of the house. Feeling oddly out of touch, but charmed by what I had just seen, I went back inside the house determined to hone my own skills of understanding when a chicken was talking. In retrospect, I don't think that aspiration ever happened!

Within a few weeks, those baby chicks were large enough for Gladys to leave them on their own. The extremely interactive, loving mother became those teenage chickens' worse nightmare. Anytime they would follow her to a food source, she would spread her white feathers, daunt a "you're gonna die if you come any closer" look, and sprint towards them. It did not take the young ones but a few days to understand that they had literally and physically been kicked out of the nest! I've thought of that story a few times when raising my three teenage daughters and even practiced the "beady eye" look, which actually looks more like arched eyebrows on me.

Seeing how fast those young chickens were growing, I overheard Jeff and Mr. T talking about what nice fryers or soup meat they would make in a couple of weeks. Jeff was instructing Mr. T to kill them a couple at a time and put them in the freezer for future use. My stomach started churning as I looked one of the larger teenage hens in the eyes and then panned down to her wings (which is my favorite part of the chicken to eat). "I CAN'T DO IT. I KNOW I CAN'T DO IT," I told the young hen as if it would change her plight. It had always been extremely difficult for me to eat something to which I had grown even a little attached.

Growing Disciples

Sekou grew up in the country of Guinea which bordered Liberia to the Northwest, but then as a teenager moved to Liberia where he contracted a severe form of malaria (cerebral malaria) that could acutely damage small parts of the brain. Thankfully, that did not prevent him from accepting Christ as His Savior, and within a year, he found his way to us in Tappeta. He wanted to attend Bible school and then take the Gospel back to his home country of Guinea.

Because of my major in English, the missionary men in charge of the Mid-Liberia Baptist Institute were glad to hand over the reins of the English department to me. In order to understand where the Liberian students were in their English abilities, I gave placement tests to every student applying to study in our Bible Institute (high school graduates only) or our Central Bible School (for those who never completed high school, but still desired to become proficient in God's Word). There was also a night Bible school, mainly for the wives of the day students. The illiteracy rate always seemed higher for the Liberian female population, due in part to the hardships of continuing their education after having children.

After giving Sekou an English placement test, it was clear that he was not ready for any of the levels of Bible training. He did not read a word of English and seemed to have a very hard time comprehending the things that I would read to him. After prayer and consulting with the other missionary teachers, I felt led to personally teach Sekou to read. Three afternoons per week we met on my porch for a couple of hours to work on his reading. Because of his enthusiastic commitment to learning, we also allowed him to audit the Central Bible School classes in the mornings. You would have thought that we had given him a million dollars; he was so excited to study God's Word! For him to learn to read was our main agenda in those afternoon sessions, but it was also evident that we needed to work on his comprehension skills. Despite it all, I could see his love for the Word and for the Savior that had saved him from a life of sin!

Out of a willing and hungry heart, God gave Sekou a divine understanding of His Word when I would read it to him. For over a year I taught him, and I must admit to you that there were days when I would literally go inside my house after a session with him and cry. Some of that crying was out of compassion and concern for his inability to recognize words, but the majority of my tears were for myself. I became so discouraged that I wanted to give up. Still, there was something in the way he held his Bible, talked about the spiritual need of his people and begged me to keep teaching him.

While teaching an English class in the Central Bible School I allowed Sekou to participate in the storytelling time. Instructing the Liberian students to become effective storytellers was one of the ways I trained them to speak well in front of people. They naturally loved to tell stories, so instead of intimidating them with difficult topics to speak on, I encouraged them to use their Liberian parables and stories from the Bible for that particular assignment. Sekou and I had worked on a particularly simple Bible story for his presentation; but when it was time to give it, he got many of the facts wrong and stammered and stuttered through the story. Unfortunately, that prompted some of the students to laugh at him. I stood up for him that day, insisting that the students apologize to him, and promised Sekou that we would not stop until he was able to read on his own.

Despite all that, it was still the single most challenging part of ministry during our first term. In 2002, during our last year of ministry in West Africa, Sekou showed up at our house in Ivory Coast. God was so gracious to allow us to see part of His master plan with Sekou.

CHAPTER TEN

Mama always said life was like a box a chocolates, never know what you're gonna get. —Forrest Gump

The Best Part

Jeff often traveled without me for various reasons, mainly because we had very small children and there was always more to pack when traveling with them. He would go on evangelistic trips with Bible school students, travel by airplane or helicopter to remote towns for special meetings, and often would be invited to preach revivals in some towns that did not have an established church.

There are, no doubt, many differing opinions about rearing children among the culture to which you are ministering, so I am not here to make a point for any particular sentiment. While I never thought that I was overly protective of my girls, I probably was a little more emphatic about their sleeping arrangements than of other things. Admittedly, when I look back, I wonder if I did the right things by the girls. Should we, as a family, have traveled together to those villages more often? The point is moot for me now, but I do firmly believe that it should be left to the discretion of each family unit.

When we did travel to the Liberian villages to minister as a family, one of the ways the villagers had to show their apprecia-tion was to cook for us and we learned to be grateful for their open hearts on our behalf. Even when Jeff traveled alone, he was treated as an honored guest. In most places, that meant that he was served the very best food they had: goat kidney or the intestine served over rice. As indigestible as that may sound, it was indeed supposed to be an honor to be offered the kidney or intestines of a goat in the soup. Jeff first ate it at a pastor's conference that he was attending during our first year in Liberia. Not only was the kidney hard for him to eat, but the soup was also laced with hot pepper that had him coughing and sweating profusely. Amazingly, God gave Jeff much grace to eat foods that seemed to us Americans as unappetizing. "Where He leads me I will follow; what He feeds me I will swallow." That little cute jingle might give the impression that all missionaries are fine with eating whatever is offered, but simply put, it was not always true—at least not for me.

We have seen a little bit of everything served up on top of delicious African country rice: charbroiled monkey's hand, anteater, deer, snake, and smoked fish. Some tastes are acquired, some are just impossible. Though I am a strong and adventurous woman, eating strange and unfamiliar foods was one of the things that I felt I could not do.

Crying On Purpose

"SAVING FACE" was a term that we learned early on while living in Liberia. The average Liberian, not having much at all materially, guarded his name and reputation profusely. He would do almost anything to maintain a high caliber character. That very fact was noted one day with an incident that happened at our airplane hangar. The hangar was centrally located on the mission compound with a small dirt road leading to it from the outside world. Inevitably, almost every afternoon you would find most of the missionary men there, working, repairing, maintaining the planes, and talking out mission issues under that metal roof. It was a close equivalent to an old general store with a front porch where all the men would gather to catch up on the week, swap stories, and file their latest complaints about world happenings.

One cloudy, humid afternoon, the Catholic clinic's small ambulance quickly wheeled up on the compound bringing a very sick woman that needed to be flown to one of the nearby hospitals. She was so sick that even before Jeff and another missionary could get her loaded into the plane, she died. It was just too late. Her husband and a couple of other people had been in the ambulance with her. Jeff said that he was startled when, all of a sudden, and with great passion and exertion, the husband of the dead woman began wailing loudly and thrashing violently on the concrete floor.

Michelle and I were in our house some sixty yards away and heard the commotion clearly. Curiosity got the best of me, so I left

Michelle in the hands of one of our African workers and rushed to the hangar. By the time I reached the hangar, I found that I was not the only one fascinated by the noise the man was making because at least fifty Africans had already gathered under the awning of the hangar. I was always amazed at how quickly a crowd could gather in Liberia–without the aid of cell phones! Their form of communication, which we were not usually privy to, was as effective as email or telephone. It was as if they had their own Facebook network!

As the man was weeping and wailing in a local dialect, I asked someone to translate for me. "I SPENT ALL MY MONEY ON YOU AND YOU DIE? WHY? WHY?" he lamented in front of everyone. In truth, we missionaries knew that the Catholic clinic always paid for any ill patients they brought to us, but the rest of the audience probably did not know that. What I found out during that incident was that it was customary for the one closest to the dead person to wail loudly so that he could never be accused later of killing the person who had died. The body of the deceased woman lay under a sheet in the coolness of the hangar for a couple of hours while the man, finally assured that he would not be held responsible for his wife's death, went to look for a truck to pick the body up.

Knowing that my very curious three-year old was probably asking a million questions back at the house, I headed home, but not surprised at all to meet Michelle on the road coming towards the airplane hangar. She had drilled the African worker until she finally told Michelle that a person had died and that someone was crying because of the death. Michelle sneaked away from the house and that is when we caught her coming towards the hangar. She just wanted to see the dead lady, she told us with those beautiful brown eyes. I just cannot imagine where she got such curiosity!

The Raisin Bran Grinch

Jeff had always loved Kellogg's Raisin Bran, but in Liberia it was very difficult to find. One day, however, while he was in Monrovia, he found the cereal in a store and bought two boxes of Raisin Bran and five boxes of another kind. That may seem extreme to you, but we had learned to buy things when they were available because the next time they most likely would be gone.

The morning after Jeff returned home with the treasured boxes, he and Michelle sat down at the table excited about having cereal to eat for breakfast. That particular morning, Jeff put a box of Apple Jacks and another kind on the table along with his beloved Raisin Bran. As Jeff poured plump raisins and bran flakes into his bowl, Michelle's eyes were drawn there. She picked out a raisin from her dad's bowl, ate it, then slid her bowl over to the box, asking him to pour her some "raisin" cereal.

The look on his face was priceless. It was one of those rare but adorable moments when men show us the little kid within. Jeff tried his best to get Michelle excited about the Apple Jacks, opening them and popping one of the crunchy nuggets in his own mouth. Michelle would not be distracted. Then Jeff told her that Raisin Bran was not really good but was just healthy for older people. Undeterred, our little redheaded beauty said, "WELL, DADDY, YOU WANT ME TO BE HEALTHY, TOO, RIGHT?" Undone, he poured a small amount into her bowl. Being in the middle of the African jungle with only two boxes of your favorite cereal certainly can bring out extreme possessiveness!

"Life" and All That's Inside It

The brand of the flour we used in Liberia was called LIFE. I'm not kidding! It was stamped all over the bags. Incredibly enough, it lived up to its name. I was taught as a rookie on the mission field that you always, always, always sifted your flour before using it. Sifting it ahead of time did no good because more bugs would find their way into the white substance almost over night; only right before using it would guarantee–somewhat–that it was as clean as possible. Not until I really started doing quite a bit of baking did I understand the wisdom of that advice. Even sealed bags of flour were literally alive with critters. Little black things would come crawling out of the white powdery grain as if in pursuit of the one who would dare break up their private party.

For the first year, I remember sifting my flour two or three times before I was convinced that I had taken all the "life" out of it. By the second year, I might have sifted the flour once. After some time, I put away the sifter and simply picked out the bugs that I

92

could see. Hating to admit this, but a few months before our first furlough, I baked the biscuits, cakes, and cookies with the "life" intact—as long as the dough was going to be dark anyway. I gave everyone the option of picking out the baked bugs if they did not need the extra protein. Remember, no judging unless you have been there, done that!

There was a joke in the missionary circle that if you stayed on the mission field longer than four years before taking your furlough, you would actually find yourself looking for bugs to put in the flour! Halfway kidding about some of that, you just need to trust me when I say that living in a remote area of the world with bugs in your flour can do things to you! You never know what LIFE will serve you!

Driver Ants Again!

One fine day, we had another close encounter with the small black Liberian creatures that God esteems as wise and worthy of observation. Always one of those people who needs at least one bathroom break during the night, I had gotten up around midnight, fumbled for my flashlight on the night stand, and found my shoes. I shuffled into the bathroom in my flipflops with a flashlight aimed purposely at the floor. As I sat on the toilet to do my business, six roaches scurried on the floor in front of me. Six of them; six very large roaches. It is not unusual to find cockroaches even in the cleanest houses, but six scurrying together around the toilet told me a different story.

We kept a can of bug spray in almost every room, so I grabbed the can and sprayed the six unwanted visitors. Tenaciously, one of the roaches kept walking toward our bedroom, so I followed it with the can of spray. As my flashlight toggled toward the edge where the wall meets the floor and where there was also ant coursing installed (the coursing was used to stop ants or termites from going to the wooden rafters of the roof), I saw more than just the ant coursing. I saw ants. Many ants trying to sneak into our home like they owned it.

Jeff was abruptly awakened out of his peaceful slumber and made aware of what was going on. He groggily slid on his boots, took his flashlight, and went outside to see what might be happening on the other side of the wall. Not too many minutes passed before I heard yelling and hollering from my knight in shining armor. My mind went quickly to what kind of creature could be on the other side of our walls tearing him to shreds, but instinctively I was pretty sure that I knew. Jeff was being attacked by driver ants. He had followed their distinct path and found them literally surrounding our house. With that many ants, it was almost impossible to turn them, so we slept with Michelle on her waterbed the rest of the night. She was an extremely sound sleeper, and I could not help but imagine what the ants would do to my little girl if they found her. Me and my imagination!

By morning, after our dramatic and sleep-deprived night, Jeff went to check on the status of the ants and found that they were mysteriously gone. Later in the day, a Bible school student who worked for us in the afternoons found a nest of driver ants burrowed deep into the ground near the edge of our yard. He forged a plan. Digging into the nest with a shovel, he then poured kerosene and gas around it, struck a match, and threw it towards the nest as he leaped backwards. The combination caused a dynamite effect and fire burned in the hole for quite some time. Ask me sometime if I was sad that we had destroyed a driver ant nest and thousands upon thousands of innocent ants. Ask me if I really thought about how we were possibly upsetting the ecosystem at that moment. Just ask me!!

Decisions, Decisions, Decisions

A couple of weeks after our ant massacre, we flew down to Monrovia for a vacation. At that point, we were still giving thought whether to have our second child in Monrovia or at our home in Tappeta with the midwives whom I had grown to love and admire. During that week of vacation, another missionary woman from our Tappi station went in to labor, flew with her family down to Monrovia, and checked herself into a local OB clinic there to have her baby. It was the ensuing events at that clinic that helped Jeff and I make up our minds about definitely having our second child in Tappeta.

The lady was in full-blown labor, forty weeks pregnant with her third child when she was admitted. After making her wait for what seemed like a very long time in the hall, an orderly came to register her. His belligerence and incompetency was evident from the very beginning. So many things happened that could have potentially put hers and the baby's life in danger. I lamented all that she had to go through, but was personally thankful that through her experience, it was made clear to us where we would have our second child.

That week, while on vacation, I cooked for thirteen people a couple of times. In my mind, I had always thought that I began cooking for larger crowds later in our ministry, but as I read through my journals, I realize that it was something that I just naturally did from the beginning. Cooking for two people or for thirty people was something easy and fulfilling for me, something that I enjoyed doing, and something that tweaked my gift of hospitality like nothing else. In our present ministry with college students I again have the opportunity to hone the gift of cooking for large crowds nearly every week during our on campus Bible studies.

Another gift that God was already sharpening for our collegiate ministry, even during our first term as missionaries, was Jeff's passions for taking time for young people who were interested in ministry. He was always willing to go beyond the expected to give them the dynamic, unexpected experiences that would help in molding their thinking towards God and ministry.

During that particular vacation, there was a 15 year old guy named Andy, who was staying with the missionary family in Monrovia. He really wanted to visit the "bush" ministries but wasn't sure how that would work out. Jeff struck up a conversation with him, finding out Andy's desire to visit our Tappi compound, so later that day Jeff asked me if we could possibly house Andy for a week or so when we returned home to Tappi. Of course we did, and even though we don't know what ever happened to him after he left Liberia, we would like to think that God used our hospitality and ministry as well as what he experienced in Monrovia to steer Andy into what he was called to do.

Not in "Venn"

As I mentioned earlier, Jeff often went alone or with other missionary men to villages on the weekends to preach. One Sunday he was dropped off in a place called Venn (pronounced "vain"). He walked thirty-five minutes from the airstrip to the village with a man who meandered out of the bush to meet him. Arriving in Venn at 10:00 a.m., Jeff hoped that he was not late for the planned services, but soon found out that it did not start until around noon. Being hospitable and wanting to honor the visiting missionary, the pastor had his wife bring Jeff a plate of potato green soup and rice at 10:30 a.m. Potato green soup is not really a brunch kind of food for Americans because of its heavy oil and strong taste. Even more so, I had fed Jeff eggs, grits, and bacon at 9:00 that morning before he left home. Always taught to be gracious and appreciative when offered food, Jeff did his best to eat what was given to him and was thankful that he had some time to let it digest before he had to speak.

The worship service went from noon until 3:00 p.m., and at the end, sixteen people were saved! A former Bible school student interpreted his message for him into the local dialect. After spending a little more time with the people, he and his guide walked back to where he met the airplane. He arrived home by late afternoon, tired, but extremely grateful for what God had allowed him to be involved in that day.

CHAPTER ELEVEN

A man's heart deviseth his way, but the Lord directeth his steps. Proverbs 16:9

Where There Was No Doctor

Before telling you the Ipecac story, I feel the need to describe our medical setup in Liberia. We were blessed to have a missionary nurse whom I have mentioned several times. Rachel Schildroth, who by the time we arrived in Tappita, had over twenty years of missionary experience in Liberia. While talented and knowledge-able, she was quick to tell us that she was a nurse, not a doctor, and certainly not a miracle worker though she did believe God was. For medical emergencies that may arise, we would need to fly to Monrovia, and even there, the medical pickings were slim. Though I had a brother who had a terminal kidney disease and I myself had gone through three surgeries by the time I was 19 years old, there was not a great deal that I knew about medicine nor how to treat anything other than elemental ailments. As our family grew, I felt the desire to expand my knowledge of the human body and how it reacted to disease and such. Assisting Rachel in the OB clinic once or twice a week both aided and spurred on the desire to become more medically literate.

One of the missionaries there in Tappita shared her copy of *Where There is No Doctor* (David Werner, Hesperian Publishing). Inside the book were valuable tips on natural and herbal, homeo-pathic, and home cures for the specific snake bites, spider bites, allergic reactions, and so forth that one might experience in that particular region of Africa. It was a fascinating book and helped me so much, especially the section on childhood ailments and diseases. The Hesperian Foundation (http://www.hesperian.org) is a great resource for medical and practical health care advice if you are visiting other countries.

When three-month old Stefanie became croupy and had a hard time breathing, it was *Where There is No Doctor* which explained to me how to make a "steam tent" by pouring hot water and peppermint leaves into a bucket. I then lay Stefanie on my lap and covered us both with a quilt, allowing the steam to fill our "tent." For Stefanie, it worked wonders as it cleared her up almost effortlessly. For me, it also worked wonders as a sauna and opened my pores in a pleasant sort of way as sweat poured off my skin in rivets.

Because of the poisonous snakes and spiders in the African rain forest, I practically memorized the sections on what to do for certain bites. I was very familiar with various rashes and fevers, particularly malaria. Using mosquito nets on all our beds and a spray down with insect repellent and long-sleeved shirts if out after dusk, I tried to balance being responsible about our health with the faith that it certainly took to live under such medically adverse situations. Cholera, Dysentery, Lassa Fever, Typhoid Fever, Meningitis, staff infections, numerous other kinds of fevers and bacteria from flies, food, and water were constant reminders that we were indeed vulnerable creatures. It really did *reach to God* as the Liberians often said. After being in America where even the worst medical emergency could be farmed out to a specialized trauma unit within minutes, it honestly took great spiritual effort to lay down those fears at the Heavenly Father's merciful feet while living in a remote part of the world. It was all about trusting God wherever we were, but it did not come easy!

Today, Michelle is 27 years old and works in a surgical clinic. When I was pregnant with her sister Stefanie, Shell would play doctor or nurse as I took my afternoon rest time. Even then I was amazed at her medical aptitude by the age of three. One day, she and two other missionary kids were going to open a pretend clinic like Aunt Rachel's in Shell's playhouse on the piazza. Michelle found the Bandaid tin (remember when they came in tin containers?) and other medical objects that I thought safe for three year old play. Jeff and I were in the process of cleaning and sorting out our medicine cabinet in our bathroom, so Michelle asked if she could have the empty cough syrup bottles for her clinic. After a while, I noticed two full bottles of cough syrup were missing, so I went out on the porch to see if our little nurse had confiscated them for her patients. Not sure if Michelle would do that or not, I felt it wise to check.

What I saw was Michelle and another young child with bottles of cough syrup bottoms-up in their mouths. The bottles were empty as they brought them away from their mouths! You may not have forgotten about the "empty" bottles I had given her just a few minutes before, but I had. While I took the other child home so that the parents could do whatever they thought best for him, I left Jeff in charge of the ominous bottle of Ipecac with explicit instructions of how much to give Michelle. For those of you too young to remember, Ipecac was a drug that people would use to assist someone in throwing up things that should not have been put in the stomach. Parents kept Ipecac in case of accidental drug ingestion by one of their children, which is exactly what I thought had taken place in that story.

Walking back to the house, I could hear the awful sounds of heaving and retching, my poor little girl throwing up everything.... except any trace of cough syrup. I searched again for the full bottles of missing cough syrup and found them–untouched–lined up in Michelle's play pharmacy inside her playhouse alongside mashed up leaves, mud, and bread pieces dissolved in water. Feeling extremely foolish but still somewhat agitated by being put in that kind of position, I wiped Michelle's face, gave her some Coke, and put her to bed.

She slept for nearly two hours, and by that evening she was ravenous, eating enough food to restock her Ipecac-ridden body. As some parents will do, even if we have mistakenly imposed a punishment, we will still try to use the incident as a teaching tool for the child. We sincerely hoped that Michelle would always remember that day if she was tempted to put anything wayward in her mouth. And, as for the mother, this was the catalyst to convict me to work on my impulsive jumping to conclusions without getting the whole story.

Michelle and the Ipecac story was the perfect example of how I had not yet balanced the knowledge of how limited we were in medical options with the truth that God was, is, and always has been in control of our lives. Being a parent of small children carries great responsibility every day. Mix that up with American parents put in the middle of the African jungle with a very rambunctious daughter who was always into something! Little did I know that He would answer my prayer to trust Him more in some definite ways in the following months.

Summed up, it goes like this: where we lived deep in the West African jungle, if there was a true medical emergency where time was of the essence, it would fundamentally be the Heavenly Father's will against the forces of nature. It was a rather uncomfortable feeling to come face-to-face with my humanity and to finally say out loud, "I am **NOT** in control at all." In America, we live with false perceptions of authority and dominance, honestly believing that we control way more than we should ever place on ourselves. To our American man made provisions and resources we have given our allegiance, and then, when it all crumbles, we lose faith in everything. Even in God. To an increasing extent, in the middle of the jungle, I was coming to understand why the African Christians had a much larger concept of God and what He could do than did I. They had absolutely nothing else but Him.

Living in the Unexpected

Our best laid plans are forever being changed and divinely interrupted by a sovereign and wise God. That is the nature of this life as a Christian. Making plans while serving as missionaries in West Africa—or being in ministry anywhere for that matter is risky business. As Americans, we are conditioned to plan out, map out, scope out and be specific with the time and places we need to be somewhere. Now, don't get me wrong; I know that the Bible speaks about things being done decently and in order, and it is a good rule to live by. But for the most part, while ministering in West Africa, our plans just never seemed to come to fruition quite like we thought. Thankfully, I became vigorously aware that when God changed our plans, it was going to be amazing though not always easy.

A perfect example of that was the planning of our wedding anniversary celebrations while in Liberia. In 1986, while I was pregnant with Stefanie, Jeff and I celebrated our fifth anniversary. A couple of the other missionary ladies and I had earlier decided that we would help each other make those celebrations a little more special by keeping each other's children and cooking a special meal for the anniversary couple. It seemed the perfect remedy for young, love-struck missionary couples that wanted to do something special while living mainly isolated in the middle of the West African jungle.

On the day of our fifth anniversary, I woke up with a horrible stomach bug. That was not an unusual occurrence for any of us, but the timing was definitely off that day! By afternoon, I was no better, so Jeff and Michelle went to the Wittenberger's home to eat OUR anniversary meal with their family. I remember lying on the couch thinking all kinds of sad and pitiful things, when it dawned on me that the very same thing could have happened in America.

The following year, on the day of our 6th anniversary, I was more determined than ever that we would have a wonderful celebration and made plans accordingly. Despite my best efforts, two things were fighting against me: my husband was on flight duty that week and our August anniversary is during Liberian rainy season.

Starting early that morning, I listened constantly for someone to approach our door and call Jeff away. It happened in the early afternoon. A rap at the door, an urgent call for a medical flight, so Jeff abruptly dropped everything and headed to the hangar to prepare the plane. The skies were ominously dark and threatening, not too unusual for that time of year, and reluctantly, we said our goodbyes at the airplane hangar with Jeff's promise that he would do his best to be back within two hours.

Fifteen minutes after he left, the bottom literally fell out of the cloud which was looming above our mission compound, taunting my celebratory plans. There was no lifting of the torrential rain for almost twelve hours! On Jeff's side of the story, after takeoff, he ran directly into a heavy sheet of rain heading straight for our compound. He had to fly a path well out of the way to get around the cloud, and while doing so, had a sinking feeling that he would not be back that afternoon to celebrate our anniversary.

There were no telephones on the compound, so the only way we had any contact with the outside world was through either ham radio or a shortwave radio that connected us to our Liberian mission compounds in Monrovia and Yila. There were scheduled "radio times" with the two other compounds at 6:30 a.m. and 6:30 p.m. each day. The missionary guys always attended "radio time" in the mornings and evenings, giving them time for making specific plans for the day, praying about various matters, or just "shooting the breeze."

Because Jeff had not returned by the evening of our anniversary, I walked over to participate in radio time with my umbrella in hand. The rain had still not relented. Those were the moments when a missionary pilot's wife, after not hearing from her husband for a reasonable amount of time, had to keep a cool head and try to exercise the faith that we taught others to embrace. Even though I really was looking forward to spending the evening with him to celebrate our sixth year as a married couple, I was praying even harder that he had not tried to come back through the menacing rain clouds. Deep in my gut, I knew that he was too smart a pilot for that.

Sure enough, as I stepped on the Watkin's piazza, I heard Jeff's voice through the static of the radio. After dropping the sick passenger at Phebe Hospital, he headed back. With a sinking feeling, he saw the relentless clouds hovering over Tappi and was forced to land in Yila, a small town located not too many miles from us. In Yila was a smaller Baptist Mid-Missions compound where two older single missionary ladies were working. Thankful to hear his voice and to know that he was safe, I knew, too, that he would be in good hands that night. That did not stop the friendly joking toward the rookie missionary wife who had planned a romantic evening for her husband, but instead had to be consoled that he would get a good meal in the company of two older missionary women in a village just thirty miles away! Rainy season widow.

I walked home in the gloomy rain fighting an even more gloomy attitude. Putting away the well-prepared anniversary dinner, Michelle, Stefanie, and I ate sandwiches and fruit. For a few moments, I dwelt on all the reasons I did not like living in the middle of that rainy jungle. But as I looked at the bright, expectant eyes of my little girls, my spirit rose and challenged me to count my blessings. This broke the spell of my present circumstances. Tumbling on the floor, reading books, coloring pictures of ducks and bears, and feeling the wet kisses from these two tangible pieces of my heart put it all in perspective.

Jeff returned by mid-morning ready for some fresh clothes and a big hug from his three girls! That night we celebrated—and I learned a big lesson. Life and love and blessings can be and should be celebrated any day!

First Church Plant

Jeff traveled by helicopter with another missionary pilot to a town of 800 people one weekend following our fifth anniversary. Upon reaching Saclepea, it was discovered that the only place to hold a church service was in the main government building located in the middle of the town. Saclepea was home to one of our Bible school students who had a burden for his town to be reached for Christ and had asked the missionaries to help him. The first Sunday, Jeff preached to 130 people and thirty-eight came forward to accept Christ. Simultaneously, while Jeff was preaching in the government building, the other missionary, James Wittenberger, stayed with the helicopter and preached to about 200 people who had come out to see the strange mechanical bird that had landed in the local school yard. That town won Jeff's heart and believing that it was ripe for a church, he felt God tapping us for that opportunity.

Excited since it would be the first ministry we would do apart from our corporate efforts with the other missionaries, church planting had always been a priority on Jeff's missions agenda. After almost a year on the mission field, we were going to really live out the Great Commission in a pointed and specific way! God and us! God sometimes asks us to be willing to work with others so that we can learn, grow, and come to understand more of what He is trying to accomplish in His kingdom.

Then there are those times when He calls us out to walk alone with Him—down paths that may seem very strange and isolated, but also potentially fruitful. Are you heading down one of those paths? If you are called out to work with others, respect them and support them, working hand-in-hand for the ultimate goal of building Christ's kingdom. If you are in a situation where you feel God wants you to go it alone for a bit, put your BIG FAITH shoes on and get going! Either way, He desires that His love and great salvation be known to all the world!

Allow Me To Deviate For a Moment

Depending on where a missionary feels he will be working can often determine what specific skills he might accrue. Jeff was a husband, father, evangelist, Bible professor, pilot, construction builder, mentor, supervisor, church planter, painter, jack-of-all trades (and might I add, master of most). If I may, would you allow me to get sidetracked from the present story for a moment and relive the days when Jeff and I began dating? Hopefully, this will divulge principles that may help someone reading this book.

After my three year struggle with God about surrendering to missions, I set my face like a flint and headed to Bible college. It was not always easy (flint-faced or not) and there were times I truly wanted to recant on my commitment to God's calling on my life. Thankfully, my spirit was more willing to surrender than the flesh was to abandon. During my initial surrendering to be a missionary, I promised Him that I would never renege on my commitment to do His will—but that certainly did not mean I would be immune from the temptation of doing so.

That having been said, I began to build my priority list for what I desired in a husband; a man that I could go anywhere with and know that he would not only care for me, but know HOW to care for me. There was a difference in my mind. One of my first preferences was that he be a missionary pilot. I had always loved to fly, so what better way to get around on the mission field than by airplane! God's Word tells us to delight in the Lord, and He will give us the desires of our hearts, and that is exactly what that means. God uses things that we have a passion for when defining our call. It was such a proviso that the man I would marry be a missionary pilot that I made up my mind to only seriously date those guys in the missionary aviation program at Piedmont. Though I strayed from that mandate twice, mainly because they were young men seemingly called to be missionaries, my soul would not allow me contentment in that. Pilot. Must be a pilot. How about the really cute one with the nice brown eyes that seems very shy?

Twice before dating Jeff, I dated two other student pilots, and the relationships advanced enough that I was ready to fly with them and scrutinize what kind of pilots they were. Both times the poor guys failed; one on a horrible landing. The other because he took crucial shortcuts when he was prepping the plane for flight. Perhaps he thought he was being cool by doing that, but he had already broken my confidence in him by the time we took off. If he would shortcut the prepping of a plane with just a girl he was dating, what would he do a few years from now in a jungle ministry—perhaps with our children in the plane with him? No THANK YOU, SIR, TAKE ME HOME, PLEASE.

Later that fall, the pilot with the memorable brown eyes, Jeff Abernethy, asked me for a date and that was pretty much the end of my singleness. Even though I knew that Jeff had captured my heart and there really was no turning back, I still asked him to take me flying because I was still curious about what kind of pilot he was. He was, however, an unbelievably skilled pilot, even at such a young age. He spent more time than he needed on the flight prep and his landing was faultless. I could not believe that God had given me–totally–the desire of my heart and the practical fulfillment of my husband list! Also on my "husband priority list" was the belief that my missionary husband should be skilled with tools and creativity. Isn't it like God to give us above what we ask or think?

Thank you for allowing me that parentheses in my story, but I felt it necessary that you understand how appreciative I am by the talents God has given Jeff. He is amazing with his hands, a hard worker, a great provider, and has gone above and beyond to make things as comfortable and practical for his family during those years in Africa and beyond. He was–and still is–my optimum soulmate and coworker in ministry!

During my first years as an African missionary woman, I was a wife, mother, chef, bed and breakfast manager, teacher of elementary and junior-high missionary kids, a barber, correspondent/writer, and an English professor at the Tappeta Bible Institute. How much is all that worth in today's corporate standards? It doesn't matter to me. The heavenly rewards are amazing and eternal and the almighty dollar has absolutely nothing on that!

When someone asks me what they should do to prepare for the mission field, I answer with a resounding, "Learn as much about everything possible!" All the little side roads that God takes us down (or even those we choose for ourselves) could be used as preparation for a specific use down the road in ministry. What you learn before you begin ministry is amazingly useful. We, as Americans, don't like to feel we are wasting our time with anything. I'm telling you, if you truly live out Psalms 37:4 and 5, step out and learn to do things that you love as you prepare for doing the will of the One you love! He is the Master Engineer!

CHAPTER TWELVE

I am thankful that our God is an ON-TIME GOD. —UNCC student

Times and Seasons of a Baby

The day I was due to deliver baby Stefanie, our missionary nurse slipped and fell in the mud, breaking her wrist as she was walking to Wednesday market. She had to be flown to Monrovia to have it set properly, and several of the missionaries thought that I should have gone with her. Thankfully, God had already shown us His will concerning the birth of our second child, and even with our nurse Rachel out of the picture, I was still content and at peace to deliver my second baby with the Liberian midwives in Tappi. Believe me when I say that it was not bravado at all, even though I imagine as I have told my story in the past, it might have been construed that way. Though always up for adventure, I was not willing to play carelessly with the birth of one of my children! God just gave absolute peace: there is no other explanation.

While the ultrasound that I had in Monrovia back in July showed the baby was due somewhere around the middle of September, one of the midwives measured my belly (the act of taking a tape measure and measuring the height of the fundus) in a less conventional way and calculated that I was not due to deliver until about the second week of October.

Stefanie was born on October 7th, so you can understand why I was both amazed and completely entrusted to those midwives. Jeff had his own ideas of why the baby was supposedly taking longer than usual to arrive. Ever since I had found out that I was pregnant, I had called the baby "TJ"—which was the name we would have given a son. In a journal dated September 6, 1986, I wrote, *Jeff says now that he is sure that it is a girl and she's mad at us for calling her TJ the whole time.*

Since Rachel had broken her wrist and was in Monrovia, I helped run the OB clinic for the entire month before Stefanie was born. The midwives were efficient and competent, and I was mainly there as a reference point. Looking back, I am sure that the responsibility of the clinic during that time served as a great distraction as we waited for baby Stefanie to arrive.

Our Little American-African Arrives

I once heard a college student say that she was thankful our God is an on-time God. So true, and even more so when it comes to the mysterious ways of babies. By the end of the gestational period, a woman is usually finished, done, at the end of herself. She has shared her personal haven with that sweet little creature long enough! It is time that the little one face the world for whatever it is worth. Even fathers are ready for the mothers to birth the baby. Everyone is ready except YOU KNOW WHO floating peacefully and contentedly inside the cozy, watery home. All three of our daughters had hung HOME SWEET HOME signs inside my belly and were sending messages for pizza delivery.

Stefanie Leigh Abernethy came exactly in God's time. I hope that I will not bore you with the details of her birth, but it was such an acutely commemorative time. After dropping twenty-six pounds, being extremely sick for more than four months, and at the same time, battling culture shock and mood swings, deep down I still knew that it was right to have that baby in the middle of the Liberian jungle.

God was merciful to the little American mommy who had only lived in the unfamiliar African jungle for ten months. I went to sleep on the eve of October 6 with tinges of hope, awaking around 1:00 a.m., filled with more than just hope, but also with a strong assurance that it was time. From that point, I never thought about being afraid nor did it stress me to realize that I would be able to have absolutely nothing for pain, no matter how hard the labor might get.

The jungle was pitch black and quiet except for the soft breathing of Jeff as he slept. Whispering my longings and petitions to my Heavenly Father who I knew was there with me, I tiptoed around, getting things ready, laying out clothes for the baby, making some hot tea for myself, making sure for the twelfth time that the bedroom where I would deliver was clean and orderly. I reveled in the exclusiveness of the early morning quietness, but was starkly aware that all would change very soon. When I could no longer delay the pointed breathing through the contractions, I woke Jeff. When he realized that it was still very dark outside but heard the urgency in my voice, his face became a mural of excitement in the flickering amber light of the kerosene lantern.

By 3:30 a.m., Jeff had gone for one of the missionary ladies who wanted to be there for the birth, mainly, in case Michelle were to wake up during the process. He also rode to the clinic and informed the two midwives that I had chosen to help with my delivery. One of them, Emma, arrived a few minutes later seeming very nervous and concerned. She told us that she had just delivered a baby about three hours earlier and that the baby had been macerated, black, and rotting as it came out of the mother's womb. Emma was still having a hard time with what she had seen. The Africans have many superstitions, and even after becoming followers of Jesus Christ, it took great effort to lay down those fallacies and begin to live out the truths given to them in God's Word. Emma felt that she should not be in the room with me because she might "jinx" our baby.

Even in the evidence of my labor cranking up, it was a wonderful time for us to talk to her, using Scripture and prayer to help release her from those fears. Nothing like getting your mind off your own situation (like labor pains) than by investing in the lives of others! Though the labor pains increased rapidly, I was still able to be involved in the teaching process with Emma, and thankfully she soon agreed to help deliver our baby. As I began the pushing process, Jeff tried for comic relief. After four hours of labor, he was concerned for me, especially knowing that there was nothing to give me for pain. So, as Stefanie's dark hair crowned, he exclaimed, "I SEE BLACK HAIR! OH, BY THE WAY, SWEETIE, THIS BABY BETTER BE WHITE!" A very cute joke, definitely, but the timing was off. The joke fell soundly to the floor as another round of pushing ensued. Poor guy!

Stefanie was born at 6:30 a.m., with the humming of the generator and about 100 curious bystanders waiting on our piazza for the news. That, unfortunately, was as close as they were getting to the delivery room, though it might have been different. When I first decided to have Stefanie in Tappita, I considered delivering at the OB clinic just as the African women did. Incredulously, I soon got wind that a couple of the midwives were going to sell a few tickets for entry into the delivery room to watch the white woman have her baby. That was enough to persuade me to deliver in the most controlled environment I knew: my house.

However, there was no way to stop the throng of people waiting on our piazza and what made it more interesting, was that none of our windows had glass in them. Only a thin metal screen was between those waiting for the white baby to be born and the sounds a woman makes while in labor. I have no idea what they heard and at the time, I am sure that I did not care.

When Emma cut Stefanie's umbilical cord, that was the last I saw of my new baby girl for almost an hour. Jeff and my Liberian midwife friend Mary swept her away to be weighed, cleaned up, and shown off. I heard clapping, singing, and shouting on the piazza, and knew that Jeff must have gone out there with our little baby. I heard later that he went out the door holding her up above his head and was praising God for a beautiful little girl. The Lion King was proud of his cub, and many of the townspeople were perplexed by the genuine pleasure they saw in Jeff's face.

In Liberia at the time we were there, a man was not really considered a man until he was able to have a son. Since we already had a daughter, everyone assumed that our second baby would have been "Teacher Jeff's" son. When Jeff walked out on the piazza, tears running down his face, praising God for baby girl Stefanie, some of the men in the crowd asked him how he could be so happy about another girl child. So, with his second beautiful daughter snuggled deeply into his arms, another teaching opportunity arose.

With all the celebrating on the piazza, Michelle did indeed awake as baby Stefanie began crying. Our beautiful, wide-eyed three year old came out of her room saying, "I hear a baby crying! My baby is crying." She went to look at the baby, but instead of wanting to hold her right away, she first needed to see mommy and to make sure I was fine. When the young nurse deemed her mommy in good health, she excitedly went out to find her new baby sister. Eventually I was able to also hold Stefanie for the first time and after eating a big breakfast prepared by one of my missionary friends, Beth Wittenberger, both Stefanie and I slept for quite a while.

Having to take care of a baby the first night without a hospital nursery was a shock for the Americanized mother. Stefanie acted hungry all night and hardly slept, so neither did we. By the third night, I was seeing the advantage of having nurses to help with a newborn baby so that the mother could get some rest. Through all the adjustments of caring for a new baby in the middle of the jungle, I was acutely aware of one thing. Having Stefanie there in the town of Tappita was perhaps one of the best things we could personally have done.

I later wrote in my journal:

> For me to have chosen to have my baby here in Tappi by their very own midwives is a compliment to exceed no other. It showed them that we love them, trust them, and want to be a part of them. So they all came to celebrate with us, that special Liberian-born child of Americans! It has been almost twenty years since a missionary woman had delivered a baby in Tappita.

Often God calls us to do unusual, uncomfortable, and unconventional things. As Americans, it can be difficult for us to leave our traditions, stepping out of the ordinary so that we can see God do the extraordinary in our lives! Do we dare allow God to be extraordinary in our lives? Today? Every day? With our children? Our possessions? With our lives?

Finding Our Normal

Within a week of Stefanie's birth, life demanded its normality. Our new little girl was one week old when Rachel, our missionary nurse, returned from Monrovia with a cast on her wrist and asked me to be her "right" hand while her wrist was healing. She could not write at all, and in the running of the weekly clinics, there was much necessary documenting of patients' care. So, Stefanie and I headed to the clinic every Tuesday morning, and while she slept peacefully on my lap or was carried around by one of the midwives, I filled out charts, made notes, and wrote prescriptions for Rachel.

Three weeks after the birth of Stefanie, my parents came for a visit. It was amazing because I knew that my mother did not like to fly at all, and here she was coming all the way to Africa to see us! It might have had something to do with the fact that I had teased and told both sets of grandparents that there would be no pictures of Stefanie sent until they came out to see her.

My parents were with us for thirteen days, and it was so wonderful to share all the things that we had only been able to write about before. Jeff's parents and his youngest sister Renee came out a few weeks later, and we were able, again, to share all the cultural idiosyncrasies and introduce our wonderful African family to them. Just rereading my journals even now overwhelms my heart with the love they all had for us and how supportive they were of what God had called us to do. They tasted the African foods, went with us to the local churches, and walked with us to the weekly market in town. Of course, I had a break from bathing the girls as the grandmothers both desired to do that. Michelle especially enjoyed having the attention of other family members. After their visits, it was so much easier to describe things to them in our letters because we knew they had a better idea of what we were talking about.

A Different Kind of Yard Sale

Near the end of the Bible school year, which in Liberia, was the first of December, it was customary for the missionaries to hold a yard sale open only to Bible school students and their families. At first I did not understand why we could not simply give away our stuff as it was obvious that the families were in great need. But after a few months, I began to grasp how the tension and jealousy would have mounted up if we were to just give our stuff to certain Bible school families. So, we continued the tradition, using one of the Bible school classrooms for our group sale. Going by only the experience of participating in yard sales in the states, I wondered how many hours we would have to stay there until everything was sold.

Wisely, but baffling to me at first, the veteran missionaries who had done those yard sales before, kept the doors locked until we had laid everything out on the tables. When the door was unlocked, whoever it was that had unlocked the door might just as well have become a doormat for the fury of how everyone entered! Walmart stampedes had nothing on those African shoppers! In less than an hour, the tables were completely emptied! It seemed too daunting of a task to charge for each individual item, so we charged them by the paper bag full and left it to the individual families to trade and barter with the others for what they really wanted.

The second yard sale in which we participated was my most memorable one. Stefanie was about 14 months old and walking. Jenny, a Bible school students' daughter who watched the girls in the afternoons, brought Stefanie over to the sale with her. Stefanie had on a diaper and a little diaper shirt which was about all she needed during that time of year. Once the sale began, we never set eyes on Stefanie again until the last item was bought. I, assuming that Jenny was watching Stefanie, concentrated on taking money from the students and sharing some good natured banter about the items they were buying. A few minutes later, Michelle called for me to come and see Stefanie. "She poo-pooed on the floor, Mommy," I was informed by the big sister.

As I looked up from the table, quickly wondering how that could have happened....I saw her. STEFANIE WAS COMPLETELY NAKED. No diaper. No shirt. Nothing but the birthday suit with which she was born. Her clothes had obviously been taken in the yard sale! Michelle later told us that several African women tried to take her clothes, too, but she ran under the table and hid. That yard sale was such a complete success that they had literally bought the clothes off my baby's back. Did Stefanie seem to mind? Absolutely not.

Cultures in Collision

One of the most ambitious desires of our young missionary hearts was to minimize the disparities between the Africans and our deeply embedded American mind set. Despite our best intentions, every day seemed to bring a new and daunting dilemma; not only with the Africans, but also with other missionaries. Should we learn the local dialect or not spend effort and time on that? Do we hire unsaved workers in our homes? Do we have our babies in Tappita or in the capital city of Monrovia? Do we dress like the Africans or as an American? Do we walk the two miles to church with our children or not? To our chagrin, there seemed to be a constant cacophony in our new lives, even though our hearts desired unity with the other missionaries and acceptance by the Africans. While those are, in themselves, noble aspirations; time and experience taught us that with fellow missionaries, unity was usually achieved when we sometimes agreed to disagree.

We also realized after the first few years, that the Africans never placed on us the fervency to be like them; we did that to ourselves. Certainly there were times when our attempts to acclimate to the African culture allowed us positive footholds that would not otherwise have been gained, but balancing it all was a heady undertaking. One of the most profound collisions of culture came during our first year when the English church moved two miles away.

If you are a churchgoer at all, you know what the Bible says about not forgetting to gather and worship with the body of Christ. It is a strengthening and uplifting time for Christians anywhere in the world. For our first year in Liberia, that was never a problem because the English-speaking Baptist church was located not even a half mile from our compound. We had but to walk down a small footpath, a cool, refreshing jaunt through the thick canopy of the jungle to attend church. Even five days after having Stefanie, I walked to church, though later I regretted it somewhat as my mothering instincts told me that it probably was not good for a five-day old baby to be passed around and held by every African woman in the church. However, to my amazement, Stefanie showed no repercussions from the experience.

By the middle of November, the English church moved two miles on the other side of town. The closest Baptist church then was the Gio church located less than a mile away, but no English was spoken except when a missionary preached. That presented a dilemma to those of us who had small children and no transportation—other than motorcycles. While I was in the process of learning Gio and did not mind going to the Gio church, it was hard to handle both Michelle and Stefanie during the long services.

When the men went out in the airplanes to preach on Sundays, it obviously left us, the mothers, with the little ones. So what was the right thing to do? Did we herd up the kids, tie the babies on our backs, grab our Bibles, and walk the two miles to English church each Sunday morning? The African women did it all the time. So, feeling the weight of that self-imposed pressure to do as the African women, I tried it, twice, I believe. Walking to the English church was mainly downhill and in the morning, we were able to enjoy the coolness of the day. Even Michelle enjoyed running and skipping down the small dirt roads, hunting caterpillars and special rocks. Coming home in the early afternoon was much different. I still remember how overwhelmed and fatigued I was. Michelle, no longer enamored with the trek, wanted me to carry her (she was only 3), but I had Stefanie tied to my back and didn't think my knees would hold up. By the time I made it home—after flagging down a money bus who transported us to the compound for a little extra money—I was in tears both from fatigue and frustration.

There was no academic or emotional preparation for those kind of dilemmas. What was the right thing to do? Were we expected to live and act just as the African women? If you were to ask five different missionary women, you would perhaps get five different answers. In those cases, situational ethics kicked in and we simply did for our families what we believed was scripturally acceptable, physically attainable, and currently available. I, along with Nancy Sheppard, another missionary woman with a young baby, decided to take turns attending church while the other one would keep the small babies at home.

When Stefanie was about one month old, I kept Nancy's two youngest children so that she could go to church with her husband for a special Sunday night service. Stefanie was one month, Nathan was four months, Melodie was almost two, and Michelle was three. It was interesting and overwhelming at times, but she did it for me the following week, so it was worth it to both of us. When the teenage missionary kids were home from boarding school, they were more than willing to babysit for us while we went to church or went on excursions with our husbands to nearby villages. Now that was the best of both worlds!

As the children got older, the three mothers with small children designed a rotating Sunday School for the young kids. Looking back, none of our kids were damaged physically, spiritually or emotionally by our decisions in those early years of their lives. We simply asked God to give us wisdom for what was the best for our children and our ministry there in the African country of Liberia for that time.

CHAPTER THIRTEEN

That He would grant you, according to the riches of His glory, to be strengthened with might by His Spirit in the inner man. Ephesians 3:16

Propping It Up

Occasionally, we were able to fly with Jeff down to Monrovia and stay for a couple of days. It was always gratifying to have a change of scenery, even though after a year of living in Tappi, I was getting increasingly used to our compound. For the first few months, I remember feeling extremely stifled if I was not able to fly somewhere or even to take a motorcycle ride in the afternoon. The four walls of our home closed in on me quickly.

Planning a trip to Monrovia with our whole family for a few days was no small thing. We had to pack up, find a Bible school student to house sit, and tie up any loose ends that might come due before we returned. As anyone knows that has ever done it, cleaning out a refrigerator is a challenge and still one job that I abhor. In Tappita, because we used a kerosene refrigerator, it was more financially beneficial to completely cut it off if we were going to be away more than four or five days. That meant completely cleaning it out and finding someone that had room in their fridge to store our perishable food items.

After everything was cleaned out, cleaned up, packed up, and farmed out, we hauled our luggage to the airplane hangar in a wheelbarrow. Sitting regally on top of our bags was our lovely little Michelle, who no doubt thought of the wheelbarrow as her very own carriage. It never failed that when it was time for a flight to take off, almost everyone on the compound would come to the hangar. There was something magical about watching the plane soar into the sky and pass over the trees as it disappeared into the African sky. The hangar was situated directly across the runway from our Bible school classrooms, and when the plane started up, all teaching had to cease for a few moments because of the noise.

That particular day, however, the plane would not start with the key. Michelle, Stefanie, and I were already inside the tiny cabin, waiting as Jeff was getting last minute lists and instructions from other missionaries. After several attempts with the key, Richard Dodson, another missionary pilot, began turning the prop by hand, propping it, prop blade by prop blade, until the plane sputtered and finally came to life.

Seeing my concerned look, Richard explained that starting an airplane that way was exactly like jump starting a car with battery cables. Ever the realist, I was not to be consoled. There was just something unnerving about having to watch the prop manually turned in order for it to start. If I would have counted my breaths during that long trip, it seemed that there were not more than about a dozen; that's how scared I was that the prop would just decide to stop in midair. Being well initiated into the exclusive Tappeta Pilot Club, my husband laughed and joked about things that were not the least bit jocular to me then.

Since Jeff had started flying solo over the Liberian bush country a few months before, I carried my own fears about him falling mercilessly to the thick canopied floor of the jungle and never being found again! It's the price I paid for having a huge imagination. That day, I almost went crosseyed watching the prop as it spun in motion with the rest of the plane. Where were the parachutes? Or just maybe a barf bag?

Betty Crocker Has Entered the Jungle

During our second Christmas in Tappita, it was obvious that I had slid into a comfortable understanding of what it took to create culinary delights in the middle of the jungle. Improvisation was key. One week, this young Betty Crocker decided to make lasagna for the Watkins family upon their return from the states. The sauce was simmering in the pot and a cake was baking in my oven, all seemed right in my tropical world until I took the lasagna noodles out of the box. Small black bugs scattered everywhere! Bugs! Bugs! And more bugs! Using my hands, I smashed all I could as they looked for another place to have their party. I then dumped the rest of the noodles out of the box only to find that some of those black bugs had thoroughly and disgustingly embedded themselves inside the lasagna noodles. Even I, a veteran cook of the jungle (of one year), could not envision putting those noodles in hot water and watching hundreds of bugs float to the top of the pot. No way!

So, again my improv skills came into play as I created my first spaghetti pie. I had never even heard of spaghetti pie, but it certainly worked well when the aromatic sauce was on the stove, cheese grated, and oven ready for baking. Our guests might have appreciated my culinary skills, but I reveled in the knowledge that those buggy lasagna noodles were wrapped in plastic laying in the bottom of my kitchen trash can.

Willing To Teach and Be Taught

One Sunday near Christmas 1986, Jeff wanted to take us to Saclepea. He was hoping that I would also feel the same burden to preach and teach in that town and win many for Christ. As no one had any specific plans for the airplane, we were able to go as a family with our wonderful personal pilot; it took about eighteen minutes, which was not bad for our young, short attention spanned family. More than one hundred and fifty people came out just to watch us land. After greeting many of the townspeople, we then walked another thirty minutes to reach the center of town where the church was meeting. I had Stefanie strapped to my front in a baby carrier, and Michelle, when she got tired of walking, would ride on Jeff's shoulders. What a sight we must have been walking down the grassy pathway heading to church. It was one of those moments when I most felt like a real African missionary woman!

The people of the church were happy to see us and were gracious to allow Jeff to preach regardless of their plans for that day. I was feeling very "missionaryish" that morning and wanted to have a children's church. As I had brought no materials with me, I thought I would try to sing Christmas songs with them. To my surprise, absolutely none of the children (nor the adults in the service) knew the Christmas songs that were so familiar to us as Americans. On the flip side, the African children taught Michelle and me a couple of Christmas songs that they knew. I felt that we had much to teach those precious people in both Word and song, but it became evident that they, too, were worthy of teaching us. Two people came forward for salvation that morning after Jeff preached and eight wanted to rededicate their lives to serving Christ and Him alone.

When we flew away from the town, watching the throng of people waving goodbye to us from the side of the dirt runway, we both felt the "divine pull" to come back—again and again. God had definitely tapped us for that town, for that time. We arrived home around 2:00 p.m., and after having quick sandwiches, we fell into our bed for a long siesta on a sunny African afternoon believing that we were exactly where we were supposed to be.

As Normal As It Gets

Probably one of the most popular questions that I have been asked as a missionary is, "WHAT IS A NORMAL WEEK LIKE FOR YOU ON THE MISSION FIELD?" In America, we are so embedded in our routines, so much that we may assume the entire world lives as we do—locked within a rigid schedule with morning and night consumed with things we must do. Most missionaries do not live predominantly by routine, though that does not mean we do not have order and organization in our lives. There were those responsibilities and ministries that were both consistent and weekly, but in West Africa, each day brought the new, the unexpected, too. Having said that, I found in my journal a span of a couple of weeks which gives a slight idea of what it was like as a missionary in Liberia on a given day. Keep in mind as you read the following excerpt that there were no pizza deliveries, no drive thru fast food, no electric dryers, no 24-7 electricity in our home. While there had to be a method to our missionary madness, many things were simply out of our control.

In January, 1987, I was asked to be in charge of the Gio/Mano Women's Seminar which ran for two weeks on our mission compound and saw hundreds of women come from the surrounding villages. Believe it or not, I taught a craft class during that seminar. If you know me at all, "crafty" is not a word you would use to describe my talents. It does seems from my journal that they were just very simple crafts like coloring pictures and gluing Bible pictures on paper to make flash cards to take back to their villages.

They were encouraged to use those pictures to tell the stories to their children or grandchildren. I always liked the image that conveyed to me!

Mondays were usually big catch up days on laundry, hanging clothes back out to dry if they had not completely dried on Friday and Saturday, making bread and other food items that would be used for that week's meals. I did a bulk of my writing on Mondays because there were no classes in the Bible institute that day. The Monday of the Women's Seminar, registration had started early that morning, even though no one arrived until around 10:00 a.m. The first week I taught the craft class from 4:00–5:00 p.m. each day. The second week, I taught a course on fundamental biblical doctrines—on a very simple, practical level. Also, on that noteworthy Monday, we had a Bible school staff meeting for a couple of hours.

Tuesday mornings was when, if not teaching in the Bible institute, I would help our nurse Rachel with the OB-GYN clinic. Becoming somewhat proficient at registering patients gave me numerous opportunities to get to know the ladies who came to the clinic. Wednesday mornings were always market days in the nearby town of Tappeta. People would bring their wares from their farms and trek from town to town, giving the feel of a traveling farmer's market. I always made a point to go, even if I just needed to get one or two things. It gave me an opportunity to practice my Gio, to build friendships and even perhaps to witness to some of the ladies who were selling.

Then there was Thursday. We've all had those days. The ones where you go from one thing to another until you finally drop in your bed at night. I taught the Health class first thing in the morning on birth control and how even women in the jungles of Africa could still practice a form of natural birth control that worked for the most part. After the class, I went home to bake coffee cake for the Women's party that night, spent time with the girls, had my other class from 4–5 p.m., came home for a quick supper with my little family, and then back over to the Bible school for a party for the women attending the seminar. We played both American and Liberian games including musical chairs. You have never played that game until you experience it with a bunch of wonderful, fun-loving, but extremely competitive, older African ladies! The older the lady, the more feisty and determined she was to win the prize.

Friday was another Bible school staff meeting and that time we were discussing some disciplinary issues: one moral and one academic. Jeff had a medical flight that day, carrying a young boy whose eyes were so swollen and red that they literally protruded from his head.

Sadly, he did not live through the night. That happened so often with the medical patients that were flown to nearby hospitals, so it was a priority to talk to those patients and their families about Christ during the flight if possible. Again, you just never knew IF you would ever see that person again.

Dog Days and Miracles

One of our Bible school students brought a little puppy by our house because Jeff had mentioned that we might like to get one for the girls, one we could also train to be a watch dog. We bought him and christened him "Tippy" because he had a little white tip on the end of his tail. For the first week, he slept inside the kitchen door on the concrete floor while we were having a doghouse built for him in our side yard.

A few weeks later on a Tuesday morning, I was at the clinic helping Rachel, when Jeff came to tell me that our puppy was foaming at the mouth and was half paralyzed; two distinct signs of rabies. My heart almost stopped as I remembered that Michelle had been playing with him for several days, and just the day before, I was outside with baby Stefanie when the puppy jumped up to pull Stefanie's socks off her foot. His little teeth had nicked her foot in the process.

Of course, my mind went into overdrive with that memory. Here we went again with the colliding fears, the potential hazards, the injuries, the diseases, and the feeling of absolute helplessness. When it came to dealing with the physical dangers of our children there in the jungle, we were, as the Africans had always been, at the mercy and power of God–and God alone. Again, God called me out to lay my children and husband at His feet.

Mr. T remembered that right before the puppy started showing symptoms, he was limping on one foot. That same day he had killed a rather large tarantula beside the doghouse. So, we put the puppy in a pen behind Jeff's tool shed and watched him. He was really sick. I prayed and held on to the hope that it was merely the spider bite that was causing that illness. But then, the way he looked that evening, I thought surely he would be dead by the morning. Amazingly, as unpredictable as anything else in life, the puppy started drinking a little water by late that afternoon, and by the next morning was still alive and seemed stronger. We offered him a small bowl of rice, and he gobbled it up.

Six days later, he was completely back to normal, and even his foot was pink and normal looking again. He had been bitten by a poisonous spider and had fought to survive. It was not rabies! I was so humbled to realize that God had showed Himself in a remarkable way...again! He was the PERFECT, FAITHFUL PROTECTOR of my little brood no matter where we lived. Tippy became a living icon to that fact, and when I would watch Michelle play with him, I felt so thankful!

Another Trip to Saclepea

As often as possible, I went with Jeff to Saclepea, especially when baby Stefanie was younger and easier to handle. Learning from my first children's church experience in Saclepea where I felt ill prepared, the second time I remembered to take flannel graph stories, a children's music cassette, and felt armed with the necessary tools to make it work. I taught them a few English songs, but was surprised to realize that even many of the small children needed an interpreter to translate what I said into their local dialect. I taught the story of Zacchaeus and gave an invitation afterwards. Several children raised their hands and we took the time to deal with them personally.

That Sunday I had the privilege of leading three young boys to Christ! Two of them said they had never heard the story of Jesus before. I was thrilled to be able to see fruit myself instead of just hearing about Jeff's experiences when he would go out preaching. In my journal, I even wrote their names: *John, Leon, and Arthur.* I mentioned that they would be the preachers of tomorrow, and that is so true! After the civil war that played itself out between 1990 and 2003, I have wondered what ever happened to them. Did their salvation experiences keep them from fighting in the war? Are they allowing God to use them today? I just can't wait to get to heaven and see them again face-to-face!

Amazingly enough, when I look back on my ministry inclinations at any point, I know that I never felt called to specifically teach children. While Jeff has always been a master at getting down on the level of children as well as expounding deeply into the Word of God to adults, I always felt like my strength and passion was in teaching teens and women. It had never been required of me very often to develop and run children's ministries–there seemed to always be others who desired to work with that age level. Still, for a short time I was able to contribute to the church plant effort in Saclepea, God using even me to reach out to the children of that town.

For the Sake of the Call

After calling Tappeta home for about a year, the missionary honeymoon was definitely over. It was thoughtful and wise that former missionaries had come to the consensus years before that missionary men newly arrived on the field should not be required to go for long overnight evangelistic trips until after one year of living in the country. That gave the entire new family time to acclimate themselves to the unique way of doing things in the jungle. By February of 1987, the concession was over for our family, and Jeff was booked for several trips, many of them lasting up to a week at a time.

Jeff had planned a trip to Saclepea to preach a week of revival meetings soon after the concession was lifted. He had been preparing those seven messages for weeks, and when it was time for him to leave, I felt like I was sending out a married rendition of the Apostle Paul. He was excited, and I couldn't help but be excited also, but sending way too much food and other items for his use during that week. It was all new, sending my husband away to a remote Liberia, West African town, and in my best efforts, I was trying to help him be as comfortable and nurtured as possible while away from me. He said not a word as I put together my bizarre, but caring package of goodies. He knew my heart was in the right place.

In my journal of February 22, 1987, I wrote:

> I sent him 8 gallons of cold boiled water and ice. Hopefully it will last him all week. I baked him banana bread to take and he even carried a container full of lasagna in a cooler, plus two cans of chicken noodle soup. He just cannot eat rice and soup twice a day. Chick Watkins said it was fish soup most of the week when he was there, which doesn't sound delectable at all. I promised to have him a big pot of spaghetti ready next Saturday when he gets home. But, you know, this is what missions is all about! Above all, we want many people to be saved and a good solid church to be established.

Reading back over that, it is hilarious to me now! We were still so young and green in our jungle living. How in the world did I think that ice was going to last an entire week in Africa even if it was in a cooler? And lasagna? What was I thinking? I am certain that Jeff probably did eat rice and soup two or three times a day and learned to enjoy it. While I did not document how many accepted Christ that week, I do know that it was a pivotal week for the foundation of the Good News Baptist Church there in Saclepea, which, by the way, is still going strong today! Only what's done for Christ will last...even if ice doesn't!!

CHAPTER FOURTEEN

There is enough time in every day to do God's work...........in God's way.
—Dr. Ted Engstrom

Understanding Our Limitations

Over the past twenty years, I have seen numerous good workers in God's kingdom burn out and fall by the wayside. Their circumstances might have been different and the reasons might have seemed viable; it is certainly not my intention to deny or condone personal reasons. There are plenty of books on the market about burnout in Christian ministry, and I will concede to those authors the right to delve deeply into all the whys, hows, and ifs. I can only speak for myself.

Anyone that knows me will vouch that I am a spirited, stubborn, passionate, outspoken woman who loves God, her family, her ministry, and other people. But lurking behind all that love, in the deepest recess of my heart, I know how truly selfish I am. At times, the overwhelming tendency to succumb to my selfishness is much stronger than any guilt I might feel about not being about my Father's business. As raw and revealing as that is, what is inside those human elements of Kim has also may have kept me from completely burning out in ministry, though there have been times I felt that I was tottering on the edge of it!

I believe that even in Christian ministry, without taking it to the extreme of being selfish, we must be protective of our hearts, minds, souls, and bodies. "Broken and spilled out for love of you, Jesus" is part of a song that has incited controversy on the left and right side of Christian service. IF we completely are broken and spilled out, then there is nothing else to give later on. While that may be a true statement, perhaps there are times when broken and spilled out is exactly what God has planned for our lives and He must be the one to do the refilling. That is the key; it must be God's will for us to be broken and spilled out. On the contrary, the pouring out and used up should not come from neglecting ourselves. It reaches to Him to either put us back together for further use in His kingdom or take us into our eternal rest. That is entirely His call. There are no kudos for overwhelming our bodies and minds because it makes us feel better to do so.

On the other hand, if we are so protective of ourselves and what God has given us, how can we ever be effective to do the things that matter for eternity's sake? We have example after example in the Bible of men and women who simply allowed God to use them—very small, seemingly insignificant people, to do very big, significant things for Him! The point needs to be made: a perpetually off-balance scale will wear out quickly just as an off-balance life and ministry will.

I do not have any secret formulas about this kind of dilemma, though I do have a God-given perspective on the difference between what God requires of me and what I selfishly require of myself. There is a huge distinction between the two, but it seems that there are Christians everywhere who cannot differentiate well between the two. It is in that distinction where we find victory in Christ and a biblical denying of self that must come to all of us. For a poignant definition of selfishness is preferring one's self over God. Only in truly grasping God's infinitude, choosing a realistic view of our limitations, and asking Him to help us discern the balance in living out the purposes He has for us, will we be able to live healthy spiritual lives. God alone knows best how that should be played out for each of us.

After a year in Tappi we were thankful that we would have the opportunity to have a small truck shipped out in a container that was also bringing radio equipment. Seeing the benefits of having a vehicle even in our jungle ministry, we had asked Jeff's dad to pick one out for us. It was around the time that Jeff was going to get our truck out of port that I could feel myself smothering, choking, crashing. No amount of ministry or busy work could deter that.

So, when Jeff prepared to go to Monrovia, I looked at him meaningfully and said, "We need to go with you. I know that it will cost more money and it will put you out a little, but I need to get out of here for a while." Respecting what I needed, he revised the plans for the trip to include us. We flew down on a Wednesday, and after a couple of days of relaxing in Monrovia, the girls and I were planning to come back in the airplane with another missionary pilot. Jeff would drive our truck back over the road whenever he had taken care of all the paperwork. I was satisfied with the thought of even two days in Monrovia and felt that it would help the funk I was in.

During most of our visits to the Liberian capital, we would take time to visit the beaches for a couple of hours. The African side of the Atlantic was rocky, rugged, and filled with rip tides. Building sand castles, dashing in and out of the waves, eating a picnic lunch on a blanket, and basking in the African sun was part of our beach-going ritual. Jelly fish were always plentiful on the shoreline and would often come rushing in with the tide. One day, Michelle had a jelly fish tentacle wrapped around her little leg and came running out of the water screaming like a banshee. I, the valiant and fearless mother of that terrified child, with my bare hands, unwrapped the stinging goop of jelly from her sweet little leg, paying for that act of bravery for many days as my hand swelled and peeled from the effects of the poison. But, I would have done it again.

On the day when the girls and I were to return to Tappi, I was again feeling the dreariness settling around me. Conveying my deepest feelings to Jeff, I admitted that I was not ready to return to Tappeta, so we stayed. The next day, Jeff received a phone call about our truck. The ship would dock around 5:00 p.m. that afternoon. Jeff went to the port, but by 10:30 p.m. was back without the truck. He was told that the truck was down in the hatch with the rice and would not be unloaded until the next morning. Sunday morning saw Jeff right back at the port again where the truck was indeed unloaded around 8:30 a.m. It looked fine, except there were no outside mirrors. He left after seeing the truck safely parked in the Firestone parking lot with the security guard, which, of course, would watch the truck for an extra fee. Basically, we were paying him not to steal it or watch someone else steal it.

On Monday, Jeff was told that the truck could not be released that day because there was too much paper work to be completed. There was also the business of finding our crate that had been packed by his parents. It was soon discovered that the crate was under 130,000 bags of rice, none of which they had even started unloading. After we had been in Monrovia for five days, Jeff could see that it was going to be a longer process than he had planned, so he called for the plane to come and pick us up. Admittedly, I did feel a little guilty by wanting to stay those extra days and then having to pay for the plane to carry us back to Tappeta; however, God worked out the finances for the trip by providing other passengers to help pay for the flight. By the time we arrived back in Tappeta, I was ready to be back. The break was exactly what I needed.

Lesson learned: take time, take a break, and understand your limitations. And be honest with yourself about the needs that you feel are taking front row. Selfishness or genuine need? Only the Holy Spirit can separate the confusion between the two. If you follow His leading, you will be better off for it....and so will your ministry!

Trucking It To Church

Jeff and our truck arrived in Tappeta four days after the girls and I had returned home. Other than the side mirrors, nothing else was missing or damaged in either the crate or on the truck. After a spaghetti dinner for my tired husband, we began our ritual of going through the boxes that had been packed in the crate, staying up to almost midnight! Most likely, it is only missionaries or those who have lived in foreign countries and received packages from the states who will understand the phenomena of smelling the inside of a box that had been packed in the States. When we would receive a package from America, every item coming out of the box would be sniffed, conjuring up a multi-sensory experience of both enjoying something that could only be found in America and recalling the smells that we miss about our homeland. If you find the whole idea of this strange, then you have never lived away from home long enough.

The next day was Sunday, and we awoke with an excitement to realize that we were no longer bound to the schedules of others and wondering who might be needing to use the plane for evangelism that particular day. We had a truck! There was a village about twenty minutes by air from the mission compound that Jeff had previously visited by plane. We decided to go there, and I must say that riding in the air-conditioned truck was a blessing for all of us—even baby Stefanie who had been born into the hot jungle and knew nothing of this convenience.

Arriving in the village, the Christians living there were happy to know that we had come to spend the worship time with them. I had brought a flash card story and told it to the congregation before Jeff preached the message. That Sunday morning, as Jeff was preaching, the town "crazy" man dawdled straight to the front of the church.

In my journal of March 29, 1987, I wrote:

> *Evidently he was Catholic or just thought he was, because he came, kneeled down, mimed a crucifix with his hands, walked and kneeled right in front of Jeff, and did the same thing again. He tried to kiss Jeff's hand and was calling Jeff the "Messiah." While the old African pastor was making announcements, the crazy man would get up and start quoting scripture. He had really shifty eyes and would always look sideways, not right at you. He seemed smart enough, but out of control. He would get upset at the interpreter, stand up, and tell everyone that the man was not interpreting right. Jeff had to finally call him down. After Jeff called him out for his behavior during the service, he spouted off a whole string of scriptures, impressing me with his knowledge but concerning me with his demeanor.*

After the service, Jeff was witnessing to a couple of people, so the deranged man came up to me and starting expounding on the condition of man all the way back to Adam. When I asked him to condense his point, he changed the subject and said, "Jesus never casts away a man in need, but your husband was trying to cast me out of the house of the Lord." After attempting to talk with him for about fifteen minutes while holding a squirmy five month old, I realized that we were getting nowhere and never would. Simultaneously, the thought crossed my mind that the unhinged man could possibly be demon possessed. That distinctly crossing my mind when I accused him of playing the devil's advocate by disrupting the church service and he simply smiled. When I started using the term "Holy Spirit" to see what he would do, he cringed.

So, I became a little bolder and accused him of hindering the Holy Spirit but stated that Jesus Christ would prevail.

Though he did not roar or scream like I had always imagined most demon-possessed people would, I distinctly remember feeling that I had been in the presence of pure evil. Jeff had felt the same way, and we prayed for his soul on the way back to Tappeta, leaving all those things that were rolling around in our minds with the all-powerful God. It didn't dawn on me until much later that I had been holding Stefanie right in front of this man who was possibly possessed by the devil. Comforting me was the fact that she was protected by her Heavenly Father. We were becoming more aware that we lived in the middle of one of Satan's strongholds and his opposition to our ministry was, at times, palpable.

A Mean Old Mosquito

When Stefanie was about six months old and just learning to crawl, she started running fevers every other day. I could tell that she was just not herself, attempting to maneuver around much less than usual. Each day that she would have a fever, it would be slightly higher than the last time. Finally, one day it went up to 105 degrees! There we were in the middle of the jungle with a very sick baby feeling totally helpless and afraid. Everything we tried did not bring the fever down. I bathed her, but at the fever's highest point she was incoherent and sluggish.

On the following morning after the fever spiked, we drove two hours to Ganta where we had been told there was an American doctor at a Methodist hospital. While traveling, I cried, prayed, talked, pondered, and yes, was scared out of my mind, as I held this precious little child for whom I could do nothing. I thought of the scads of African mothers that had been through the same thing, holding their weak and sick children, but perhaps having no monetary means to provide proper care for them. Again God asked me to look to Him only and tenderly reminded me that Stefanie was never really mine, but always His. Trying to grasp the awesomeness of that, the trip seemed to take forever.

Upon arriving in Ganta, we were able to see the American doctor who was on a short term stint in the country. In the midst of this trying situation, more cultural collisions bombarded me. Because we were American, we were automatically taken straight into an exam room ahead of African patients who had been waiting for hours to see the doctor. I remember hesitating, looking around at the other women holding their babies, seeing something unexplainable in their eyes, and taking a step back. But the nurse who had called for us to follow her would have none of it. We needed to come with her right now! Looking into the feverish incoherence of my baby girl, I had no strength to comprehend the colliding feelings inside me as we followed the nurse down the hall.

The doctor quickly did a blood test, and while getting acquainted with baby Stefanie, he noticed her umbilical hernia. Stefanie, to this day, does not like to talk about that condition that she had until age three. Her belly button, at one point, protruded more than two inches because of the hernia. The doctor did not seem very concerned and said that he had seen many of them. He also told us that they usually take care of themselves by the age of five. When the blood test came back, we were somewhat surprised that Stefanie had tested positive for malaria though the doctor was not. He gave her a chloroquine injection and some baby aspirin right away with instructions on how to give the chloroquine syrup to her for the next two days.

Of course, I went through all the emotions of feeling like a mother who had failed her child. Why had I been so careless? I beat myself up mentally for allowing my baby to become so sick. The word "malaria" had such a scary and negative undertone, especially to new missionaries not familiar with it. On our way back to Tappeta, we tried to recall when Stefanie would have been exposed to mosquitoes which, out there, was every day, and though there was a mosquito net over her crib, it was impossible to protect her or ourselves from every mosquito.

By the third day after our trip to the doctor, she was back to her normal, happy, playful self, and we were thankful. Because I had been nursing Stefanie, I was told that she was getting all the malaria prophylactic that she needed until she was weaned. However, what I had not deduced was that she had recently been drinking out of sippy cups and taking more bottles because of my erratic ministry schedule, decreasing the amount of malaria medicine she was getting from mommy's milk. So, we started giving her chloroquine syrup each week when the rest of us took our tablets. Yum, yum, quinine syrup is so sweet and lipsmacking. Not! Try pouring bitter tonic water down your baby's throat and you'll get an idea of how fun each week was when we gave Stefanie that medicine.

Because of that incident with Stefanie, I was able to process a little more my growing empathy for African mothers raising children in this part of the world. Thinking back at how easily (comparatively) we were able to hop in our own air conditioned truck and travel to the hospital, waltzing directly into an exam room, I allowed my mind to see the many mothers walking along the side of the road with their babies on their back, sick, tired children walking beside them. Then I cried. I cried for the mothers sitting in the waiting area of the hospital constantly fanning flies away from the parched lips of their very sick little ones. I made myself remember the cries of the weak babies and the desperate eyes of those mothers as they watched the white woman walk past them into the safe confines of the hospital. Should I have sat on the terrace with those mothers holding my sick little one? Would that have made them feel better? Made me feel better? The perpetual collision of cultures constantly brought me to my knees.

CHAPTER FIFTEEN

And the things that thou hast heard of me among many witnesses, the same commit thou to faithful men, who shall be able to teach others also. Thou therefore endure hardness, as a good soldier of Jesus Christ.
II Timothy 2:2-3

Building His Church in Saclepea

Jeff continued to go almost every week to Saclepea and the rest of the family went when we could. With Stefanie getting older and moving around more, we decided to take Jenny, the girl who helped me with my little ones during the week. This would free me up to be more involved with the growing ministry in Saclepea. That was the first time that Jenny had ever flown, and it was so much fun to watch her as she saw her country from a much higher perspective.

The church there was growing a very strong core group, and it was with them that we spent extra time teaching, encouraging, and praying. Though some of the church leaders were spiritually immature and weak, God taught us so much by watching Him work in their hearts exactly where they were. It dawned on us that we were still growing and learning too, and that God was good to use us in spite of ourselves.

One particular story that vouches for the amazing growth that God was performing in the hearts of the church folks in Saclepea was when Jeff called for a special offering. With the numbers in the church increasing, the consensus was that it would soon be time for the Good News Baptist church to build its own place. Someone had already given a piece of land located on the outskirts of the town, but the land would need to be surveyed and documented correctly before it would be wise to start building.

My journal reads:

> *At the end of the service Jeff asked them to take a special offering to help send someone to Sanniquellie with the money for our church land survey. It would take $4.00 for*

someone to travel there and back. The offering was $4.60, so Jeff showed them how God could provide through them and give them even more than they asked. A plate of rice and soup could be bought for 50 cents at most cook shops, so whoever took the trip could also have money for a meal. It would have been extremely easy for Jeff to have placed $5 in the offering plate to take care of the trip, but the church members needed to see that God could and would provide through their obedient giving.

It was a huge lesson for the young church that morning to see that God was willing to use them! This lesson would prove to be part of the staying force for this church which, to this day, still exists. Long after the civil war took us away from Liberia, the church did build a meeting place which still stands as a reminder of God's faithfulness to them—even when the white man was not around.

As missionaries, it was so easy to be control freaks especially with our own "pet" ministries. Desiring things to be exactly up to par, we sometimes felt the need to do things ourselves in order to make sure they were done right instead of allowing those we were training to be involved in the important learning process. Even though I was not particularly apt at building a children's ministry, it was still hard for me to hand over flannel graph stories and other materials to those in the church who felt called to teach the children. Part of me assumed that they would never tell the story like I would nor would they take care of the teaching materials as I would, but I really tried to lay down those prideful thoughts. Of course, they would not do it like I would, but by God's grace, do it better!

Months after handing over the children's ministry to a Liberian couple in the church, I went with Jeff for a visit. It was so heartening to see how the ministry was growing, and I was amazed at what natural gifts this couple had with the children there. Who was I to say who God would and could use just because they did not do it exactly as I would? This was a launching pad for much of our ministry as it took on the face of strategic mentoring and has remained to this day....making disciples and teaching them to do the same!

Still, it has taken a daily and purposeful letting go of any ministry in which God has allowed us to be a part so that He could work out His purpose in our lives and in the lives of those we were called to teach!

Missions in the Raw

The weekend finally arrived where I would see if riding over the road to Monrovia was as interesting as flying there. Other than the strategically-placed military checkpoints and the unnerving peering of the soldiers with their AK47s hanging off their shoulders, it wasn't too bad. I was happy when we hit paved roads in Ganta, which was the same town where we had taken Stefanie about three weeks before when we had found out she had malaria. Traveling on dirt roads for nearly three hours seemed to shake my brain into mush.

Our business manager's family in Monrovia was leaving Liberia permanently, and Jeff had worked out details to buy his ham radio equipment. That was our main reason for taking the trip to Monrovia. We arrived on a Friday afternoon, and had to stay with the business manager's family because all the other houses were full. That night was one of the hottest nights we had ever experienced in Africa as the thermometer in the house registered 103 degrees at two-thirty in the morning! No one slept very well that night.

We left Monrovia on Sunday afternoon, more grateful that our home was upcountry where, thanks to the moist rain forest, the temperatures always remained a little cooler. Saclepea was on our way back to Tappi, so we decided to stop there for the Sunday evening service. By the time we arrived in Saclepea, we had been in the truck for over four hours, and the girls were irritable and fidgety. Knowing the futility of it, I didn't try to take them into the service. So while Jeff went into the building to greet the church folk and preach, the girls and I stayed near the truck.

I had been needing to go to the potty for quite some time, but wasn't sure what to do with six month old Stefanie whom I did not want crawling around in the dark while I did my business. First, I had to find a secluded place to do this business. Why didn't I just go to the public toilets, you ask? Well, there were none. Okay, there was an enclosed building on the other side of town, but even then it was just holes in the ground, and I could not, in my mind, see how I could do that with two children, especially in the dark. I eventually found a place that I thought would work, and asked three-year old Michelle to hold Stefanie long enough for me to do my business. Halfway through, Michelle started screaming that she was going to drop Stefanie, and it was very likely true since she was practically squeezing her around her neck. They both started freaking out, Michelle because she could not hold Stefanie anymore and Stefanie because she could not breath, but I was in no position to stop at that point, so I gently tried to coax Michelle into calming down and not to choke the life out of her sister. We all survived the episode with only slight leftover trauma. That was truly an example of missions in the raw!

The following Sunday we again returned to Saclepea and found out that the church members had prepared a feast and a special program. For the past four visits, they had not fed us per our request. We did not want them to have to look for extra food every time we came to worship with them. I brought, as I had in the past, one large thermos of drinking water for our trip, which had always sufficed for those short visits. However, that day they had prepared a gravy soup which was mainly made up of palm oil, onion, and a type of meat. The meat of that day was goat. Now, Jeff had eaten goat several times over the past year, but this would be my first time and I was not looking forward to tasting my first bite of goat with dozens of eyes watching me.

Remembering that honored guests were served the intestines and kidneys of the goat, I steeled myself for the inevitable. How wonderful that they wanted to honor us with the best food. I really tried to be thankful and bask in that honor, but as I gazed at the mushy meat perched on top of a perfectly good plate of rice, I lost my resolve. Moving that honored piece of meat around my plate while I laboriously chewed the rice, I focused on visiting with some of the ladies around me and then handed off the rest to some hungry children standing near me.

As if that was not enough for my stomach for one day, they had prepared the soup with so much hot peppers that the pungent smell trailed the steam off the plate. After taking just one bite, our noses and eyes began to water. At the time, I was the only one in the family who ate hot things and usually enjoyed them, so it was not for myself that I was concerned. Jeff had an almost zero tolerance for hot foods, and I knew that he must be going through agony while trying to smile, talk, and swallow that pasty fire. Michelle was not able to eat any of the soup, so I pulled out some plantain chips that I had brought along as a snack. As the chips were salty, Michelle began to gulp the water we had brought in the thermos like we had a whole barrel of it.

It was at that moment that I lost (just briefly) the capacity to feel my child's thirst. Jeff and I were experiencing such fiery mouths that we weren't sure if the burning would ever stop, our stomachs turned nauseous from the intensity of the peppers. We took very small sips of water, but our mouths were crying out for gallons. I became immune to Michelle's whining about being thirsty. I know it sounds cruel, but don't judge a person's actions until you've swallowed the same pepper as she has.

Then a miracle happened; an absolute miracle, I'm not kidding. After we graciously, but quickly thanked the church family for their hospitality, we took our leave, desperately trying to find a small store where we could buy a Coke or something to quench our thirst. Liberia was still under a pretty strict "blue" law so all stores were closed. As I reached into a smaller cooler to get Stefanie and Michelle a cookie, out of the corner of my eye, I saw something glistening. Wet and cold. Certainly it was a delusion. But, no, in the corner of the cooler was a small plastic bag of ice! I did not even remember putting it in there! Lesson? Don't underestimate God's ability to do anything, even sending ice from heaven to refresh His weary and desperate servants in the middle of the jungle! The four of us each sucked on a piece of frozen heaven as we made our way back to the airstrip.

To Kill a Scorpion

Later that evening, my mouth, though feeling raw, at least was not burning. Jeff had gone into town to the evening service, and I was putting the girls to bed early. While setting Stefanie down on the living room rug, out of the corner of my eye I saw something moving on the floor beside the dining table. Looking closer, I saw that it was a scorpion! Sauntering straight towards us, I tried not to panic and as calmly as possible asked Michelle to go into the kitchen and bring a cooking pan. The only problem: I forgot to tell her why. That did not work with my inquisitive Michelle. She stood there and asked me what seemed like a thousand questions about what I was going to do with a pan in the den.

As I watched the ugly black thing come closer to Stefanie and me, I tried again. "Michelle, listen, there is a scorpion on the floor...." That's as far as I got with that explanation. She ran and jumped up on the couch like the scorpion was only after her! I appealed to her, "Michelle, please, honey, mommy really needs you to go and get a pan so I can kill the scorpion. I need to watch where it goes. PLEASE BE BRAVE. I won't let him hurt you!" After what seemed the longest time, she finally jumped down and ran off to the kitchen, coming back not with a heavy frying pan, but a baking pan. At that point, I was not going to be picky. I strategically placed the pan on top of the scorpion as it defiantly raised its pinchers towards me like a banner. It remained trapped under the pan until our "Braveheart" returned from church. Then–CRUNCH TIME!

Spontaneous Funeral

On another Sunday, Jeff and another missionary flew to Saclepea for the day. It had become much more difficult to travel with Stefanie who had learned to crawl and was getting into every-thing. Having the truck at my disposal and after leaving Stefanie with Nancy Sheppard who was staying home with her kids that morning, Michelle and I went into town to the local Baptist church. During the song service, a group of men came and stood at the back of the church along with two soldiers. Following the eyes of others who were distracted at the uniformed visitors, I could not imagine what was going on.

At the end of the song, the pastor stood up and announced that *Old Lady Murceo* (though it may sound insulting to you, it is seriously a term of great respect in the Liberian culture) had passed away in Monrovia. Because she had been a longtime member of the

140

Tappi Baptist Church, one of her last wishes was to be brought back to Tappeta for her burial. The pastor told us that the body of Mrs. Murceo was in a car outside the church, and if everyone would please ready themselves, the church would now perform the funeral service of this elite member right then.

Before my eyes, the church was transformed into a house of mourning. The same choir that had been singing praises and admiration to Jesus with a jubilant spirit did an about face and began to sing a different kind of song. When everything was cleared from the front of the church, the men solemnly rolled in the casket and parked it right in front of the pulpit. Some of the women sitting around me started mourning and wailing which scared Michelle. With wide eyes of intrigue, she clung to me while the church continued their transition from praise to lamentations. It was West African fashion to mourn loudly even if you did not know the person, perhaps out of respect for that person's life.

After the pastor preached what I supposed was a fine funeral message because it was in dialect that I was still learning, the casket was opened and everyone was expected to file past and pay their last respects to Old Lady Murceo. Not really sure at what to do at this point, but feeling that it would be rude to sit in our seats, Michelle and I queued up along with the rest of the congregation to pay our respects.

Holding tightly to Michelle's hands, because I knew how fascinated she would be seeing this kind of thing, I didn't put it past her attempting to park herself in front of the casket and gawk for a while. Quietly I reiterated to Michelle that she must save ALL of her questions and comments until we were out of the church and in the truck. Not knowing how long this woman had been dead and certainly not wanting the smell to give me the answer, we filed by as quickly as the procession would allow. I was relieved to see that there was a glass partition over the body which made it somewhat more palatable, but it was still pretty evident by the way the body looked, that she had been dead for quite some time. On the way home from church that morning, Michelle did not disappoint me: she asked dozens of questions about what we had just experienced.

Another day, another lesson about this fascinating country where my cultural perceptions were constantly being challenged with graphic reality. In Liberia, you just never knew what to expect when you went to church. From crazy men spouting scriptures to animals rambling around the first fruits at the altar to impromptu funerals. Life in Liberia was definitely an adventure!

Jeff, a Rat, and Preaching in the Streets

During our second year in Liberia, Jeff participated in a week-long pastor's conference in the larger town of Ganta. He and Chick Watkins stayed for the entire week while the other missionary men flew back and forth during their days of speaking. Jeff was given the topic of soul winning and visitation which he taught twice a day for four days. Over thirty-five pastors attended from all over the country, giving Jeff a great opportunity to meet many for the first time and to have some sweet fellowship with Liberia's greatest spiritual leaders.

When feeding large crowds in Liberia, the cheapest meat to use was dried fish or other dried meats. In America, this would be like buying a can of Spam to make ham sandwiches instead of buying the fresh deli slices of ham. Dried meat in African soups was even hard for Jeff to handle. Shriveled and charred, dried meat had a pungent, vinegary smell that was always unpleasant to me.

One day at the conference they put dried monkey in the soups which had been prepared for the visiting pastors. Trying to get the newest missionary to eat the hand of the monkey, some of the more mischievous African pastors laid it prominently on top of Jeff's rice! While it was a great thing to experience the camaraderie of his African brothers, Jeff still could not eat the dried monkey hand. I am not talking about beef jerky, though in a sense, I guess it was like that. MONKEY JERKY just doesn't have the same appeal.

Anytime that Jeff went into a village to sleep, he always carried a mosquito net. Without it, he would be sharing his bamboo framed bed with the creatures of the night. Often he would wake up and sense that a rat was trying to chew through the mosquito net or roaming around the room looking for bounty. I knew by hearing Jeff's stories that I was not ready for those kind of adventures yet!

142

On the last night of the week-long conference, Chick Watkins encouraged Jeff to go out on the streets and just start preaching while the conference was finishing up inside the church. Jeff had a liberating time just opening his Bible and proclaiming God's truths on the streets of that town. He saw several people come to Christ through the effort. Through his teachings and passion for giving Liberians the Gospel of Jesus, Chick Watkins fast became one of Jeff's heroes in the faith. He enjoyed that week of watching Chick witnessing, counseling, and encouraging the Liberian pastors. Mentors are so very important in whatever our life's work is. Being able to see your mentor in action was the best kind of learning! Jeff came home from that conference extremely tired from the nocturnal company that kept him from sleeping very soundly, but very encouraged by the results of the week and all that he had learned from Chick and the African pastors.

CHAPTER SIXTEEN

Even from a dark night, songs of beauty can be born. —*Maryanne Radmacher-Hershey*

Ring-a-ling!

Our first Christmas in Liberia was somewhat a blur considering the few short weeks that we had been there. However, by December 1986, when our second Christmas in Liberia rolled around, we were a little more established, felt a little more confident with a year of jungle life under our belt, and had added to our family just eleven weeks prior with baby Stefanie. Both sets of grandparents had already booked tickets early in the fall, and we were in high expectation of spending time with them in our African home, watching them with both our little girls, and introduce our African friends to the ones most precious to us whom we had left in America.

My parents came around the first of November and stayed for two weeks. They were able to celebrate Stefanie's first month birthday with us as well as participate in a couple of the Bible school festivities planned during that time of year. Within ten days of their departure, Jeff's parents and baby sister came to visit. Thanksgiving coincided with the Abernethy's visit, so that was fun. They returned to the States on December 9th, leaving us with a longing to go with them, to go where it was familiar and easy. After the birth of Stefanie, four weeks of family visits, and then experiencing our second Christmas in West Africa; well, it took some spiritual stamina and God's amazing grace! God IS incredible all the time, but in those times when our flesh seems ready to overpower us with sadness, loneliness, and want, His presence is always enough!

A Story in Itself

Today was a story in itself, was what I wrote in my journal on December 18, 1986. The Liberian school year went from March through mid-December, making the months of January and February their summer break. During those two months when there was typically no rain, the Liberians prepared and tended their rice and vegetable farms. On that particular December day that my journal referenced, Jeff was scheduled to speak at the Ziah Mission School graduation—a school that had been established many years ago by missionaries. Ziah was a small town not even twelve miles from Tappita, but the only way to get to it was on a two-track road in unpredictable condition.

Jeff and I decided that the girls and I would go with him since it was only intended to be a short day trip. He chartered an old, rusty, weathered fifteen passenger money bus for $40 to take us straight to Ziah with no stops. Otherwise, we would have stopped every mile or so along the way to pick up and drop off passengers. That could have potentially added two or more hours to our twelve mile trip! Stefanie was just eight weeks old, and though she had been an easy baby, I felt a little insecure about going deeper into the jungle with my two small girls. Nonetheless, I refused to succumb to my fears as our family of four boarded the money bus about 9:00 a.m. that morning. We brought our own boiled drinking water and some snacks in a small cooler along with extra clothes for Michelle and Stefanie.

As we traveled out of town and zoomed past scores of people plodding down the road in flimsy flipflops, I started feeling guilty about the scores of women with baskets on their heads, babies tied to their backs, and little children with no shoes walking beside them. I conceded that we really were millionaires compared to them, and that was why my family and I were seated on a money bus all alone heading to a nearby town. There were times when I hated the way I stuck out like a sore thumb and struggled with how the Africans might have perceived us. While bouncing along the rough dirt road, I imagined what it would be like to walk the twelve miles with my children and husband, smiling and chatting with the Africans whom we would pass on the dusty road. It was a beautiful image, but the bubbly notion soon popped out of my head when I also remembered the time I tried to walk just two miles to church with my two children in the heat and dust. *THE COLLISION OF CULTURE CONSTANTLY PLAYED LOUD, MINOR NOTES IN MY HEAD!*

As we turned off the main road onto the Ziah two-track, I forbade Michelle to hang her head out the window because of the proximity of the trees and branches to the bus windows. Six miles into the trip, we came upon obvious road construction, and I tried to remember if we had passed any signs that would have indicated "ROAD CONSTRUCTION AHEAD" or "DETOUR." Ahead of us, a crew with a bulldozer had torn out a wooden bridge and had just started placing the pipe for the new bridge. On those small roads it would have been impossible to turn around except if there had been an area delved out for that purpose. We were nowhere near any area like that, so there we sat along with several other vehicles, and waited.

Needless to say, Jeff found plenty by which to be entertained, even involving Michelle with facts that kept her from getting bored and whiny. Thankfully, Stefanie slept, ate and slept again. I took my Bible out of my tote bag and tried to read as I shooed flies and averted dozens of curious little eyes gazing unashamedly through the windows at the white woman sitting alone on a large money bus meant to hold at least thirty people.

When Michelle had enough of the curious bystanders trying to touch her red hair, she stomped onto the bus and sat close to me. Jeff tried politely to shoo away the children gathered around the bus, but it was futile. The novelty of seeing a practically empty money bus reserved by four white people was just too much. Such was the plight of being a white person, especially a child, in an African culture. And that never changed. Our children had to grow up learning to deal with the constant staring and sometimes heckling by the African children anytime we traveled.

Around 1:00 p.m., the last pipe was laid, and the construction crew deemed the bridge safe. Hold on! Where was the supervising engineer to make that call? Everything in me wanted to scream, "LET'S GO BACK! PLEASE DON'T CROSS THE BRIDGE!" But I knew that would only cause the driver to have a good laugh at my expense. Jeff tried to reassure me that those pipes were probably safer than the wooden bridge they had just taken out. Probably? Holding tightly to baby Stefanie and to my breath, I watched wide-eyed as we crossed the deep muddy ravine below us. I did my best not to panic, but that was what happened when a very dramatically-inclined white American woman followed a compelling calling on her life to go wherever God had chosen. Even if that meant across a newly-laid bridge deep into the jungles of West Africa.

Knowing that the graduation was supposed to have started at 10:00 a.m. that morning, I asked Jeff why we were still going to Ziah. Surely it was over by now. However, my wise husband, who had traveled far more extensively in Liberia than I had, knew something that I did not. Liberians did not care as much about time as they did for quality. To them, Jeff was a quality speaker, and they had all the time in the world.

In the States, what would happen if a speaker was late for a graduation ceremony? I think we will agree that no American high school senior would dare wait for over three hours to receive his diploma! MAIL IT TO MY MOM, SIR—I'M OUTTA HERE! Not in Ziah. The whole town had waited for two basic reasons: they knew we would come and they also knew how unpredictable travel was. The delay we had just experienced was commonplace to them. Their acceptance of things that could not be changed or others that could change in an instant inspired me!

Sure enough, when we arrived three and a half hours late, the townspeople were happy to see us and did not, in the least bit, seem put out or inconvenienced. In fact, they had not even started the graduation. It was evident from that amazing scene that few Africans died of stress-related heart disease. The incident reminded me so much of the soon coming of Jesus Christ, and how we are to be faithful until He does come. Some were sitting in the church building patiently and expectantly, others were about the business at hand, but no one seemed to doubt that we were coming.

So thankful were they that Teacher Jeff had brought his family, they placed two extra chairs on stage for Michelle and me in their unique and beautiful way of honoring us for sharing their special occasion with them. I was falling in love with the African people over and over. All went well during the program until Stefanie woke up and decided that she wanted to eat. As she "rooted" for her food, the audience collectively turned their eyes to me. Unwilling to share this feeding time with over a hundred curious spectators,

I discreetly attempted to walk off the stage and found privacy in a nearby hut.

For me, the actual giving of the diplomas was the most exciting part of the three-hour program. When her child's name was called to receive his diploma, the mother would dance down the aisle, drop a few coins in the teenager's hands, singing and dancing joyously back to her seat. It was a big, big deal—this graduation thing.

Embodied in the heart of this story are some of the things I miss most about living in West Africa. The Liberians knew how to enjoy the little and big things in life with passion, fervor, and celebration! Come to think of it, I did feel a little like that on the nights my girls graduated from high school! Well, except for dropping money into my daughters' hands! Nope, I wasn't that happy!

After the intriguing program, the church hosted a celebratory feast for the graduates and those in attendance. Michelle and Jeff gobbled down the potato green soup cooked with some kind of undisclosed meat, but I was mainly thinking about the ride back in the money bus and how I would tell the driver if I needed to stop because of the oily potato green sloshing around in my stomach. Playing it safe, I just ate dry cooked rice.

On our return trip, we witnessed to the driver of the truck whom we had hired to take us back to Tappeta. He asked us many questions and really enjoyed arguing about whether the Bible or the Koran was more accurate.

A good lesson for any of us who are Christians: never knowing if we would ever see a person again to whom we are witnessing should inspire us to say everything that needs to be said the first time. Sure we may feel shy or unsure of ourselves or may even slouch under the possible rejection of the person to whom we are talking. But, it is not us that they are rejecting; it is our precious Savior. We are only guaranteed that one chance, that one time to share Christ. Oh, to always be bold enough to say what we need to say! Such was the case with that Muslim driver. We never did see him again during our years in Liberia, but we can only pray that the verses we read to him from God's Word and our testimony of Christ's love would have brought him to that saving grace which can alone take him to heaven.

Silent Night in a Faraway Village

After returning from one of the most unusual experiences of my African missionary career, I was very tired. Despite the fatigue, I felt somehow more connected with the African people because I had shared that special event with them. Since Michelle had played with baby goats in the village all afternoon and Stefanie had been held by dozens of women during the festivities, a long, warm bath was in order. Squeaky clean and fed a snack, I tucked the girls in bed.

Feeling tired but extremely melancholy, I sat in the living room and looked at our Christmas tree. It was not the plastic blow up tree that we had used the year before, but a tall artificial tree we had brought in our container of belongings, beautifully decorated with lights and shimmering ornaments.

While sitting there, it dawned on me that I had not seen a single Christmas tree nor any colored lights in the town of Ziah that afternoon; still there was very much a "SENSE" of Christmas, a spirit of hope and praise. Strange how I had always thought that to make the season bright, there had to be a Christmas tree, Christmas music, and Christmas presents. Indeed, that Christmas of 1986, was a turning point for me, and even though we have been ministering back in America for more than eight years now, I have never forgotten what I discovered that night faraway in the quiet Liberian jungle.

His Spirit bore witness in the hearts of those who would probably never sing Jingle Bells or eat cranberry sauce or pumpkin pie. After some years of ministering to those precious African people, I began to understand that Emmanuel had also come to them, and they, far better than I, understood how to give back praise to Him in their own way, own manner, own language, and own unique rhythm!

In the silence of the cool African night, my heart bent towards Jesus Christ much like the shepherds must have that starry night in a place just as quiet and unassuming. EMMANUEL! Shhhh! Listen, HE IS STILL WITH US....no matter where we are. IN THIS PLACE. IN EVERY PLACE

It's Beginning To Feel A Lot Like Christmas

As Liberia was located only about six degrees above the equator, there was no such thing as snow or frigid Arctic air blowing. Every year during late December and early January, the temperature would drop slightly and a cool breeze would blow in from the Sahara Desert. According to my journal of December 21, 1986, it was the first time that I remembered wearing a sweater in Africa. That the cool weather came right before our second Christmas in Liberia was a special treat.

My journal reads:

> *It's been a real cool, refreshing day. No one in the States would believe how we are sleeping under three blankets or walking around wearing sweaters and jackets in the morning and late evenings. It's only 66 degrees at 11:00 p.m. By 6:00 a.m., it has gotten down to 56 degrees. During the day it has never gotten above 78 degrees and the humidity is down to around 65 percent. My lips are feeling chapped. It's been wonderful, but at night, we do not have the luxury of closing our windows. So under the blankets we go.*

Since we only had screens on our windows, there was no glass to close out the coolness or the heat. Finding a few blankets in an old packing barrel from a previous missionary tenant, I washed them up and gave them to my Liberian friend, Mary, for her family. Blankets were something that I would never had imagined that I could have given away in a tropical climate such as Liberia, but that cool time was somewhat unusual, and I felt bad for the Africans trying to deal with what to them was extreme cold. Never did I think that we would experience chilly weather as we did that year in Liberia.

For over a year, we had been in the habit of making chocolate milkshakes in our blender before the electricity went off, but during that "wintry" period, we made hot chocolate for our family and enjoyed sipping it while sitting around the tree singing Christmas carols with Michelle. Incorporating some of our American traditions into the simplicity of the African Christmases was the best way we knew to give our children the best of both worlds.

151

The Making of New Traditions

Being missionaries in West Africa brought constant new lessons, new discoveries, and new uncertainties almost daily! Every missionary pilot rotated on a weekly flight line (on call) status throughout the years. This meant that if there were medical or supply flights needed, the "on call" pilot must be available to make those flights. During Christmas week of 1986, Jeff happened to be the pilot on call, and sure enough, there was a summons for the plane on Christmas Eve. Since our anniversary incident when Jeff was forced to stay on another mission compound because of bad weather, I was always concerned that other circumstances would keep Jeff in Monrovia overnight. Thankfully, he was able to return by 4:30 that Christmas Eve afternoon ladened with mail, packages, and groceries for everyone on the station.

Christmas Eve of that year, I started a custom which continued for all the Christmases we would spend in Africa–away from family traditions in the States. I made lasagna and the girls would open one gift. We had a fun family time extolling the beauties of the season and teaching them of the real significance of the holiday. In my mind's eye, those are some of the sweetest memories I have of spending time with my children on the mission field. They grew up sensing that our little family unit was important and was sometimes the most secure place they had. That realization has certainly carried into their young adult lives. We have remained very close and our traditions, while not sacred, and forever changing as do families, are intermingled with sweet tastes of days gone by and promises of more to come.

Carolina Pit Cooked Pork

Mixing the ingenuity and astuteness of African outdoor cooking with the principle of "pit cooked BBQ" from the Carolinas, Jeff and a couple of his African guy friends designed a cooking pit in our backyard. So successful had we been in our culinary efforts with pork during the past months that the station as a whole elected to purchase local pork, and that the Abernethys would cook it for Christmas.

Now, burning or ruining two or three pounds of your own pork is quite different from being responsible for 32 pounds of pork bought by someone else. The pressure was on! Filling the barbecue pit partially with fire coal (a type of charcoal), we wrapped the seasoned pork in yards and yards of aluminum foil and placed it prayerfully in the pit. Several moistened banana leaves served to seal the pit for cooking. I do not remember how many hours it took to cook that much pork, but it did turn out very well. What a relief to be able to present to those hungry, expectant missionaries that scrumptious BBQ for our Christmas feast.

A Very Long Moment In Time

Christmas 1987 would be the last Christmas we would ever spend in Tappeta, Liberia, though we had no way of knowing that at the time. On December 13, 1987, my first major missionary moment happened. A *missionary moment* is an event that heightens the reality of what God has called us to do and defines our commitment to that call. I will delve in and out of my journal in the next few paragraphs in order to best tell the story.

Sunday, December 13th, started just as any other Sunday does out here. We ate breakfast about 8:30, then Jeff got ready to go out on a preaching expedition in the airplane. That particular Sunday, he and two other missionary pilots were going out in the Cessna 180 to three different towns to preach. Jeff was going to be dropped off in Saclepea, of course, then the other two would go on from there.

> *The day passed quickly for me. By 1:00 p.m., I had lunch ready, and when Jeff had not returned, I went ahead and fed the girls. An hour later, I had put both girls down for their naps and was reading a book. I do not remember exactly when I knew that something was wrong, but subtly the sense of panic and what if came. The airplane was not equipped with a radio that could signal us here on the mission station and cell phones were years from being available, so there was simply no way that I could know anything until someone came and told me.*

Before Jeff and I ever married, I told the Lord that I had to be able to surrender Jeff to His hands and never worry about his flying. So far, I had been able to do this for the most part. I was very thankful that the Lord had kept him safe and that He had helped me to have peace of mind every time Jeff flew off in the airplane. But this was a bigger test....a test of ultimate surrender. At 3:45, I was on my knees speaking fervently to God. Yes, I was afraid, but there was still the "PEACE THAT PASSETH ALL UNDERSTANDING" shrouding me.

My journal that day cites: "*However, I knew what I had to say ALOUD to God. 'Father, even if Jeff is down in the bush somewhere dead or terribly wounded, I know that I can still trust you. Help my unbelief.' After that prayer, I struggled to rest in God's will and not my own.*" Putting feet to my faith was often the hardest part, especially when there were other people involved. I had to walk the talk; there was no other way out of this situation but to keep looking up. If I looked around at the situation, I felt that my heart would explode and everything felt out of control. Looking up was best choice. IT ALWAYS IS.

I so desperately needed that unexplainable peace that God promised. And He gave it in abundance when I asked in sincerity. At 4:15, Beth Wittenberger came down, and we went to see Millie Dodson. All three of us were without any news of our husbands. They had been gone since 9:45 that morning. Chick Watkins came over at 4:30 and said that he would take the Cherokee up and fly around the towns where he knew they might be. We could tell that he was worried, too. I came home and tried to think about feeding the girls some supper. My mind and ears kept listening for anything that sounded like an airplane! "OH, GOD, TEACH ME WELL THIS LESSON OF WAITING AND TRUSTING. I DON'T LIKE IT, BUT I DO NEED TO LEARN IT. GIVE ME STRENGTH TO FACE WHAT MIGHT COME TO ME IN THE NEXT FEW MINUTES."

A little after 5:00 p.m., a money bus drove up on the mission compound towards the Wittenberger house. I knew that it was news of the airplane and remember how my breathing quickened, but I did sense God holding me close. Soon Beth came down on her motorcycle with a worried look on her face. "They're all right," she said. "James had an accident with the airplane, and Richard and Jeff are probably still waiting in Saclepea." The strip where the accident happened was narrow and short, a huge challenge for even the best pilot, which James was. A limb of a tree caught the right wing just as he was taking off and slung him around and then down. The plane was in pretty bad shape, but the men were all safe!

My heart was singing! I thanked God for the men's safety and then asked God, "Did I pass the test, Lord? Did I trust you enough?" Soon after talking with Beth, I heard the Cherokee coming in for a landing. Running on the energy that sheer relief brought, I dashed to the airplane hangar with my little girls in tow. As Jeff got out of the plane, I gave him a big bear hug which I think might have embarrassed him in front of the others, but I really did not care. My heart was so thankful that God had shown His mercy to our guys and that I could hold Jeff in my arms again.

A Christmas Camping Experience

The infamous Christmas camping trip with another missionary couple, four missionary kids and two other teenagers visiting from the States on a short term missions trip was my first experience into the deep bush of Liberia without Jeff. A group decided that they wanted to go on an all-night trip into the bush, but they needed several adults to go with them. Jeff had been on many of those hunting trips into the bush, so he was more than willing for me to take the truck and go with them. He would stay with the girls at the house and sleep in our comfortable bed. I ragged him about that, at least until the next morning when I thought of crawling red-eyed and aching from weariness into that comfortable bed.

We had a big tent, pots and pans for cooking, and several spotlights for the hunting part. Finding a clear place to camp, we unloaded our supplies and then several of us headed out to find fire wood as the others went hunting. Later around the campfire, we had a wonderful time sharing testimonies and hearing a devotional by the short term missionary. Around 1:30 a.m., the first of the hunters came in with their bounty: two wildcats, one flying squirrel, and three sofley-sofleys. I had absolutely no inclination to gaze at any of those bloody, dangling creatures of the wild!

Soon they wanted me to transport them further up the road in the truck. Two Liberian teens along with the two missionary guys were on the tailgate of the truck with a spotlight. When they would see something up in the nearly 100-foot tall trees, they would holler and beat on the truck for me to stop. After hearing shots and feeling that they had hit one of the creatures, they would take machetes and chop through the bush to find where it fell. We arrived back at the campsite around 3:30 a.m., and I was starting to get sleepy. Trying to stay awake a little longer, I watched William Farr (one of our Bible schools students who today is one of the Liberian professors) sear the skin off the wildcat, turn it in the fire, and then cut it open, pulling the guts out. The last straw came when I heard one of the guys talking about how "sweet" (very, very good) that the meat was going to be when it was cooked.

I went inside the tent and lay down, trying to make my stomach calm down from the thought that it might have to eat some of that wildcat. No part of me could imagine eating rice and wildcat soup at 4:00 a.m.–or any time of day–for that matter! At 6:00 a.m., I woke up and had some strong coffee to drink while those that had stayed awake the entire night teased me about missing the meal.

We arrived back on the mission compound around 7:30 in the morning, and I dreamed of a piece of toast and my warm, soft bed. What I got was an excited greeting and syrupy kisses by two bright-eyed little girls who were happy to see their mommy and ready for the day to begin! Jeff came out of our bedroom stretching and looking very satisfied with himself for getting a good night's sleep. Despite the relentless fatigue, I wouldn't have traded that Christmas memory for anything.

CHAPTER SEVENTEEN

Not by works of righteousness which we have done, but according to his mercy He saved us, by the washing of regeneration, and renewing of the Holy Ghost; which He shed on us abundantly through Jesus Christ our Saviour. Titus 3:5,6

Reflections

When focusing solely on the thousands of Liberians that lived in remote, hard-to-access villages in just a hundred mile radius of our mission compound, it felt a little overwhelming. Often the "clash of cultures" that I have spoken of before would bombard me with an irrepressible desire to reach those around me but also plague me with an aching sense that I was not culturally equipped nor physically adept to plunge headlong into the dense jungle with a Bible in my hand like Mary Slessor.

So common is it for us to be tempted to set our sights predominantly on what we think is the bigger picture, the incredibly brave and adventuresome calling that others seem to enjoy. That is where we think, if we were totally honest, that God's favor hovers. Nothing could be further from the truth. God delights in making the common, ordinary things in our lives uncommon and meaningful.

In those early years of being an African missionary, working in my home, occasionally teaching in the Bible institute, caring for my children, preparing meals, and assisting in those things that would help the other missionaries began to feel like not enough. I compared my calling with those around me and those "great" missionaries about whom I had read. When Satan can prompt us into comparing ourselves and our efforts to others, he can succeed in distracting us from the eternity-reaching results that can be realized right where we are.

Discontentment is a sin. Basking in the dissatisfaction of where we find ourselves can only accelerate the arrival of other sins. Anger, bitterness, envy, and an absence of joy in our lives. If you have never studied the Fruits of the Spirits and compared them with the fruits of the flesh, the books of Galatians and Ephesians will guide you on that journey. Though I try not to live in regret of past sins, one of the saddest things in my life is to wonder about all the lessons I missed, differences I could have made, and memories lost of watching God be extraordinary in the places where I found myself drowning in my discontent.

No doubt I was quite a work in the making and certainly still am! There was the side of me that tried to be mindful of ministry burnout and would sometimes feel the need to step off the compound for a few days. Then there were the times when I told God that He had not given me enough to do, that I wasn't feeling I was making a difference. Discontentment, plain and simple. It was one of my sharpest vices and I hate to admit it.

All I can do as I reflect on that dual image of myself in early ministry is to thank God for His unconditional love and patience! Today my daughters are all young adults and just in the past few years, in listening to their memories, their stories and the lessons they recount, has helped to wipe away any idea that I could have possibly done anything better than teaching and training them when it seemed other missionaries were doing "greater" things.

While I do not have the direct experience of trudging through the jungles and proclaiming God's Word to remote villages as Jeff did, I realize that he was able to do all those things for God's glory because his heart safely trusted in me to care for the things back home. I was just as much a missionary in every essence except perhaps in my attitude of not being content in where God had placed me!

Things Domestic

The only wringer washer that I ever remember seeing before coming to Liberia was in the "smoke house" on my grandparents' property, but never in my life had I ever experienced the joys of using a wringer washer to wash clothes. Add that to the fact if I wanted to wash any of my clothes in hot water, I had to first heat the water. Thankfully, I was able to take a bucket out to our work shed where the washer was located along with a heating coil. There were two galvanized tubs: one for the rinse water and one for the wet clothes after they had gone through the wringer for the second pass. It took me a few weeks to get my system down about clothes washing in my new surroundings, mainly because I usually had one of the guys do it for me on Saturday mornings. However, after Stefanie was born, I was compelled to wash diapers during some evening hours.

"There has been no rain today. Eight loads of clothes on the line and they all dried! Very unusual for rainy season." Two short, seemingly insignificant sentences in my journal entry for a day in July 1987, but it was a big deal. If you remember, I told you that we mainly washed clothes on Saturday morning when the generator was on for three hours. With a family of four, you can imagine the amount of dirty clothes that would mound up during a week's time. Sometimes it would be necessary to wash some of Stefanie's clothes (mainly cloth diapers) during a week night, but it had to be a real need because usually there were always too many other things to do inside the house during those three hours of electricity.

Our wringer washer was out in a storage building about a hundred feet from our house, and if I washed at night, the clothes would have to sit in a basket overnight until we could hang them up the next morning. Saturdays were just the better time to catch up on all the washing, so that is why there were eight loads of clothes drying on the line that particular day.

During rainy season, it was an ordeal to make sure that our clothes were taken off the lines before the rains would bombard us in the early afternoon. Most of the time, the clothes would not be completely dry when the rains arrived, so if there was enough daylight left when the sun came back out, we would go through the process of hanging those pieces of still damp clothes back out again. Frequently, there would be a good amount of clothes that would have to be rehung for a day or two in a row before we could deem them dry. We had a term called "rainy season dry" which meant we could still wear them, but they were definitely not crispy and fluffy dry.

There were those times, too, when our clothes had dried nicely during the time we took our siesta after lunch, then unheeded, the rains would come in full force. The violent beating of enormous rain drops on our zinc roof would always act as an alarm to us, kicking our resting bodies into gear. Dashing madly to the clothes-line in an attempt to save the dried clothes, we usually conceded that the rain had won. And the drying process started all over. If a load of clothes had to be hung out too many days in a row, they would begin to "ripen" which would initiate the need to be washed again.

Another Lesson in Trusting

Over and over God prompted me to consider how tightly I tried to hold on to my children instead of releasing them daily to Him. From snakes, scorpions, spiders, and malaria, He took me into the realm of even more physical dangers. Jeff's motorcycle had a basket attached to the back of it where he would carry items from place to place–or more times than not–where he would carry little girls begging to ride with their daddy! Stefanie was probably nearly eleven months old when she took a ride OUT of the basket while riding with Jeff. Deciding to stand up in the basket and before Jeff could talk her into sitting down, the motorcycle hit a bump and out Stefanie flew! Thankfully she hit no stumps or hard objects; only dirt....and lots of it! A little squirt of no more than 20 pounds, she just sort of bounced off the ground without really getting hurt. Nonetheless, you can imagine the fear that Jeff must have felt as he watched her fly out.

So many things could have happened, but they didn't. We live too often with the "what ifs" when God would have us live in the present with Him, the Great I AM. Every day, every moment, our children, our lives, and possessions, our very steps, must be given to the One and only One that holds them tenderly in His hand.

Refining Fire

This next story is not light reading. Undoubtedly, this is one of the most spiritually evocative times in my entire life. Have you ever had one of those times that changed you completely from the inside out? That challenged and stretched you beyond what you would have ever believed you could handle? A defining moment. This is mine.

160

In the predawn hour you could hear the jungle chatter building to a monumental crescendo. It was no different that morning, except that I was not listening to it snuggled contentedly beside my husband in our bed. Instead, I was sitting on the edge of a small hospital bed in our mission station's OB clinic. The voice of one of our Liberian midwives came plunging through the soothing jungle melody. "Missy, she fini" (interrupted *She is dead*). There was a kind of unbelievable awe to those words; a moment of denying the truth of it, even though I knew the midwife was right. She was a 30-year old Muslim woman named Mayummu who had been attempting to deliver her third child.

Our nurse was in Monrovia because of a medical emergency, so I had been left in charge of the clinic mainly as an administrator. The well-trained Liberian midwives were quite capable of handling routine deliveries and minor medical issues with our maternal patients. Beyond that, I was instructed to send any patients that the midwives thought would need extra care to a nearby hospital by plane or by road. It was evident within a few hours of Mayummu's arrival that her condition was definitely in need of professional medical care. She had been admitted to our clinic at 6:00 a.m. the previous morning with excruciating pain in her stomach, not all seeming to be due to labor.

It was a very cloudy day, intermittent with strong downpours of rain; definitely not conducive to safe flying, so we encouraged her family to take her to a hospital by money bus. They insisted that the road was closed, accentuating the fact that it was the middle of our rainy season and not at all unusual for the road from Tappi to the hospital to be impassable. Sometimes there were areas where the mud puddles were one-fourth to a half mile long, making it all but impossible for a vehicle to pass through. At those times, the only way to cross the mammoth mud hole was to walk through it or around it to a car on the other side.

Knowing that Mayummu's husband was the owner of a money bus, I pleaded with him to try to transport his wife to a hospital before any serious complications took place. Laughing at my suggestion, he cited in his dialect that she was merely a third wife and he would not spoil his truck for a third wife. They could easily be replaced, but trucks could not. It was a very good thing that he had left the room before the midwives interpreted what he had said. My flesh desired to lash out and give him a piece of my mind. Thankfully, the Spirit of God in me kept me from doing that though the reality of this husband's words stung me.

Leaving the care of Mayummu and the others at the clinic, I went home for a couple of hours, returning to the clinic at 7:30 that evening thankful to see that a medical worker from the government clinic had come to check Mayummu. Having a limited knowledge of maternity issues, I did not feel capable to handle this alone so was glad to have his opinion on her condition. He said that the baby's heartbeat sounded as if it was in distress, and it was obvious that the mother was quickly losing strength. At 9:30 p.m., her contractions completely stopped. She was very tired and just wanted to sleep.

I carried some of Rachel's obstetric books to my house to read, trying to find answers. In the middle of reading, the Lord helped me. I knew that the cessation of her contractions was not normal since the baby's head was so far down into the pelvic area. Something very serious had happened. I also remembered that her contractions were never regular, more spasmodic and very hard. Her blood pressure was very low and her temperature was only 94! According to what I had read, it seemed that she could have had a ruptured uterus from the pressure of the baby's head in the pelvic area. Perhaps the baby's head was too large to pass through or maybe the placenta had dropped below and lodged the head of the baby. Which one, I just wasn't sure!

Having already tried to witness to the woman, her sister had repeatedly told me to stop talking to her about Jesus. Still, I gently talked of Jesus because I did not feel at peace to be quiet. Mayummu knew she was dying and had begun her feeble prayer to Allah. Her sister, sitting on the other side of the bed, begged me not to talk my religion to her. "LEAVE HER SOUL TO MOHAMMED," she cried, rising from her chair to fling her body over her sister. At that moment, my heart knew an overwhelming burden for those Muslim women. They really had no hope of eternal life in heaven, and I thought how differently it would be if it was one of our

162

Christian women who truly knew she was on her way to live with Jesus! I silently watched Mayummu slip further from life and closer to hell. The awful reality of it stung me with a heavy turmoil in my heart and soul. I began to cry quietly as I prayed.

Within fifteen minutes or so, Mayummu was slipping in and out of consciousness, and her sister, thinking her death was imminent, began the terribly morbid but musical African death wail. My skin tingled as I listened to the futile prayers for this woman. She called to Allah, but I knew that he was not the Father of Jesus Christ, the Savior of the world. That God they did not accept at all! If only she knew what she was saying! I went home at 10:00 p.m. feeling helpless. The midwives promised to call me if they needed me.

At 5:15 a.m. that call came as a soft, but urgent rapping on our door. The woman, I was told, had been struggling with her breathing and was very weak. This could only mean that there must be fluid buildup (perhaps blood) and it was moving near her lungs and heart. I knew in my heart that we would lose her soon, but I still prayed that it would be a sunny, clear morning and that Jeff could fly her to Phebe, wanting desperately to get the burden off me for many reasons. But God had other plans. After arriving at the clinic in the foggy gray of the early morning, I climbed on the bed, sat with my back against the headboard, and the midwives slid Mayummu so that she was propped up against me.

Her temperature was still 94, but we could not get a blood pressure. Her pulse was weak and she was cold, clammy, but sweating profusely! We had lost the baby's heartbeat several hours before. Mayummu was in pain and struggling for breath. I tried to talk to her again about not putting trust in Mohammed, asking her how could he save her if he were dead himself? I told her that Jesus Christ was alive and could save her soul, even if He chose not to save her life. For the first time in my life I prayed for an anointing to speak in tongues, but more so that the words I was saying could be understood supernaturally by her in her own language. I quoted John 3:16 vigorously into her ears over and over, taking advantage of the time that her sister had left the room, so I could talk with her in peace.

She knew she was dying. She just wanted to lie down, but we tried to keep her sitting up to help the breathing. At around 6:25 a.m., she went comatose, but was still slightly breathing. The midwives and her sister all panicked. At that very moment, God allowed me to envision flames licking around her body as she traveled faster and faster into hell. I remember physically squeezing her, trying to pull her back against me—as if that effort would keep her from crashing into hell. It was an overwhelming moment.

God held me as I held her, so I stayed there. I knew that this woman would die in the next few minutes and that I would be sitting here with her. All I could think about was, "OH GOD, SHE'S GOING TO HELL AND I CAN'T STOP HER!" Out loud I said, "Please, Mayummu, why don't you listen to me? Jesus Christ is your only way to heaven." She stopped breathing at 6:30 a.m., and I tried artificial resuscitation—but I think it was more for me than anything else.

Her husband came in the room while I was doing CPR and was watching me with eager eyes. I had done everything I knew to do and actually did get her breathing again for about a minute. She looked right at me and I saw terror in her eyes. She mumbled something and I almost collapsed with the pain of it. Then God reminded me of her baby, and that it was already safe in Heaven with Him. If the baby had been born, it would have had little chance of ever knowing Jesus Christ.

Rejoicing in that, it was not long before I heard the death wail begin outside. I cannot even begin to describe an African death wail. It was blood-curdling and agonizing. If the words "ABSOLUTE HOPELESSNESS" had a sound, this death wail would be it. Melodic in a harsh, minor key. Sadness and terror and grief wrapped in a blanket of chants and inhuman sounds.

Moved deeply by the grieving intonations outside the door, I turned to her husband and said, "I'm sorry. God gives life and He takes life. There's nothing else I can do for your wife." He knew I had done everything I could and saw the tears in my eyes. Stepping outside in the midst of dozens of Muslim mourners was a sight for which my mind was not ready. Some of them were tearing their clothes and rolling in the dirt in complete hysterics. I felt like throwing up, but I chose to stay and brave the death scene no matter how much I wanted to flee! I sat down on the front steps of the clinic amidst at least fifty people that hardly knew I was there. Their eyes glazed over—they had gone somewhere else in their minds. It was easier that way, I guess, when there was no hope.

The tears came to me in a rush. I sobbed uncontrollably from grief, from sorrow, from desperation of the bondage of sin that I observed around me. Then I heard Mayummu's sister close by chanting a song to Allah as one of the midwives interpreted for me. She was asking him to be kind to her sister, and as if Allah needed reminding, that she had been a faithful Muslim, and to please make a good place for her in heaven. It stirred an anger in me that I did not quite understand! I went to her and took her chin in my hands. In English, which I knew she could not understand, I spoke of the hopelessness of her religion, telling her that the same thing would happen to her if she did not accept Jesus Christ. I was crying very hard again, but she just looked at me with despair and a forlorn look in her eyes. That look will never leave me.

I WILL NEVER BE THE SAME!

CHAPTER EIGHTEEN

Life can only be understood backwards, but it must be lived forwards.
—Soren Kierkegaard

Over the Road and Through the Mud

What possessed us to commit to a marriage and family seminar in October near the end of rainy season, I cannot say, but Mark and Nancy Sheppard and Jeff and I accepted the opportunity to do a one-day seminar on Marriage and the Home in the town of Ziah, where the infamous high school graduation program had taken place some months before. While we were still young missionaries and relatively young parents ourselves, we still knew that more than anything, those people needed scriptural guidelines to help them build strong Christian families, too. Godly principles are the same no matter the country, but the cultural tweaking is what makes it unique to a certain people group.

We were to leave on the afternoon after the death of Mayummu, from which I was still physically and emotionally exhausted. Nevertheless, life marched on, and there was much to do before we could depart for the seminar. Our African "nanny" Jenny and one of the missionary's teenage daughter, Becky Watkins (now Messer), were going to stay with our two girls at our house since we would be gone overnight. Though Ziah was only twelve miles away, it might as well have been one thousand since there was absolutely no way to stay in contact with our little girls. With hearts held tightly by God's promises, we kissed our girls goodbye and left with the Sheppards. The roads were not in good shape, so it took us an hour to travel those twelve miles.

If I remember correctly, this was Nancy's and my first time staying in a bush village. In the opinion of Jeff and Mark, the house we were given in Ziah was much nicer than some of the others in which they had stayed before. There was tile on the floor, the beds were decent, and there was no evidence of rats that I could see.

Unique would have been if the house had been built with an inside toilet–which it hadn't! That's not so bad during the day, but I had always been one to rise for an early morning "tinkle"–and there was the rub. It was still dark outside, but I could stay in bed no longer without paying the price later.

Though I dreaded to find the outside toilet facilities alone, I took pity on Jeff and let him sleep. I knew that the toilet house was an enclosed, nicely thatched building on the other side of the church, but in the darkness, my memory was not kind to me. I walked by several houses–all of them looking alike–and noticing several fires that had been started and where women were chatting softly to their neighbors. After walking past the same block of houses about three times, two of the women started laughing, rose from their fireside chat, and took me by the hand. One on each side, chatting with me in their dialect and pointing with their other hand. Feeling not a bit comfortable at the moment, I was grateful when they gently shoved me towards the blessed building where the toilet was waiting. I gave them a sheepish smile and even tried to thank them in their own dialect. They laughed all the way back to their houses. It was another one of those moments when I felt very white and very American.

The seminars were very well attended and seemed well received. Finishing up by late afternoon, we promised to come back again and continue the teaching in a few months. Because of heavy rains that had fallen during the night, the roads appeared in worse shape than the day before, and after getting stuck in the mud three times, we finally arrived home almost two hours later! Thankfully all was well with our kids and after much hugging, kissing, and hearing stories of their adventures, I cannot even begin to tell you how good it felt to take a long nap in my own bed that afternoon. I am almost sure we had omelets or sandwiches for supper, and most likely, went to bed as early as we could get the girls to bed.

Sometimes I think of those people in Ziah and wonder how many of them still even remember the things we taught them. After thirteen years of civil war, I don't even know how many still live there. But, God has promised that His Word will never return void and it is indeed a promise that He has often allowed us to confirm with our own eyes! It is that privilege of being a part of seeing God change lives and giving a little of ourselves to others that meant so much to us—and still does!

When Things Go Bump in the Night

Our mission compound generator ran on diesel and our planes used aviation fuel, so every six months or so, one of the men would have to make a trip down to Monrovia to order more diesel or aviation fuel. More than once in the past years, at least a couple of hundred gallons of fuel had been stolen before the truck arrived on the Tappeta compound. From that point on, it precipitated that one of the missionary men would need to travel back with the fuel truck each time. Though a long, tedious, and bumpy ride, somebody had to do it. During one of the times that Jeff was making a fuel run, I had my own rendition of things that go bump in the night!

As was my ritual before bed, I had been reading a book when I heard noises right outside our bedroom window. Jumping out of bed took a little effort since we slept under mosquito nets on a waterbed, but as fast as possible, in one fluid motion my feet hit the floor and I grabbed the flashlight that I always kept on my bedside table. I shined the light outside the window and called out, "Who's there?" Bump, bump, rustle, and my eyes caught a glimpse of two figures running into the bush. Our long wooden ladder was against the house where the attic door was, so I supposed the thieves were after something up there. It would have been extremely difficult for them to enter the house because of the thick steel security bars that were in every window.

Still not sure what I should do, I just walked around the house shining the flashlight inside and out. Suddenly I heard Mark Sheppard's motorcycle just fifty yards from our house as he was returning home from somewhere. I called out to him, and he quickly came over and carried the menacing ladder to his house. He also drove around the yard for a few minutes just to discourage the possible thieves from coming back. There was really nothing else I could do and was thankful that neither of the girls had woken up during the ordeal. Tucking myself tightly behind the mosquito net, I read and claimed Psalms 3 and 4, then cutting off the lights,

I lay listening to the sounds of the jungle. I couldn't help but feel so small and vulnerable in the midst of that incredible tropical maze, but I was also in awe that my Heavenly Father knew exactly where I was.

Four days later, after Jeff and a young man on a short term trip from the States had returned from Monrovia, we had a recurrence of that bumpy night. The sounds in the attic made us think the thieves had already scaled the house (without a ladder) and were in the attic. It felt so good to be vindicated and know that I had not imagined those two visitors a few nights before. Jeff and Ken bravely decided to go up and see what our thieves might want from our attic. They retrieved the ladder from the Sheppards storage shed where it had been since Mark had taken it, climbing up to have a look. What they found was unexpected if not a little disturbing considering that we had children in the house. It was a wildcat. A young wildcat that had taken up residence in our attic, possibly feeding off the nocturnal creatures that I absolutely refused to think lived above us!

Remembering that the Watkins family had been missing their pet wildcat for a couple of weeks, we assumed that it was probably him. Could it be that the thieves of four nights ago had known there was a wildcat living up there–had seen the eyes or seen it roaming around–and decided to take it for their soup pot? That assumption was much more comforting to me than to believe that two Africans were trying to spy on us in our house! No one had ever had that problem before.

Our idea of respecting each other's property and always asking before taking something off someone else's property was not particularly in groove with the West African culture. They lived much more in community than we do as Americans. As I have noted before, if any of our fruit trees were producing, the local children would come in our yard (uninvited) and partake of the ripened fruit. This presented another cultural collision. How much should we have pushed the Africans to ask before taking fruit from our trees or capturing a wildcat that lived in our attic? What was the balance? In their culture, they had boundaries, of course, though they were a little more communal than our American ones.

We continued trying to teach the African children to come to our door or window, asking before they took mangoes or avocado (butter pears), but after the first couple of years, we stopped rushing out to scold them quite like we had in the beginning. After seeing the "pecking order" of eating in their culture which deems that children eat only after all the adults have finished, we knew that the children were probably hungry. We chose to bend to the primal needs of the children instead of our own "rights" to proprietary matters.

The only varmints that we never got used to stealing our mangoes were the fruit bats! Mainly because they did their stealing at night while we were sleeping and occasionally would drop a ripened mango on our asbestos roof as they hightailed it out of the yard! That mango hitting our roof would raise the dead–and it always jolted us from sleep! In the jungle or elsewhere, I imagine there are some creatures to whom you just cannot teach manners!

Our Own Rikki Tikki Tavi Named Robbie

Before we even arrived in Liberia, my paranoia of coexisting with snakes was out of control! I prayed earnestly that I would never see a snake in my home in Africa, and I must say that in looking back, I do not remember experiencing the trauma of having to deal with a slithering shadow of a snake in any home we lived in. Without even realizing it, my praying muscles were growing, as I brought to my heavenly Father those things that threatened to undo me. He answered according to His will and my asking.

A few months before Michelle got her mongoose, she and John-Mark were outside playing with his. Jenny had baby Stefanie out on a blanket, and when Michelle and John-Mark decided to run and play a bit, they put the mongoose under the blanket for safe keeping (or so they thought). Taking a break from my afternoon duties, I walked out to where Jenny and Stef were. Before Jenny could stop me, I had plopped down on the blanket beside them! Realizing almost instantly what I had done, I slowly and painfully peeped under the blanket. There the little fellow was lying straight out–almost flat–with tongue hanging out, barely breathing. I put my hand to my mouth and tears filled my eyes. How was I going to tell

John Mark and Melodie that I had killed their mongoose by sitting on him? I felt awful. Unable to delay the inevitable, I went inside to get a towel in which to carry him back to his owners. My mind was in pain just remembering the look of that dying mongoose! When I walked outside, Jenny was shaking her head and smiling, and there beside her was the mongoose, walking around...a little bit in shock and limping, but definitely alive! For Michelle's fourth birthday, she had prayed that she could have a mongoose like her friends had.

One day before her birthday, some little African boys came by selling a baby mongoose and Michelle just knew God had sent it to her. So we caved. Those dark chocolate eyes looking at us with so much excitement and faith was just too much! She named him "Robbie" because she missed her cousin Robbie back in the States.

Reginald Ascue Lennon III (alias Robbie) became a part of our little family and fared well for as long as he was a juvenile mongoose. He ate all the cockroaches (making a nice crunching sound and if you dared watch him, you could see the legs and antennas hanging out the side of his little mouth), bugs, lizards, and anything else that was brave enough to enter his lair. Terminex could not have done any better! He liked to take trips outside, too, and hunt around for a few hours.

One of his favorite and funniest spots to loiter outside was by our dog Tippy's doghouse. He would get inside it and then not allow Tippy anywhere near it. One afternoon, it started raining really hard and Tippy wanted to escape the downpour by getting in his house. Well, Robbie was already in the little house and absolutely refused to share it with the dog. There is a cute picture somewhere of baby Stefanie and Robbie the mongoose sitting at the door of Tippy's doghouse. The poor dog was lying mercilessly out in the sun while the two young ones played in the cool of his house.

Around sunset, Robbie would have had enough of outdoors and would waddle to the front door on the piazza and nudge it open with his long and powerful nose. He was really cute and fun to have around–like I said, until he became a full-fledge adult, and then it was a different story. He became mean and ornery and was difficult to handle. Even Michelle was getting to where she was afraid of him. So, it was outside he went. We had to lock our front piazza door for a while because he would still try to "nose" his way in at night. I did feel sorry for him (slightly), but he had exasperated us so much. It occurred to me that there are some animals in the wild that simply cannot be completely tamed. Within a couple of weeks, we did not see him coming around anymore and perceiving what might have happened to him, we were not surprised to hear from some African friends of ours how "sweet" he had tasted in African soup. Such is the way of creatures in the jungle. I comforted myself by realizing that we had likely added a year to the mongoose's life by taking him in.

Adding It All Up

Often I lamented that I did not feel I was doing enough for the Lord our first few years in Liberia, but the more I reread my journals, I just have to laugh. What WAS I thinking? Hindsight is everything when the truth is revealed!

Missionaries should arrive on a ministry field with strong biblical training. That is a given. Besides that, what makes each missionary unique are the other occupational trades, talents, and inclinations that they possess. Thinking you might want to be a missionary? Learn all you can. Love what you do. Think of the practical skills you can acquire.

For the sake of helping you perhaps see that you can never underestimate what you can do if you have to and if there's a need to, I will give you an example of my own missionary trade experience. I became a "gourmet" cook, an English professor, a school teacher of other missionary children besides my own, an assistant in the medical clinic, an assistant to the midwives in delivering babies, chief barber and beautician (cutting the hair of the youngest girls and even some of the missionary men on our compound), and a couple of times was a wedding coordinator, helping some of our young Christians in the local church to have nice weddings. Other than my major in English, I really had no training in any of the other duties that came knocking on my door, but usually had a spirit of adventure to at least learn.

As to my being a wedding coordinator, it came by proxy. Paul was one of our Bible school students and had worked for us when we first arrived in Tappi. We had established a very strong relationship with him since that time, and I even remember the day that he brought Rachel, his betrothed, to meet us. Paul and Rachel wanted a church wedding in the Tappi Baptist Church and wanted us to help them with it. Beth Wittenberger and I decorated the church, fixed a kneeling beach, and made a unity candle area.

The Friday night before the Saturday wedding, we assumed that we would have a nice, quiet rehearsal with just the wedding party–just like you would have in the States! Wrong! There were nearly a hundred people standing at the windows peering in and making noises of all sorts. Regardless of what I thought should have happened, the wedding the next day went beautifully! A couple of years later when Paul and Rachel had their first daughter, they graciously named her Michelle. Our Michelle thought that was pretty special!

As for teaching other children, it was certainly something that I never planned, but it seemed to completely and naturally become part of my daily duties. During our second year on the Tappi mission station, I was voted to be the station treasurer. Any of you that know me very well may be laughing hysterically, because it is no secret that I have never gotten along with math very well! Even when I was in college–and before online banking–my mom would have to balance my checkbook for me.

So, I deferred the title of station treasurer to Joan Watkins, who is an absolute whiz in math and everything to do with accounting. We made a deal that I would take most of the responsibilities of teaching her daughter Becky, who was twelve years old and in seventh grade that year. That was more my speed!

It also happened that when our young children became school age, we missionary mothers created a teaching schedule that put the children together for several subjects and helped lighten our individual loads.

On the Job Training

Over those nearly four years we were in Tappi, Jeff taught several classes on soul winning to the men in the Bible Institute, and in lieu of having them write papers, he decided to take them out to nearby villages and let them use what they had learned.

Probably some of the most effective teaching was the specific on-the-job-training.

I decided to incorporate the same techniques when I taught Speech courses to the Bible Institute guys or the Central Bible students. In class, we would practice reading a chapter out loud, then memorizing scripture passages and quoting them in front of the class, and I also gave them assignments of storytelling. As they gained their confidence, we expanded what they had learned to the villages around them. Giving them the tools and the mandate to practice standing up and clearly communicating to others, they were required to go for at least one weekend to a nearby village where they would teach a children's church or Sunday School lesson. I preferred sending them out in pairs so they could learn to (fairly) critique each other as well as themselves.

My heart so desires to believe that there are still Liberian men and women using those communication skills we taught them during our time in Liberia. Through that teaching, it is my prayer that they are proclaiming the truth of Jesus Christ in the depths of the Liberian jungle and even into the larger towns–and that they are also teaching others to do the same. Since the Liberian civil war, missionary friends and African pastors have told us how the Gospel has powerfully gone forward through the efforts and passion of many of those we trained in Tappeta some twenty years ago! This reminds me of what Isaiah 55:11 says: *"That God's Word will not return void."* Where else in life will you consistently be guaranteed a 100% return on your efforts?

CHAPTER NINETEEN

The ultimate measure of a man is not where he stands in moments of comfort and convenience, but where he stands at times of challenge and controversy.
—Martin L. King Jr.

When the Shadow of Death Looms

Death in any form: sicknesses, viruses, accidents, chronic ill-nesses, even suicides, is mysterious to us. Cancer may have come to your family or perhaps you have experienced the tragic accident of a loved one. Death or the possibility of death is never welcomed except in the absolute despondency of the disease-riddled ones that can only hope the pain will soon end. I saw my brother reach that point near the end of his life enshrouded with a terminal illness that finally consumed him. The Liberians embraced death in a dif-ferent, more up close way. Facing death, not necessarily in a morbid way, a Liberian did realize it as an integral part of life. This philoso-phy forced them to accept their vulnerabilities and fragility in a way that more medically progressive cultures refuse to do.

For example, when a Liberian baby was born, there was an unspoken axiom that refrained the parents from naming their newborn baby until between the third and tenth day after birth. If the child lived that long, the belief was that he would most likely be strong enough to continue in his given walk of life.

Though there was always jubilant dancing and singing as the African women encircled the building where the miracle of birth had taken place, the naming of the baby always was withheld for those numbered days. I enjoyed dancing with the women that would sway with celebrated fervor around our clinic when a baby was born. In retrospect, I do not believe that initial commemora-tion was as much for the new life brought into the world, as it was simply out of a thankful spirit that the mother of that new life had come through childbirth safely.

On a personal level, God continued to show me how tenderly and ably He held the lives of my children. So, it should not have surprised me when it was time for me to be tested with the same lesson concerning my husband. I never even knew that I had a false security when dealing with my husband's mortality until my Heavenly Father asked me, quite succinctly and suddenly, to lay it all down at His feet. Give your husband to me. Trust me to take his life or sustain it. That experience marked me for life and was a solid platform for reminding me how powerfully God always wanted to work in my life.

It all started on a Tuesday morning, a week when Jeff was on flight duty. I was at the OB-GYN clinic helping Millie Dodson and our midwives with the more than two hundred pregnant women who came for medical care every Tuesday morning. A truck spun its tires in the mud as it dashed up to the airplane hangar and came to a sudden stop. Such a quick and abrupt approach to the airplane hangar usually meant that there was a need for a medical flight. Quickly a crowd gathered around the hangar as those in the first truck lifted a man wrapped in a dirty blanket from the backseat, and within minutes, a money bus filled with some of this man's family also arrived. Before the vehicle could even come to a stop, we heard crying and moaning from inside. The mournful sounds set the stage for the grave situation developing.

As it turned out, we knew this very sick man. Sammy Barkpea was one of the finest Liberian Christians we had ever known. An excellent mason, he had single-handedly spent more time and worked harder on the building of our mission's radio station than any other man in Liberia. Besides that amazing effort, thousands of hours of masonry work had been done gratis for churches all around Liberia. Because of the great need for his specialized work and his indefatigable, spirited choice to use his skills for God; in my mind, he was in the league with a lay Apostle Paul. Sammy, while never educated enough to attend Bible school, was certainly used to spread the Gospel of Jesus Christ in his own unique way. That's one reason why this story is so sad in our human comprehension of it.

It was obvious even at first glance that Sammy was very sick. He had been brought from his hometown which was only about 25 miles from Tappi, having fallen deathly ill while reaping some of the new rice on his farm. His sickness, sudden and acute, was characterized by fever, backache, sore throat, and malaise. Thinking that it might be a severe kidney infection, the Catholic clinic had sent him for us to transport. Jeff had earlier started an oil change in the Cessna 180 which he quickly finished, preparing for the thirty minute flight to Phebe Hospital. Helping the African men load Sammy into the back seats of the airplane was no easy job. Sammy was a hefty African man, so Jeff and the others had to work hard to situate him as comfortably as possible inside the cockpit. Because of his dire condition, Sammy's wife was invited to fly with them to the hospital.

Later that afternoon, when Jeff arrived back on the compound, he told me that he did not believe Sammy would live much longer. He also said that Sammy's wife said nothing particular to him during the flight mainly because she did not speak very good English. She just moaned and muttered in her dialect, obviously from a broken heart. Grief contains the same explosive, breathtaking emotion anywhere in the world; however, its outward manifestation is as diverse and cultural as the people experiencing it.

Two days later, we heard by radio that Sammy had died and that the family was asking for the body to be brought back to Tappi. As Jeff was still on flight duty, he went for the body in the early afternoon. Hearing the airplane returning a couple of hours later, several of us made our way back to the airplane hangar, finding dozens of townspeople also waiting. Sammy's wife was with Jeff, and she looked so pitiful and broken as she was helped down from the cockpit, collapsing into the arms of a couple of women waiting there for her.

Then I noticed as they were taking the body from the plane, that it was completely covered with thick pieces of cloth and black plastic. In the few times that I had seen a body being transported back by airplane, never had I seen the body bound so tightly. Something was different here, and as I caught Jeff's eye with my question, he handed me the report that the hospital, by law, had to provide in such a case as this. LASSA FEVER.

I had never heard of Lassa Fever before, but it was obvious by the wrapping of the body and the solemnity of the medical report that it was not a fever of a generic nature. What I later learned about Lassa Fever was that it could become a killer in quick, epidemic proportions. First noted in Nigeria in 1969 after an older missionary woman died in the town of Lassa, it was determined that rat particles (dust falling from bodies of infected rats) in some parts of West Africa carried the deadly virus. Other ways of becoming exposed to the virulent disease were by contact with saliva, urine, or sweat of the infected person or by eating the meat of an infected rat.

After speaking to the family and friends who were grieving Sammy's death, we walked slowly back to the house. I noticed that Jeff was very quiet, and then he asked to talk to me in our bedroom. He showed me a cut on the palm of his right hand. He explained that the cut had happened minutes before he helped put Sammy into the airplane two days ago. Jeff had carried Sammy under his armpits which were dripping with sweat. Not taking time to cover the cut which he had gotten during the oil change, we were now facing the unknown. Was that cut exposed to Sammy's sweat enough to expose Jeff to Lassa Fever? No one knew for sure, but from all indications in the medical manuals, body fluid was a definite way to contract the virus.

We did know that the incubation period was 7 to 14 days, and that there was absolutely nothing else to be done until then. I slept with Michelle on her bed, and Jeff did his best to stay away from physical contact with any of us. No kissing, no touching–and you can imagine how hard that was for the girls to understand. To add to this, twelve year old Becky Watkins was staying with us for six weeks while her parents were in the states. Hard enough to realize that your own family possibly had been exposed to this powerful virus, we felt so badly that she too had been potentially exposed. The pressure on us was great!

It might be helpful to clarify why Jeff stayed at the house with us after we felt that there might be a chance for him to be infected. First, he had already been with us for two days after possibly being exposed to the virus. Furthermore, where else would he go? There were no other buildings, houses, or hospitals that would take someone who "might" have contracted Lassa Fever. We were living in a remote part of Liberia on a mission compound. Unlike here in the

States, there were no places of quarantine. So we did the best we could to live without physical contact.

My journal of October 3, 1987, reads:

> *I keep thinking that this is bizarre! I can't believe it is happening. I was just getting over the Muslim woman dying at the clinic, now this! I am glad that God knows me and how much I can handle. I don't want to be strong. I don't want to deal with this. I just want it to go away. Living in Africa is taxing enough without these added fears. My whole soul rebels against this new trial, but the only thing I can do is to trust God to do what is best for my spiritual growth! I MUST rest in His sovereignty!*

A couple of days after Sammy's body was brought back from the hospital, he was buried at a graveyard near the end of the runway because the Tappeta town chief would not permit the body to be taken into town. In that same week, another man from the same area where Sammy lived was flown to the hospital by Jeff. The man also died a couple of days later. Lassa Fever was a fearful word to anyone that knew of its menacing power. In the next four months, during the dry season, several people in surrounding villages died of Lassa Fever. It seemed to be a virus that was particularly potent during the drier times in Liberia.

You can only imagine the daily scene in our home for the following two weeks. While I tried not to make every little thing about the disease, it seemed to take on a life of its own. I would imagine that this is much like the reality of dealing with cancer and waiting for the debilitating symptoms to start. Every headache, every touch to his back, every bead of sweat of his brow, was scrutinized by me. I probably drove him crazy with my concern! On day thirteen of Jeff's incubation period, a "strange" virus went through our house. Becky Watkins, the 12-year old missionary kid, woke up with body aches and fever. She was sick for almost eighteen hours.

The next day, I was beginning to feel achy and tired, more likely from the stress of waiting and watching. Michelle followed a few hours later, very hot with a fever and sluggish. By that night Jeff and Stefanie also had come down with fevers. I was feeling somewhat better by the next morning, and the girls followed suit by the afternoon. Interestingly enough, Jeff was the sickest of all of us. He was restless and his fever went up to 102 for a couple of days. It was a long two days! I continued to pray and try to give my fears over to ADONAI every time they threatened to consume me, and was blessed with an immense peace and strength to deal with the uncertain days. My little girls, my husband, and sweet little Becky all were in God's hands. I had no power to save any of them nor myself.

Interestingly enough, we found out a few days later that Lassa Fever was a generational virus; that is to say, that the person initially exposed to the virus by direct contact with the rat or its dustings would become the sickest. The person developing Lassa Fever from the first person would have a less serious case of the virus. I really believe in my heart—and so did some of the others there on the compound—that we had all been exposed to a type of Lassa Fever. Because Jeff was exposed as a second generation victim, he was the sickest. The girls and I were exposed as third generation, and from there the virus strain had weakened greatly. I may be all wet as they say, but this is what I believe. God exposed us to protect us—particularly Jeff as he was constantly staying in houses in smaller villages where the danger of Lassa Fever was greater. In exposing us, we were then immune to the virus. You could say, it was something like a supernatural immunization.

No matter what the case, I was elated but exhausted after the waiting and watching and dealing with this sickness that came to my entire household. But God had shown Himself more than enough! Little by little, I was understanding that I could trust Him wholeheartedly with my family—no matter where we were—no matter what the dangers might be around us!

Fruit To Encourage My Heart

Earlier I mentioned buying soft, semi-sweet bread from two Ghanian sisters in town. Admittedly, the first few times I met them I was much more concerned about the sanitation of their baking process than I was about their souls. While I was still working in the prenatal clinic helping our nurse and midwives, both of the sisters became pregnant and registered for maternity care. It was then that I really got to know them and became more attentive to the God-given burden for their spiritual condition. Sometimes when I would go for bread, I took them baked goods or little treats that I had brought from Monrovia. An easy friendship developed, and they finally asked me more about why we had become missionaries there in Liberia. Through their questions, I was able to share my faith and it was evident that their hearts were wide open! Within a couple of weeks, I was able to lead both sisters to a saving knowledge of Jesus Christ. It was balm to my weary soul. Having dealt with so much heartache and sickness and fears in the previous few weeks, seeing two new souls coming into the kingdom brought back the encouraging realization and proper perspective to my life there in the unpredictable, but God-controlled jungle.

When our truck was not being used on Sundays for out-of-town evangelistic trips, I would pick the bread ladies up and take them to church with the girls and me. Whenever possible, I visited their home and told them Bible stories, also teaching them some of the basic Bible doctrines. Within a few months, they moved back to Ghana with their husbands, but before they left, I encouraged them to spread the news of their salvation to their family there. If I really think about it, this is exactly how the Gospel spread from the heart of the Middle East to places all over the world! God is still in the business of doing that!

Teenage Girl Fun!

I have always had a burden for teenagers. As soon as I was no longer one myself, it seemed that God gave me a compassion and understanding for this infernally difficult phase of growing up! My very first ministry in a church, after Jeff and I were married, was as an assistant teacher in a junior high Sunday School class.

After being in Liberia for almost eighteen months, Jenny, my day time nanny for Stefanie, asked me to teach her the Bible. Through this opportunity, I felt God prompting me to step out a little more in ministry even right inside my own house. Dragging blankets, snacks, lemonade, and Bible materials to my shady, peaceful side yard, we began a small teenage girls class. We started by inviting the Bible school students' daughters. On any given

Saturday, I would have anywhere between five and eight girls who attended, and for three hours, we would sing, have a Bible lesson, do exercises in a work booklet, compete in Bible trivia, and eat!

Michelle and Stefanie often would join us, and I loved that I was able to do ministry with my daughters by my side. Some years later, when Jenny was married and had children of her own, she visited us in Ivory Coast, and told me about the impact I had on her life. We relived the times we had in those girls' classes and she told me that she was trying to teach the things I had taught her to teenage girls in her own village. Pass it on! The Gospel is made just for that!

Living It Out Loud

A short while later, Jenny and one of her friends were helping me cook a meal for another missionary family who was returning from Monrovia. I was the station hostess for that year which meant that it was my responsibility to care for the needs of any traveling missionary family, especially as they returned home from a trip. There were no fast food places or Dominos to call for pizza delivery. If another missionary woman did not graciously prepare something for you to eat as you and your family returned to Tappi, you would need to quickly unpack and begin the task of preparing an "always from scratch" meal right away. No time to be tired, to rest, or to relax. Families always had to be fed.

Since all three of the other families that lived on the compound had been gone and were coming back within two days of each other, I was preparing three different meals for them. Jenny asked me why I was using all of my food for those other missionary families without having to be begged for it.

In her culture, one asked for anything and everything. You hardly ever just gave something without being begged for it. It was a great opportunity for me to talk to Jenny and her friend about giving freely of ourselves and what we have, reminding them of the promises in the Bible about that. I read Malachi 3:10 to them and then quoted Luke 6:38: *Give, and it shall be given unto you; good measure, pressed down, and shaken together, and running over, shall men give into your bosom. For with the same measure that you mete withal it shall be measured to you again.*

It seemed to make a big impression on them, simply because they saw me doing it, not just talking about it. You can never imagine what lessons you may be teaching with your life! LIVE OUT LOUD—and when necessary use words.

Life Lessons

While Becky Watkins was staying with us for a six-week period, one of the challenges I found particularly daunting was dealing with five and two year old girls and then interpreting the unpredictable ways of a preteen. In hindsight, Becky was an exceptional twelve year old, hardly showing any of the idiosyncrasies that my three daughters displayed at that age. Then again, I was not Becky's mother either, and that always makes a huge difference!

Becky had already meshed into our family easily as she had helped so much in watching our two little ones when we needed to be gone from the house. I gave her the freedom to experiment with her cooking and "playing house" with a real house, real children, and real food. She was a joy! I know that she missed her parents when they left, and there were those times when I wasn't quite sure what to say or do when she was in one of those moods. (Oh, yeah, after raising three teenage daughters, I understand that so much better now!)

I tiptoed around many things that, if she had been my own, I definitely would have hit head on. Until one day. Becky had an unusual pet called a tree bear whom she affectionately called "Bear." I don't even know how to describe a "tree bear" to you. A tree bear was like a small teddy bear with a more pointy face or perhaps like a small koala bear with four feet. Coarse brown fur with a white streak down the back like a skunk, the fur would stand on end when the animal was mad. It had soft, padded feet and no claws and made a very interesting trilling sound that was meant to throw off enemies as to their location. The trilling would start off muffled and low, but would increase in volume at each sound, giving the illusion that it moved from tree to tree rapidly. However, nothing could be further from the truth. A tree bear moved extremely slow and had to be one of God's more curious creations!

185

One night it was my turn to feed the station guests for supper, and I had decided to make some homemade chocolate pudding. Pudding from scratch is not really hard, but it is very time consuming, for you must commit to stand by the stove and stir, stir, stir. Using my French crystal dessert dishes that I had bought for a "song" in Monrovia, I filled the dishes with the delectable dessert, then placed them at the top right of each dinner plate.

I was in the kitchen finishing up the last of the meal when I heard the sound of glass shattering and things awry at the dinner table. Simultaneously, I heard Jeff and our two dinner guests just reaching our yard. Looking at the table, I went into a complete, but silent conniption fit. That does take talent, ladies and gentlemen, for remember, our windows had no screens, so any LOUD conniption fit would have been heard by our approaching guests almost immediately. "BECKY, BECKY," I screamed whispered, flailing my arms and trying not to start crying. Bear had decided that he did not like the chocolate pudding on the table, so had pushed two of the dishes to the floor and had walked in the others. There were "pudding" tracks around the tablecloth, on a chair and on our concrete floor towards Jeff's study. In a very smart move, Bear had chosen to hide himself from the irrational white woman.

I honestly do not know how Jeff knew to delay entering the house with our guests, but I think somehow he must have sensed the embarrassment and indignation I was spewing out at that moment. Did his acute hearing pick up my whispered screams? No matter, the three men, amazingly, made a detour toward the storage building, giving Becky and me enough time to reset the table with a new cloth, clean up the "pudding" prints, and set everything back in order. I re-dished the chocolate pudding with what I had left, and was standing at the door smiling calmly (on the outside) when the three men came in.

Becky was quiet that night at supper, and I knew that I had probably really hurt her by some of the things I had said while we were desperately cleaning up everything. Ah, I hate that! How I have learned over the years that words cannot be taken back and that we should be mindful of what and how we say something. In retrospect, it was more my pride (of having everything looking perfect) and my fear of man (wondering what the men would think of me), that caused me to react. How funny it might have been–and what a neat story for them to have been able to take back to America with them! Oh the things we learn!

Unfortunately, we were not finished with the saga of the tree bear. The very next day, Bear decided that he would pretend our refrigerator was a tree in the jungle; the only problem with that was a $10 glass jar of Jiff peanut butter sitting on top of the fridge. (About three times a year we would go to the American Food Store in Monrovia and splurge on a large jar of American peanut butter.) The one on top of the refrigerator had just been bought the week before, but did not stop Bear from somehow sliding the jar off.

We heard the strange, muted thud and went to investigate. Bear was peering down at the shattered jar of peanut butter as if to say that it shouldn't have been up there in the first place. That was it! I could take no more of the tree bear, but then again, I certainly couldn't send Becky home with him either. So we made a deal that he would have to stay in her bedroom unless she was going to be watching him very carefully. Becky was very afraid of me for a few days; after reading this and remembering the situation, I really don't blame her!

When I recently asked her what she remembered about the Bear incident, she wrote:

> *I remember that tree bear. He got into so much trouble. I felt really bad. I think he even broke a special doll that your mom had given to Michelle. He broke a Peanut Butter jar and I don't know what all else. You were VERY patient to even allow him to be there in the house (I'm sure you only did it out of love for me!) That would drive me nuts at this point. I remember him stealing a chicken breast off the plat-ter when it was all ready. You picked him up and THREW him across the room. Too bad he lived through it! Ha ha. I think I'd have sent him packing into the bush that very night.*

Since Becky has become a mother, she certainly understands some of the frustrations I had during that time, but I am thankful that she did not hold any of my reactions against me.

CHAPTER TWENTY

Ye are of God, little children, and have overcome them: because greater is He that is in you, than he that is in the world. I John 4:4

When In Doubt, Read the Manual

One Sunday we were planning to travel by airplane to Saclepea in our continual effort to be a part of God's church building plan for that town. For some reason, baby Stefanie and I were not able to go, so another missionary couple traveled with Jeff and Michelle. After sharing in a wonderful time of worship with the church folk, the four of them loaded up the Cherokee 6 and began that eighteen minute flight back to Tappi. About halfway through the trip, the engine started sputtering and Jeff noticed that the plane was slowly losing altitude. His first concern was that the prop could very easily stop in midair which is NEVER a good thing, so he asked the other two missionaries to pray.

Pilots are trained for many different scenarios and this was one of them. Wisely having had memorized the manufacturer's check-list for when the (one and only) engine started skipping, he mentally checked off the troubleshooting suggestions. Electric. Check. Fuel. By the indicator, there was plenty. On the Cherokee 6 there were four positions for fuel, two located in varying places on each wing. Thinking that there may be a problem with the tank presently being used, he quickly flipped the fuel indicator switch to another tank. The engine immediately stopped sputtering. Check. And, above all, thank you Heavenly Father, for giving him wisdom to remember his training!

Back in Tappi, the pilots grounded the plane for crucial and necessary maintenance. Because of the nature of the incident, they went directly to the fuel indicator and fuel tanks to find the cause. They were not disappointed. Found on the chrome ball that was part of the selector system was a large area of rust, and a small flake of that rust had broken off and clogged the fuel line.

What spiritual insight can be gleaned from this story! Memorize the Word of God so that in times of doubt, tragedy, fear, and uncertainties of life, the Truth will prevail. Be aware of the sins that settle into our souls causing rusty areas that can weaken us and ultimately become our downfall! What great reminders from the log of a bush pilot in Liberia.

Two Doses of Soda

A few days before Christmas of 1987, Mark Sheppard found two baby kittens at the airplane hangar. He brought them back to his children, but they decided to let Michelle have one. She chose a beautiful black and white kitten, and we named him "Soda" (which in the Bassa dialect means cat). From the very beginning, I could tell that this kitten was weak and sickly. He slept so much and had a very scant appetite.

Within three days, he was very weak and could not even meow. I started to prepare Michelle then for the inevitable: Soda would not live much longer. I was not sure how she would take the death of her first pet. It was one of those hard things in life from which we would love to protect our children, but parental instincts tell us that it is something they must learn to face at some point in their lives.

When Soda died, Michelle was indeed sad and cried for a couple of minutes, but I could tell that she was really trying to be strong. Ritch, a high school guy who was staying with us for a few weeks, decided to help with her grieving process. He made a nice little bag, put the kitten in it, and he and Michelle had a small funeral for Soda. That seemed to help her deal with the loss.

The next day, Mark found another kitten at the carpenter shop which was located right behind the airplane hangar. It was most likely from the same litter as the two original kittens and he gave Michelle the beautiful yellow-striped kitten which we promptly named Soda King because Melodie Sheppard had named her kitten Princess Lea. Michelle enjoyed playing with him for the next few months, but we were not sure what to do with him when we left for our one-year furlough in the States. Graciously, a Liberian Bible school student named Paul agreed to take care of Soda King until we returned the following year. We felt good about this, and even

Michelle seemed to be satisfied with that plan. Little did we know how that plan would go awry.

The months of January and February were customarily hard ones for the Liberians who depended solely on the rice that was produced on their own farms. Most of the previous year's rice had been eaten and it was not yet time to harvest the new rice, so the Liberians become very creative and sometimes desperate in how they fed their families. Our cat was living happily among Paul's family in a house close to the mission compound and seemed to be thriving. About three months after we had left for furlough, "hungry time" hit the local families.

As Soda became fatter and fatter, Paul's grandmother, who was becoming hungrier, decided that the cat would be eaten. In a Liberian family, whatever the matriarch says...goes. So, when we arrived back a few months later and found out that Soda had been put in the soup pot, it was quite the culture shock! Paul felt so badly, and though we blamed no one for it, we decided that we would not tell Michelle the raw truth until she was old enough to be able to discern what really happened. We told her when she was about fourteen. Then she laughed!

The Things We Do For Love

As Becky Watkins and I were hanging sheets all around our piazza to enclose it for privacy, we drew quite a crowd of onlookers. What in the world were those crazy missionaries doing now? As I think back at some of the shenanigans we cooked up while living in Liberia, I can only imagine what the Liberians thought as they watched us.

Becky and I had been planning a Valentine's Day banquet for four months. I prepared four pans of lasagna and garlic bread. Other ladies brought pies, veggies, and a fruit salad. To make our "little restaurant" more authentic, we placed candles on the tables and hung kerosene lanterns from the beams. Using as many card tables as we could borrow, we set several tables for four. Becky made place mats and menus, all cut out with hearts. Becky and Rachel Wittenberger were our waitresses and served the whole meal to us adults.

After the delightful meal, we came inside for our program. Starting out with each couple sharing a song of love that was special to them, Jeff and I actually sang *The Wedding Song* which was sung at our wedding in 1981. Following all the song sharing, we played the *Newlywed Game*. Still newlyweds of six years, Jeff and I answered correctly only four out of the ten questions! Concluding our evening, Rachel Schildroth gave a moving devotion on God's love with a couple of songs intertwined. Over the four years that we lived in Tappeta, we planned birthday parties, plays, cantatas, and just times where we could unwind and have fun–even in the midst of the African jungle.

The following week, I hosted a tea for the missionary women and the two Lebanese ladies in town whom we all had a burden to see become Christians. It was so pleasant to sit and visit with them, no matter if we were of different ages, different seasons of our lives, and even different nationalities. A few weeks after that tea, the Lebanese ladies came one afternoon and I showed them how to make pizza. Before supper time, Jeff went into town to pick up the husbands and we all ate together. We had some open and interesting discussion about Christianity and they commented on our obvious love for Jesus Christ. They had moved with their families to the bush of West Africa to make money; we had moved with our family out of an unexplainable love for Someone we couldn't even see! Ah! It seemed they were getting the picture. We kept praying.

A Different Kind of "Society"

Since the beginning of time, Satan has found ways to control, manipulate, deceive, prod, and intimidate human beings. In some parts of the world, his tactics may seem subtle while in others, where there is less of a Christian presence, he lives directly in the face of the people in the darkest of ways! Years ago, I remember hearing Africa called the dark continent, and I am not sure what the original intent of that meant. Perhaps it was because, decades ago, Africa was predominantly unfamiliar, unexplored, unknown, and unevangelized in the Christian sense.

It did not take us many weeks after arriving in Liberia to come face-to-face with the stark reality of the power of the Liberian

Devil Bush Society. The Society was part political, part cultural, embedding itself into some of the basest of Liberian society while parading the mask of education, health, and welfare concerns onto its platform. Nothing could be farther from the truth when one entered the nether regions of the Society. At its core, it was purely satanic.

When President Samuel K. Doe seized the country from President Tolbert in 1980, the presupposed belief that Liberia was a "Christian" nation definitely shifted. When we had been in the country only four short months, we heard our first disturbing news of Society activity.

My journal of April 3, 1986, reads:

> *Last night at our station prayer meeting, we became privy to some disconcerting news. Seems there are stories that President Doe has been attending some Society meetings, which is the Devil Bush (satanic doings), but now it has taken on the prestigious name of the Society. That's how fast and easy this kind of thing is growing here in Liberia. We had already heard months back about Devil bush men having meetings with Doe about the Christians and missionaries, and their concern that we were all trying to change the Liberian culture. The Society's argument is that we are bad for the pride and growth of Liberia as a country. Now we hear that Doe is attending Society meetings himself. And in Bong County, soldiers have actually gone into Christians' homes and taken things, harassing the people.*

This was persecution in the purest form of the word, and the government was turning a blind eye to it. In the 1980s, Bong County was the headquarters for the national Devil Bush Society, so it was reasonable to think that the persecuting would start there. We had been told that when the Society had someone killed, there were many ways of disposing of the body. One disturbing way was to take the body to a stream or river, dam up a part of the water, dig a grave in the riverbed, bury the body, and then let the water run normally again! As you can imagine, in those kind of conditions, it would be difficult to find a body because you would never even see a grave.

This all became personal to us as missionaries in February of 1988 when a young pastor from Bassa County named Alexander ran breathlessly onto our mission compound. He told us that the Society had kidnapped his wife, tied her up and had beaten her. Alexander had recently been preaching against the Devil Bush, even revealing some of their sacred secrets. Notably, this was a serious offense, and so the Society leaders chose to retaliate by taking his wife. He did not know where else to turn, and it spoke soundly of Baptist Mid-Mission's long time reputation of caring for the people of Liberia for him to seek us out.

Alexander stayed on the mission compound for a couple of days until three men arrived to take him away. Never showing them to us, the men said that they had official documents, which did not surprise us because we had also found out that the three men were trying to be initiated into the Society and were given the charge to bring Alexander to Bong County for his punishment. If they could do that, they would have proven themselves worthy of becoming part of the Society. Soon after we sent those three men away without Alexander, we heard that two government soldiers were coming to take Alexander. He was then advised by some local Christians that he should hide until it was found out exactly what those soldiers wanted with him. Unfortunately, the soldiers were able to find him.

Days later, Alexander was released but mandated to go to Monrovia if he desired to be cleared of any charges. He flew down in the airplane with a couple of the missionary men who hoped to speak on Alexander's behalf. Ultimately the government officials in charge of this case ordered Alexander to go back to Bong County and take the Society "mark" (yes, I did say mark) for his punishment. When a man was given the societal mark, it meant that if he ever stepped out of the boundaries of what the Society believed, he could be killed.

While Alexander was still in Monrovia, Chick Watkins, Mark Sheppard, and two of our Liberian Christians went into the village from which Alexander had come. It was like a ghost town. Deserted. They were told that four other men from Alexander's church had been taken and beaten as also was the case in a town that Jeff had recently visited for a pastor's conference. My journal does not speak about who found Alexander's wife and children, but they were brought back to Tappeta with Mark and Chick and reunited with Alexander after his return from Monrovia.

Jeff also heard from Christians in Saclepea that a girl from a nearby town had been taken, put into the Society, circumcised, and had died shortly afterwards. It was not unusual for young teen-age girls and boys to be sent or taken against their will to the local Society stomping ground. Parents of those unfortunate children only knew of the death of their child when they found a large bowl of rice placed outside their door during the night. If the parents were not Christians and under the fancy of the Society, they believed the "devil" had taken pleasure in their child and had kept her. While, to us as Christians, it seemed a warped way to deal with the pain of losing a child, it was also extremely heartbreaking to imagine parents having to live like that.

The eventual death of this young girl was not the only detrimental influence that this forceful circumcision of women had on society. This unwholesome practice sometimes caused women to have trouble in delivering their children (of which I had seen first-hand) and changed the whole element of sexual relations inside a marriage. Satan had his hand deep into the practices of the Society and it was his plan to use it to weaken and control families and marriages all over the country.

The Society claimed to be a positive place for budding Liberian teenagers to learn to become responsible citizens, good husbands and wives. There was talk of classes about marriage, home economics, and of course, indoctrination into Society beliefs. To this day, the Society doings are dark and hidden. It is not certain what part the Society has played in post-war Liberia, but I do pray that its chains have been broken by the prayers of Liberian Christians all over the country!

Paint the Devil Red

Jeff had the opportunity to visit many surrounding villages with some of our Bible school students during our four years in Liberia. It was by far, one of the most effective ways to train the Liberian

Bible school men to be servants for our Lord, and a direct result of Paul's example given in the book of Acts and throughout the Epistles. Most of the villages did not have buildings (huts or mud-brick) that could hold more than twenty people, so church services usually were held outside. There were times when many of the townspeople would bring their kerosene lanterns to the "outdoor church" and as far as the eye could see, there would be amber-colored flickers of light drawing darker shadows on the already dark faces of the townspeople.

If the village was accessible by road, the missionaries took a small portable generator and would hang strings of light–weaving their "white man" magic (which was basically a term used for anything that the villagers could not explain from their own knowledge), bringing brilliant sparkling light that overlaid the golden lights of the lanterns. It was a festival come to town! Can you imagine the excitement and interest something like that would draw to a town never exposed to electricity before?

When it would rain, the services would have to be postponed or canceled as there was simply no other option. Jeff said that lying in one of those simple grass huts during a heavy rainstorm was an adventure in itself. Though, by intricate design, the roofs on many of those huts were amazingly tight, the powerful African deluges were persistent and penetrating. He learned to fall asleep, many a nights with the gentle rhythmic drip, drip, drip of the raindrops finding their way through the small cracks of woven thatch.

During this uncertain time for Christians across the country of Liberia, Jeff came face-to-face with the prominence and intimidation of the Society. Like many other times in the previous three years, he, along with several other missionary men, took the Bible school students and headed deep into the African jungle for evangelism. Choosing remote back roads, Jeff would drop off missionaries and Bible school students in towns along the road. The town where Jeff finally stopped greeted him warmly and he had good meetings Monday night.

On Tuesday around noon, two Bible school students that he had dropped off at a town only a couple of miles away, walked into town to find him. They told Jeff about heavy Devil Bush Society activity in that other town and that they had not been allowed to preach. Jeff drove the men back, going with them to talk to the town chief about having a service. The town chief agreed to the church service for that one night. Feeling the excitement and curiosity of the villagers, Jeff and the students started preparing for the evening.

Soon there was heard a far away chanting, rhythmic drums, and the clacking of sticks. It was obvious that whatever the commotion was, it was headed for the town and the villagers began to run to and fro. Many of them cast fervent and worried glances at Jeff and the Bible school students as they chatted earnestly in dialect about the impending situation. Children were thrust inside the safety of huts. Chickens and goats scattered to the edges of the thick bush.

Jeff remembers that the hair stood up on the back of his neck as he raised his eyes and saw one of the most unusual sights he had ever seen. A man walked purposefully down one of the paths leading into the village decked out in a red suit that was stunningly similar to a Santa Clause outfit. Covering his face was a wooden mask imprinted with an evil caricature. As the odd procession continued toward the village, Jeff noticed that this interesting character was shrouded by several men carrying machetes, long sticks, and faces of steel.

By the time Jeff and the students saw this entourage, some of the Christians in the town were frantically trying to explain (in dialect) that the white man must leave NOW! If a white man ever looked on the Red Devil, he would die. The Red Devil's men would kill him. When this was interpreted into English for Jeff's sake, he had but a split second to make a decision. His flesh took comfort in the feel of the hard steel of the truck keys in his pocket, so while keeping his hand in his pocket, he silently prayed for wisdom. Much rode on his decision. He did not want to endanger the lives of the Bible school students nor did he want the wrath of the town chief on him. In weighty contrast, he also did not want the doors closed so that they could not minister in this town. His spirit sought clarity from above.

Jeff knew that the Bible school students were watching him. However, this situation promised to teach a much more important lesson than could ever be relayed to them in the safe, sterile settings of the Bible school classroom. What did God want to do here? Jeff does not remember feeling like a gladiator or anything exciting like that. It should not be a Christians desire to fight toe to toe with the devil, though there are times when it is necessary. But nothing can be done in our own strength. Jeff knew that. He checked his heart and only remembers a calm assurance and confidence that he was to stand still and to know that God was there. To trust God and to watch Him.

When the Red Devil and his men saw the white man standing by the only vehicle in town, they abruptly stopped. It was, in the most realistic way, good versus evil in paramount color. As the Red Devil pointed towards Jeff, he curtly bellowed out orders to his companions. Two of them, machetes in hand, walked slowly over to where Jeff and the two Bible school students were standing as the Red Devil was whisked away to the confines of a nearby hut. If what followed could be projected onto a screen and seen with spiritual eyes, I believe it would be much like the battle described by Michael, the archangel, who was sent to bring an important message to Daniel. However, Michael was delayed because of an incredible battle with the evil angels.

All around those followers of Satan in this remote Liberian town sparsely aware of the Gospel of Jesus Christ and the three men who stood in the power and blood of Jesus Christ, a spiritual battle was being fought. Jeff realized that this was much bigger than he. While words continued vehemently to be thrown from one side to the other and were interpreted for Jeff, things looked humanly dire. He remembers that his palms began to sweat as he deemed himself to stand calmly in the face of his accusers. "The white man must die! He cannot look upon the Red Devil. It is commanded and let is be so," was the decree. The Bible school students, in the most important fight in their Christian lives to that point, stood tall and spoke fervently with those men who had learned the power of manipulation and intimidation while God continued to encourage Jeff to watch HIM and Him alone work.

Incredibly enough, after a very long few minutes, the town chief approached the group and intervened for Jeff. He told the devil man's cronies that the white man had arrived first and had already asked permission to have a service in town. Since the Red Devil had not announced his entrance into the village prior, they were not properly prepared for him at this time. He recapitulated that the white man knew nothing of the Society's customs and would need to be exonerated from the charges laid against him. A master of jungle politics, the town chief insisted that the white man be able to preach from the Bible that night and by the next morning, he promised that Jeff and the Bible school students would be sent away in order for the Red Devil to have his moment in the village.

After conferring with the Red Devil, his companions brought word that it would be as the town chief had decided, but the white man and his men would need to be out of the town early the next morning. The lines of power muddied when comparing the far-reaching influence of the Society and the timeless authority of the local town chief. If the town chief was under the intimidation spell of the Society, he would most likely give in to the whims of the red devil.

This particular town chief placed himself in a precarious situation by placing the proclaiming of the Gospel on top of the Society's agenda. What an opportunity God had set before Jeff and those two Bible school students. And they took it!! As the moon was reaching for the epic blackness, oil lanterns and chairs began to be placed around the town's meeting area. Under the stars, Jeff lifted his voice and began to preach a message that came straight from the Holy Spirit. Verses that he remembered committing to memory as far back as sixth grade were cited. God's power and love was proclaimed for all to hear. He was simply an earthen vessel being used by his Creator and Savior.

In the hut where the Red Devil assumed he had taken refuge from God's presence, the Gospel seeped through the cracks of the mud and thatch. Outside the hut, two of his the devil man's body guards kept watch as if the Christian men would wield some kind of magic of their own and harm their leader. But it was the unseen Power that won in the end. When the invitation was given, those two body guards who could not drown out the sound of the Gospel and its power and could not deny the Light bidding to enter their souls, walked away from the darkness in which they had been living and willingly chose to follow the Light of the world. It was an extraordinary evening of watching God's magnificent and compelling love draw those whom had been waiting for this moment all their lives.

And all because a white man and two African Bible school students determined to stand still.....and let God be God!

CHAPTER TWENTY-ONE

Great opportunities to help others seldom come, but small ones surround us everyday. —Sally Koch

The Thoughts of a Child

At the onset of rainy season which is usually around mid-March, the spiders and snakes come up for air without fearing that they will be scorched from the hot, parched weather that is prevalent during the dry season. It was the time of year where diligence in cleaning, shaking out, and peeping under was beneficial. One night I almost stepped on a two-inch scorpion in our bedroom. Jeff and I spent the next thirty minutes trying to figure out where it had gotten in. That was a mystery usually never solved.

During the same night the scorpion appeared, some disturbingly large brown spiders started appearing around our house. One spider was obviously a female because when I lifted it up to carry it to the toilet, about thirty little baby spiders came from her sac. Michelle was amazed as I frantically stomped, squished, and slid across the floor trying to kill all the baby spiders!

A few days later, Michelle saw yet another brown spider and asked me if it was "prek-a-net" too. She then said, "Huh, why do these spiders come to our home to deliver? We don't have anything to 'liver their babies. We're no clinic! We only have one crib but that's for Stefanie, and they would need tiny small cribs anyway. They shouldn't come here to 'liver their baby spiders, right, mommy?" Out of all the many tasks that missionaries performed on a daily basis, now you know that we absolutely were not a "spider delivering clinic." That's where we drew the line.

Short Sticks, Long Snakes

While missionaries in West Africa, I often joked to Jeff that the most exciting things happened when he was not home. As I recall, this was the first of many of those kind of incidents. Jeff was away preaching at an Easter conference one year, and as I usually did when he was gone, I took his motorcycle and drove the girls around the mission compound. One afternoon we were turning to park the motorcycle on the piazza when a sudden movement caught my eye.

A five-foot long black cobra had been sunning itself exactly in the spot where the motorcycle usually was parked. Watching the snake slither into the bushes beside us, I called out for Mr. T to come. I insisted that the girls stay seated on the motorcycle with me in case we needed to make a quick getaway or something! I really don't know what I thought was going to happen, but the motorcycle seemed safer at the time. As we watched, Mr. T took a three-foot stick and hacked at the bushes. Angry and in obvious defense mode, the cobra came hissing out of the bushes, standing almost straight up on his tail with his hood flared! While the snake swayed vehemently in front of us, I watched in amazement at the adept speed Mr. T used in knocking the snake to the ground on its belly.

I tried to keep my hand over Stefanie's eyes and told Michelle to cover her eyes, too, because of all the things I had heard about the hooded cobra and the distance they could throw their poison spit. We were all three too mesmerized to take seriously the danger in front of us. It was National Geographic in living color–right before our eyes: a black hooded cobra in our yard. I almost felt proud.

What was most impressive was Mr. T ability to outwit the cobra and bring it down in one final rap of the stick. When I felt sure that the snake was dead, I allowed the girls to get off the motorcycle as I parked it on the piazza. As I turned back to see what the girls were doing, I was shocked to see 18-month old Stefanie headed towards the crumpled snake with a stick in her hand. Evidently, she felt that she needed to help Mr. T finish the snake off. It scared me to think that she had absolutely no fear of snakes and spiders at such a young age.

We could not wait until Jeff returned home the next day to tell him about our excitement with the big black snake with the hood and how Mr. T had been our hero and killed it with a very short stick! As always, I was reminded of God's goodness to us through that incident.

Sad News From Afar

Jeff had recently received his ham radio license and his very own call letters, so we were able to stay in more frequent touch with our families back in the States. One afternoon we reached our families in the States and heard that his "Nanny" Overcash was very sick and probably would not live much longer. This was the last of his living grandparents and a very hard bit of news for Jeff. It is difficult to describe all the emotions that go through your mind at a time like that.

Today, it is a little easier to go online and find a flight to take you anywhere in a relatively short amount of time. In the late 80's and early 90's, it was not so. We lived almost 200 miles from the capital city where we would have to travel to even purchase a ticket. Flights only went in and out of Liberia on certain days, besides the fact that it was expensive to make an impromptu trip to the States. That did not take away the pain from experiencing the loss nor the guilt of not being able to be with family during the time of death of a loved one. Death is never an easy creature to deal with no matter where you may live. We struggled often with what the right response should be in situations such as these.

My journal of May 2, 1988, reads:

> Sunday was a very sad day for us because we received the news that Nanny had died Saturday night. Jeff knew that it would probably happen soon, but it still did not prepare him for the shock, helplessness and emptiness he felt after the phone call. He cried really hard for a while, but then got okay. You'll never realize the feelings that go through you when you're away from family at a time like this. The devil can really make you feel guilty for being so far away. It's such an agonizing, helpless feeling. There's nothing we can do except to try to imagine what was happening there and hope that people understand why we are not there. I know Nanny never begrudged us for the work we are doing. We will miss her tremendously, especially when we go home, and she is not there.

Building Bridges Where There Is No Water

Never having any sisters, I did have one younger brother Eddie. Since he was thirteen, he had been fighting a terminal kidney disease, and at the age of 15, my mother gave him a kidney. Back in 1976, when we knew that Eddie would need his first transplant, I had just graduated from high school and was getting ready to start college. The summer before my freshman year, my mother, father, and I went to Duke University Hospital to be typed as potential kidney donors. There were several complicated tests that revealed whether a person was a good match or not to the ailing person. I matched my brother perfectly in five out of six of the necessary prototypes. My mother matched four of them, but my father matched hardly any.

Loving my brother deeply and having always felt helpless in the onslaught of the disease affecting his young body, I offered to give him one of my kidneys. Finally something that I could do for him besides play checkers and paper football on top of his hospital tray. Not being a mother at the time, I did not understand why my mother rejected my willingness to give my brother my kidney. I wanted to do that for him so desperately, but my parents were adamant. Now, after being a parent for nearly twenty-seven years, I completely understand and would have done the same thing that my mother did. She gave her son a kidney. Within time, they both recovered beautifully!

Because of the nature of his disease (it traveled destructively and exclusively through the blood stream), it was inevitable that it would, at some point, also destroy the transplanted kidney. True to its prognosis, in late 1985, just a few weeks before my little family was to leave for Liberia the first time, my brother received a second kidney from an unknown deceased donor. Saying our goodbyes while he was still in the hospital in the midst of a long, uncertain recovery, I battled, almost daily, the fact that he could die without me being able to get home quickly. Those years in Liberia were a battlefield for my soul.

My flesh fought angry duels with my spirit on whether I should really be sitting in the middle of a jungle while my family back in the States dealt with such a tenuous situation. I battled the guilt and frustration, and often wondered whether I was living according to God's will. As a woman who had always harbored a somewhat smug satisfaction at thinking I was able to be in control of my life, the reality that God was asking me to be completely and totally in reliance on Him was overpowering.

As I have already established, I am a woman with a huge imagination and when I dwelt on my fears, they took me further than I ever needed to go spiritually or physically! Building bridges, assuming the worse, I would think of what would happen if my brother was to die. If I could not say goodbye to him. If I could not be there for my parents. Satan used the guilt, the fear, the panic to weaken my resolve of being a missionary in West Africa. The nights were long and unforgiving–prompting me to visit places in my mind where God's grace did not reach, simply because I was not supposed to be there.

Rest assured, God's grace is already in EVERY PLACE that He asks us to travel. It is when we choose of our own device to travel roads we have no business being on that we find loneliness and despair and hopelessness. *Any road traveled according to His will– no matter how painful and overwhelming it may seem–will always be paved with unexplainable peace and grace.* In the early years of being a missionary so far away from my family, I had not yet embraced that truth.

A Gunshot and a $1.00 Beer

Because we were one of the only decently staffed and equipped medical clinics for miles, it was not unusual to have cars race up to our compound with people in extreme emergency situations any time of day. Though we did have, at times, two extremely capable missionary nurses and an airplane to fly some of the more severe cases to nearby hospitals, not all patients lived through their ordeals. One day, a government vehicle came careening onto our property.

One of Liberia's greatest natural resources was its forests filled with rubber trees, mahogany trees, and other valuable hardwoods. Placed strategically around the country were saw mills, usually owned by foreign companies. At the saw mill nearest our mission compound, there was a small restaurant/bar, a pool, and other ame-nities for the elite Liberians and foreigners that might pass through the area. Located right next to the saw mill was an immigration office. An officer had been having a beer with one of the saw mill workers that afternoon and decided that he wanted another one. Finding he had no money, he asked the mill worker to buy him a beer. The worker replied that he had no money to buy any more beer. Feeling frustrated, the officer demanded that the worker go inside the saw mill building where he worked and steal $1.00 so they could continue drinking beer. When the worker refused to steal the money from his employer, the immigration officer became very agitated, stood up, pulled his gun out of his holster, and shot the man in the side.

Feeling remorse over what he had done and fearing that the man might die, the officer and his coworkers brought the bleeding man to our clinic. Rachel and Joan were able to stop the bleeding, clean the wound, and give the wounded man a pain shot and an antibiotic injection. Calling for the airplane to fly the man to the Ganta hospital, they had done all they could do. Thankfully, that man lived, but we do not believe anything was ever done to the immigration officer. Sometimes it was very hard to stay neutral in those situations and not say what we were thinking. If you worked for the government, it seemed there was immunity for almost any-thing, even asking someone to steal money for a beer!

A Declaration of Insanity

Submitting is not something that a very independent and stub-born girl like me wants to do, but by the grace of God...I have asked God to help me, knowing that it is His will for my life as Jeff's wife. But there was one time when I went directly and purposely against my husband's wishes–in front of the entire missionary family there in Tappita. Most likely, that daring move saved his life.

Ever had one of those days where, at the end of the day, you are not where you would have expected to be when you woke up that morning? May 9, 1988, was a day such as that! Around 3:00 a.m., Jeff woke up with a sharp, acute pain in his lower right side which only became increasingly worse as the sun edged up to the horizon.

He was unusually quiet that morning and said that he was having severe gas pains. Right after lunch, instead of lying down for a short nap as we usually did in the hottest part of the day there, he climbed on the station tractor and cut the grass airstrip. Later he told me that he was really trying to get the "gas" pains to dissipate.

By 3:00 p.m., he was in the bed in obvious discomfort, so I sent for the two missionary nurses to come and check him. They both agreed that it looked like appendicitis and that we probably needed to get him to the hospital in Monrovia before dark. Richard Dodson was on flight duty that particular week, and he was put on alert that he might be flying late that afternoon. However, Jeff tried one more time to put off the inevitable. What if it was just intestinal gas and we spent the $180 (which was the cost to charter the airplane round trip) for nothing? He was working through the potential embarrassment of flying down to Monrovia and it not being anything serious.

Richard said that to travel safely, we would need to leave by 4:30 at the latest. At 3:45 p.m., Jeff was still wavering. The rest of us were pretty definite that it was appendicitis and growing very concerned. I remember being afraid of the possibility of Jeff' s appendix rupturing in the middle of the night–in the middle of the jungle–and the fear that help would then be too late.

So, I did something that I had never done before and have never done since in our married life. In front of the other missionaries, I declared Jeff insane and in too much pain to make a rational decision. For that span of time, I took the reins of the household and became the head. I told Richard to get the plane ready and that we would be ready for departure within 30 minutes. With help from my missionary friends, I was able to pack clothes for both Jeff and me, grab the necessary paperwork and other materials that we might have needed, and put the two girls in the hands of other families for a couple of days. We all felt that it was best if the girls stayed in Tappita until we knew if their daddy would require surgery or not.

Though Jeff was still anxious about the outcome, I do not recall that he fought my decision. By that time, the pain was becoming excruciating; I could see that on his face. Just getting him into the plane was an ordeal. My heart felt torn between quickly getting my husband the help that he needed and leaving my two little girls looking confused and apprehensive that we were leaving so quickly. My heart pounded with guilt at leaving them looking so sad and anxious, but I could only lift my concerns for our little girls to God, and be whisked away in our Cessna taildragger with my sick hubby and Richard, a very capable pilot and friend. I lamented again, for the thousandth time, that there were no phones so that I could stay in touch with the girls after we arrived in Monrovia.

Our business manager met us at the airport and carried us straight to ELWA hospital where Jeff was seen by an American doctor on call that evening. Jeff had a temperature of 100 degrees and his pulse was also 100. We were both anxious about the possibility of surgery here in West Africa, and beyond that, Jeff had never had any surgeries of any kind before outside of a tonsillectomy. Obvious to his medically-keen eyes that Jeff had advanced appendicitis, the doctor scheduled immediate surgery. As they were prepping Jeff, I filled out some papers and was asked about anesthesia preferences. Not being sure about the training of the anesthesiologist, Jeff and

We both agreed that we would prefer an epidural instead of him being put under completely. By 8:00 p.m., surgery was complete and Jeff was in a room resting quietly. The doctor told me that it was a good thing we had brought him in when we did because there was already some perforation and by the following morning, it most likely would have ruptured. All the concerns that I had had in Tappi earlier that day were justified by that news. I must say it: I felt vindicated for declaring him insane and taking over as head of the household for that little bit of time. I jokingly told Jeff that I had "saved his life."

They always say that it is about who you know and that is true in most cases. Making a call to a friend who was also a lab technician there at the hospital was the best thing I could have done. Knowing that I would be staying with Jeff in his room that first night, she brought me a pillow, sheets, flashlight, towel, washcloth, soap, and some oatmeal cookies. What a blessing it was to be cared for like that! The first morning, after a long night of no sleeping (anyone who has been in the hospital or stayed with anyone knows how futile it is to try to sleep), my friend Sue brought me an egg, two pieces of toast, and a spiced drink. It was just what I needed to start the morning! Sometimes we have in our grasp the simple things that could make another person's life so different, so much easier. Food, a pillow, soap? How often do we think about how we could bless someone else with those "little" things?

The week that followed, during Jeff's recuperation time, our missionary friends in Monrovia ministered to us in amazing ways by preparing meals and making sure Jeff had his chocolate fixes with cookies and ice cream! The day that Jeff was discharged from the hospital, we sent for the girls to travel on the next flight down. We just wanted our little family together again. When we were reunited, both Michelle and Stefanie *oohed* and *ahhhed* over Jeff's "ouchie" and gave him many sweet kisses which certainly accelerated his healing.

After having been in Monrovia for a couple of weeks, it was time for us to travel back to Tappita. I drove our little family to church Sunday in our truck, and you would have thought a celebrity had come to town for all the attention and excitement of seeing Jeff. They even announced it from the pulpit and thanked God for bringing Teacher Jeff back safely and in good health. That afternoon, there were no naps for the weary family. Liberians do a great job at extending their concerns in person, so we literally sat through visits with almost thirty people within the next two days. We laugh now at the brave move I took in declaring Jeff insane and taking over his job as head of our home. But he has told me several times that he appreciated how I cared for him through this incident. Just another "normal" day in the life of the Abernethys, right?

Splish, Splash! I Not Like the Bath!

After Jeff's surgery and we had returned to Tappi, he was not able to do many of the things required of him, so I, being a helpful wife, offered my services. Because we had the only pickup truck on the mission compound at the time, there were quite a few requests to use it for moving and hauling things. One day while Jeff was still recuperating, I drove the truck to help one of our pastors move a piece of heavy equipment used to make mud blocks to the construction site of a church building. While sitting in the truck waiting for the men, a government soldier and another man walked up to the truck and tapped on my window. Not feeling any reason for alarm, I rolled down the window and innocently greeted them.

- **Me:** *"Hello, sir"*
- **Soldier:** **(no smile)** *You know what you did?*
- **Me:** *"No, what did I do?"*
- **Soldier:** *"You did something bad-o!"*
- **Me:** **(and now I'm not smiling)** *Please tell me, okay?*
- **Soldier: (showing me two very small water spots on his trousers)** *You splashed water on my pants when you were passing on the road. Look at the spots on my pants!*
- **Me:** *Well, sir, I'm very sorry, but I never saw you—*
- **Soldier (interrupting me)** *—You never saw me? What do you mean?*
- **Me:** *I mean that I NEVER saw you standing by a water puddle. I guess I don't understand your fashion. What do you want me to say or do?*
- **Soldier (speaking harshly)** *That's all you can say after what you did? You have no right splashing water on my pants and then you did not stop to say, 'Never mind'!* (I'm sorry)
- **Me:** *Well, I never saw you, but I'm sorry if I splashed you.*
- **Soldier: (glaring at me)** *You are really asking for trouble by your actions. If you do not understand our fashion, you should not be driving here.*

Mercifully, the pastor and three church members walked up about that time. The harassment lightened up as the pastor recited the same story which I had just spoken. Neither of us had seen the soldier and the other man standing on the side of the road. We also found out later that one of the men was the government "revenue" man stationed in Tappita which would be much like an IRS official. In Liberia, anyone in a capacity with some authority could be proned to have the BIG MAN syndrome. That syndrome is not unique to Liberia though as I am sure you are well aware. There are people everywhere that see themselves more important than they really are.

The soldier and the "revenue" man wanted to talk to my husband about allowing me to drive his truck. Up country, away from the capital city, it was unlikely to ever see a female driving a vehicle. Though the incident unnerved me somewhat, I did not let it stop me from driving into town. However, I did watch more carefully as I went through mud puddles, being mindful of anyone that might be standing on the side of the road which was quite a feat considering the many puddles and that the majority of the Liberians in those small towns walked. An independent American woman learning the ways of a strict man's world in Liberia was a hard thing, but I did desire to have a good testimony everywhere I went—with or without my husband.

Later that afternoon, Jeff needed two more bucketsful of rock for a sidewalk we were laying between our house and our storage building. So he conned me into bringing the rocks in the tractor bucket and asked two Bible school men to shovel the rock into the bucket. After the humiliation of the soldier and the mud puddle incident in town that morning, I then had to endure the gawking stares of anyone within a two-mile radius that literally came out of the bush to watch the white woman drive the tractor and haul rock for her man. I must have looked like some kind of modern day hero to them, I guess! We laughed about the commotion it caused for days. Who would have ever thought?

CHAPTER TWENTY-TWO

The spirit of the man is the candle of the Lord, searching all the inward parts of his belly. Proverbs 20:27

Put On the Spot For Jesus

I continued to pray for my Lebanese friends, and though there were only about four months before we would leave for our one year furlough in the States, I tried to trust God for His timing. One day, without warning, God's timing came and I missed the clues. As she had done several times before, Suode sent one of her workers to give me a note saying that she would like me to come for coffee the following afternoon. Arriving at her house, I noticed several motorcycles and cars parked in front of the house.

If you remember the story about how I watched the Muslim woman die as she gave birth, you know that I mentioned the profundity of that moment for me as a young missionary. Just as it redefined my image of missions in an extremely personal way, this following event with Suode reverberated the truth that we must always be ready to share the Gospel. Always. But we must know it before we can share it. This experience shook me deeply, making me feel vulnerable and inadequate, while at the same time, declaring and articulating the total efficacy of the work of the Holy Spirit-alone. All by Himself, He is amazing and powerful!

Suode met me at the door and we hugged warmly, then she looked me straight in the eyes and said, "Kim, I have been moved by everything you and the other Baptist missionaries have told me. I see you live with a joy that I do not understand. My heart wants to believe you, but my mind still is not sure. Today, I will be sure. Don't be afraid or angry at what I am asking you to do for me." Feeling a knot in the pit of my stomach as well as in my throat, she led me into her dining room. There I saw four men sitting, expectantly, as if they were waiting on someone. I soon realized that it was me. But why?

Around the table was the local Catholic priest, a cousin of Suode's husband who was the Jehovah Witness guru, another pastor from a local church with strange doctrines of which I had never heard, and a representative from the Muslim community. Each of them had a Bible or some point of reference in front of them. I touched my hands together as I realized that I had not brought my Bible with me that day. Sometimes I brought it and would leave it in the car–just in case, but not this time. Suode explained to the men that she believed that I carried my faith close to me and would be able to answer any questions presented by them, but that she needed to be sure that the God I said that I believed in was true and big enough to outshine the religions they represented.

If I was not the one having to sit at the table with those men, it would have been intriguing to watch how God took care of His own reputation. He needs no one to defend His name, though we certainly have the honor to do so. However, since I was the one tangibly seen as a representative of Jehovah God, I simply whispered a prayer that I would just get out of the way and let Him work. I did not feel prepared for this and I fought the fear that was rising in my flesh. It was an extraordinary moment where I distinctly <u>knew</u> the Holy Spirit exactly as Romans 8 describes Him.

Over the next hour and a half, the Holy Spirit coated me with knowledge of Scripture that I did not even know I possessed. Questions were fielded to me from the men, all four of them determined to find a place of weakness in what I believed. I pulled from all my Bible school training, my mission doctrinal statement preparation, and years of personal devotions. But, most of all, I just spoke from my heart. Honestly, to this day, I cannot remember much about the details of that meeting except that God showed up and did everything He had always promised He would do. When I was weak, He was strong. When I was floundering, He was my Rock. When I was afraid, He was my shelter.

Finally, with a satisfied smile, Suode dismissed all the men who protested their unhappiness as they left, then turning to me, she said, "Take me to your God. I want to know Him as you know Him. He sounds wonderful and strong and faithful and good." So, I took her to the cross. It was a beautiful zenith in my life, and even now,

I can remember her prayer, knowing that God embraced both of us at that moment. When my family left Tappita four months later and I said farewell to my Lebanese friend, I knew that most likely I would never see her again on this earth. To this day, I do not know where she and her family live nor if they are safe and well, but I do know that I will see her again in Heaven. That is the hope we have in Christ Jesus as believers! We are part of His eternal Kingdom!

Facing the Clouds

During a July trip to Monrovia for our last vacation in Liberia, we experienced one of the scariest flying incidences that I can remember. We were packed and ready to travel on a Monday morning, but it literally rained all day. By noon on Tuesday, the rain had let up enough that Jeff and the other pilot felt that we could make the flight to Monrovia, but as we took off and began to fly away from Tappi, the pilots started discussing the best way to go around some of the larger rain clouds they were watching in the distance.

More than halfway through the trip, we found ourselves facing a cloud that there seemed no way around. It was thick, solid to the left and to the right. Feeling that there might not be enough fuel to get us back to Tappi, the pilots pulled up to about 10,000 feet into the clouds and went IFR (instrument flight rules) for a bit. That was a scary feeling especially in a little four-seater plane. After about five minutes, we found visibility and sunshine, and everyone was clearly relieved. But it was not until we had to face the cloud and go through it did we find the sun on the other side of it! The sun is always there. We just sometimes forget that truth.

A Foreshadowing of a Future Home

As a writer, I have always been aware of foreshadowing in literary pieces, but it is hard to believe that in June of 1988, I attended a high school graduation at the very school from which my oldest daughter would eventually graduate some fourteen years later! I fell in love with the school, with the town, with the country of Ivory Coast and its Frenchness long before I even realized that living there was more than a possibility! Looking back, I am in awe and in love with the way God often intersects us with something or someone that will eventually be a big deal in our lives. Foreshadowing is not just a literary definition; it is often a beautiful means by which God "prepares" us to move in a certain direction in the future.

As I've said before, Jeff has always seemed to understand my need to expand my horizons, to have a change of scenery, to do something a little different. Two of our BMM missionary kids were graduating from the International Christian Academy in Bouake, Ivory Coast. Traveling with a couple of missionary families who had children graduating that year, they had invited me to attend the festivities with them.

While in Bouake, I stayed in the dorm with some high school girls, and had a great time! International Christian Academy (ICA) was a boarding school run by several different mission organizations. Though some younger missionary children were sent to boarding school (as early as 7 or 8 years old), most were sent over in their junior and senior high school years. As our little family was still very young, we had not given a whole lot of thought to their high school education. I did know that I would home school them for as long as I possibly could while not compromising their very important secondary education.

The education of their children is one of the greatest enigmas of missionary families, and with that said, you can imagine the opinions on what is best run the gamut! While I could not fathom how a mother (missionary or not) could agree to send her second grader away to boarding school so that she could be available for ministry, there was a particular mission agency that in the past (though regulations have been changed) required that. It was impossible for me to understand how God could be in that decision. For me, it was hard to believe that I could even send my daughters to boarding school when they were in high school, but yet, there I was sleeping in a dorm full of girls. It was enlightening for me in many ways.

My journal of June 30, 1988, reads:

> *These boarding students seem so much like a family because they are sent here at a very important time of their lives. I was impressed overall with the spirit and independence of the kids. Most of them had good attitudes about their*

216

parents' ministries. That really made me feel better. I felt right at home and would gladly come over to be dorm parents or an English teacher if God ever opened the door. I love to be around teenagers like that!

So, God was directing my paths, my thoughts, my desires. In 1988, we were still living in our first African home, but by 2001, we would live in Bouake, the city I had visited in 1988. Though not as dorm parents, I did teach a sixth grade English class at ICA during the time we lived there. From my first African home to my last African home. Who would have ever known....except God?

The Fall of a Lifetime

I was so glad to be back with my little family after being away from them for almost a week. Jeff was quite the super dad to have traveled five hours in a truck on muddy roads with a five year old and a 21 month old just so that they could be in Monrovia when I arrived! That still seems unfathomable to me that he would do that. After our little family was reunited, we went for a quick meal and then it was time to get some sleep. The next day, Jeff took Michelle and went into town to do some shopping. The mission compound was eerily quiet, and except for the business manager, Tim Bos, Stefanie and I were the only ones there that afternoon.

Our Stefanie had always been a climber, ever since she discovered what her legs were for! The main building of our Monrovia compound was two stories. Upstairs were two apartments. Downstairs was the business office and another apartment to the left of the office. At several points in the past few months, Stefanie had observed the bigger kids climbing and sitting on the railing by the upstairs apartments. As she grew taller, she wanted to be like the big kids and started trying to climb on the railing. Of course, we disciplined her. We knew that she was no where near balanced or strong enough to climb up and sit on the railing, but she thought she was!

Earlier on that fateful day, I had already reprimanded her twice that day for attempting to climb up on the railing. In the afternoon she and I had been playing in the sandbox when Stef said that she was thirsty, so we walked up the stairs toward our apartment hand in hand. The details from that point are fuzzy, even though I have relived them over many times since then. Supposedly, I still was holding her hand when we opened the apartment door and went inside. From there, I walked into the kitchen to get her a cup of water, assuming that she was behind me. It jolted my senses when I heard the screen door slam and took only seconds to realize that was not a good thing! Dashing out the door I called for Stef to come back to me, but as I opened the screen door, I instinctively looked toward the balcony railing. Almost instantaneously I saw her feet slide over the railing and heard her cry for me. Within seconds, there was a sickening thud and the Liberian day guard who always sat by the gate was shouting something incoherent.

The cry of a child for its mother is a precious sound, and to that mother, it renders emotions that prompt her into some sort of action. Understandably, the cry I heard Stefanie make as she plunged to a concrete pad eighteen feet below wrenched me so deeply and so sharply that I could not breath. Words cannot describe the emotions that fleeted through my mind as I rushed down the steps. Part of me wanted to stand still and deny what had just happened. But questions plagued me. WAS SHE ALIVE? WAS SHE PARALYZED? WAS SHE MANGLED? COULD I BEAR IT? My mother's heart forced me to go and get my baby!

The African guard was tenderly holding Stefanie in his arms as he said to me, "Missy, the angel turned her! She was falling straight down but the angel turned her." As I took her from the fretful guard and assessed her condition, I remember thinking that she looked normal, no blood, still conscious, but obviously winded, laboring for every breath. I had no way to reach Jeff. This was before cell phones, and knowing that we could not wait until we found him, I asked Tim Bos to take us to the ELWA missionary hospital, a ministry of the SIM organization, where Jeff had recently had his appendix removed.

We had to get help quickly! My journal of July 4, 1988, reads:

> *All the way to the hospital, I wrestled with myself and how I was going to give her up. I thought she would surely die. That was too far to fall and not have fatal consequences. She was disoriented and breathless, whining steadily, but not*

crying with gusto like she usually does. I was so concerned about neurological damage. I thought so many things during those minutes it took to get to the hospital. But I can say that I did receive peace to give her up if God saw fit to take her from us. I know that God's grace is sufficient WHEN we need it.

After numerous tests and x-rays, the American missionary doctor was able to determine that there were no broken bones and seemingly no neurological damage other than a mild concussion. We were instructed to not allow her to sleep more than two hours at a time for a couple of days and to watch for any signs that could indicate that the brain might be swelling. He was as amazed as we were that Stefanie had not received more injuries from a fall such as that. Being a Christian doctor, he paused to pray with us and thanked God for protecting this little one. I remembered again the words of the guard who had seen her fall. The angel turned her! She was falling straight down but the angel turned her. Turned her indeed...of course He did!

This is a story of a sovereign God and how He used a little quilted backpack that was stuffed with a baby doll, some little toys, and a blanket. For you see, Stefanie was wearing that little backpack when she fell off the balcony. According to the guard who witnessed the entire thing, Stefanie fell headfirst but quickly was flipped to her back and that is how she landed. Completely on that quilted backpack. There were no bruises or cuts to the head. It was absolutely a miracle how God allowed her to fall, provided an angel to flip her over on her back, and then another angel certainly cushioned her little head as she made contact with the concrete. If this seems silly to you and you are wanting to make this a lesson more in physics of how Stefanie fell and ultimately landed on her back, then go ahead! Me? I choose to believe that my Heavenly Father did as He pleased. Through this traumatic event, He showed Himself to be exactly what He says He is–THE GREAT I AM.

Now for the mind games that surely come after such a traumatic experience. I played those mind games in my head over and over for months. Even now, as I write about this incident that happened some twenty years ago, I cannot fathom how I, one of the most proactive mothers I know, could allow something like this to happen! Immediately following the incident, I was so busy tending to Stefanie and watching for potential problems, that I did not really take the time to deal with it properly. That is often the way it is: we stay busy with the necessities of the moment and choose not to deal with our emotional needs. After a while, I struggled with the doubts, the anger (towards myself), and insecurities (that I was not a fit mother). Eventually, I had to move past all that. Go on in the amazing grace that God was perfect even though I was not.

This stubborn and independent young mother was learning some hard lessons about the fragility of life and how very little I did control. Control is an illusion with which we as parents tend to comfort ourselves. After an event such as watching Stefanie fall off that balcony with no physical consequences, I bent my knee a little more to the One that holds in His marvelous Hands SIMPLY EVERYTHING.

Over the years, as I have watched my children grow and spread their wings, make good and bad decisions, and stretch my patience and faith to an unfathomable limit, I have always remembered the truth that He holds the lives of my children—NOT ME. I will not always be there for my children, and even when I think that I am there, right there beside them, that will never be enough. I must rely on our Heavenly Father to do what I cannot.

CHAPTER TWENTY-THREE

A time to get, and a time to lose; a time to keep, and a time to cast away; a time to rend, and a time to sew; a time to keep silence, and a time to speak; a time to love, and a time to hate; a time of war, and a time of peace.
Ecclesiastes 3:6-8

Packing it All Up

Missionary furloughs are both needful and interruptive, much like a long awaited vacation is to most families, only on a much bigger scale. From the time that my little toe was first placed on Africa soil, I looked forward to the day that I would be able to return to the States, visit with family, and relive some familiar cultural experiences. It is not to say that I did not want to be in Liberia and was just biding my time, but there was the realization of a "pause" button that would be pushed nearly four years down the road; just for a little while. A pause for refreshment, renewal, reporting, and reconnecting. However, since it was our first furlough, we really had no idea what was expected of us on either side of the "pause" button.

During that July vacation when Stefanie had fallen from the balcony, we bought our tickets for a late October departure to the States to begin our first furlough. After that, life started moving a little faster. Not realizing how embedded we had become in the ministries there in Tappi, it was a daunting task to start pulling back and placing our responsibilities into other missionaries' hands. What would we do with our house while we were gone for a year? Would we have someone stay in it? What about our dog? Who would teach the English courses in my place? Could I get the material ready before we left? How would we pack up the things we wanted to preserve? What about the kids' toys and clothes? What important papers and items should we take back with us?

It was an exhausting three months working out the details of those questions and more, but God walked us through this time of uncertainty as He has in every place. Another missionary couple just happened to want to spend a year in Tappi, and it worked beautifully that they would stay in our home. That settled much of the issues about what to do with our things. They, too, had children so we left out most of the toys and they also would take care of our dog. In the midst of the whirlwind of activity that any departure causes, my missionary friend, Nancy Sheppard, helped me sew matching dresses for Michelle, Stefanie, and me. I had envisioned the moment we would disembark from the final flight knowing everyone would be waiting anxiously to finally see us. I thought it would be really neat if us three girls were dressed alike for the arrival.

This would be Stefanie's stateside debut, and we wondered how she would do with all the new discoveries she would make that year in the States. Michelle was living off all the things we had told her about her American family since she was only two when we had first come to Liberia.

Balancing Our Friendships

Saying a bittersweet goodbye to our new missionary family and ministries there in Liberia, we turned our hearts and minds to the furlough ahead. We knew that we had changed in those three years and had so many stories of God's provision and marvelous works to share; also we wondered how hard it would be for us to acclimate back into the American culture–even if it was for just a year.

We missionaries always feel like "strangers and pilgrims" no matter where we are. While in Liberia, we knew that we were not like the Africans, and realized that we would not completely be accepted, but we asked God to use us in spite of that. While in the States, we knew how fast a year would pass by, and there was the tendency to not want to delve too deeply into old friendships or nurture new ones. *Goodbyes, for foreign missionaries, are ever present* and despite what many may think, we never get used to them. Living in that reality long enough unfortunately transformed us into people who usually stood along the edges, never really feeling we had the emotional energies to dive in deeply. That was really difficult for me because I was a woman who lived with passion and depth in most everything I did!

Saying all that, God has blessed us with many friends who have bolstered our lives in so many ways! Now that we are stateside missionaries, our mentality has changed somewhat, and we have been able to step into some relationships without that WHAT IS THE USE? WE'LL JUST HAVE TO SAY GOODBYE mentality. Still, because of the unusual demands and consuming essence of our campus ministry here in the States, many of our friendships are still somewhat stilted. I have often wondered if those that know us and see us often think that we choose to not invest in our friendships more than we do. Hopefully, that is not the case. We do care, but feel like we live in another world that is hard to explain even through prayer letters and presentations. *MISSIONARIES ARE CREATURES WHO LIVE IN THE CREVICES BETWEEN TWO WORLDS.*

Arriving back in America after our first term in West Africa was an emotional experience for us rookie missionaries! As we stood before the custom agent who soundly stamped our passport, and as he looked up and said, "Welcome home," I almost crumbled in a blubbering mess. After almost twenty-two hours of traveling and numerous layovers, we had landed in Charlotte exhausted, but our hearts beating with excitement. Stefanie was a little hesitant, for she really did not know those people or this country.

After sweet reunions lathered with teary hugs and kisses, we retrieved our luggage and headed straight for McDonalds, per Michelle's request. There is a picture somewhere of Stefanie sitting in McDonalds for the very first time looking a little out of place and not really sure why she was supposed to be so excited about this place anyway. My heart went out to her and I kept her close to me until I felt she was ready to explore. In a way, I knew exactly how she was feeling. I felt almost shy around those that I had known so well before. It was like becoming reacquainted all over. That year, Stefanie experienced her first snow, her first escalator and elevator, and her first USDA "snake" (steak) which she asked for repeatedly.

The Year Zoomed By

Between visiting churches, family, and reacquainting with friends, we stayed on the road more than we were able to stay at home. There is a false assumption by some that furlough is actually just a year-long vacation for missionaries. Nothing could be further from the truth, I assure you! When a missionary comes home on furlough, one of the biggest concerns stateside is: "Where will we live?" Jeff's grandmother had died just six months before we came home, and her house sat empty. Jeff's mother and Aunt Stretch decided that it would be the perfect place for us to call our stateside home. They cleaned, decorated, and prepared it for this tired little missionary family coming right out of Africa. It was a gift of love, never to be forgotten, and we were just amazed that God had taken care of our housing requisites long before we needed them.

Michelle attended kindergarten at Northside Christian Academy in Charlotte, North Carolina, during our furlough year, and enjoyed making many new friends. We loved spending the holidays with family and catching up with so many people that we had not seen in a very long time. Most of all, we traveled to our supporting churches, enjoying numerous missions conferences, meeting new people wherever we went.

The last three months we were in the States, we checked off our list, shopped, packed, and ate! If you've ever heard of the "Freshman Fifteen" which is supposedly what the average college freshman will gain in that first year, the same can be said for furloughing mission-aries! Everyone wanted to feed us and help us to catch up on our eating. It took us two or three furloughs before we really learned how to pace ourselves with all the food offered to us.

Saying those dreaded goodbyes again for the second time was just as hard as the first. There were a couple of dynamics in those goodbyes that we did not experience the first time. One being that we were taking back three sweet little ones that time. I was four months pregnant as we boarded the plane that would carry us back to our "other" home. Promising my African friends before we left Tappi that I would bring back "belly" when we returned to Liberia, I was thankful that we had held true to that word. This, most likely, was of great concern to our family, but they were brave, also learn-ing to trust God with our lives just as we were with them.

Another dynamic was the disconcerting news that on Christmas Eve, 1989, a rebel leader named Charles Taylor had led an army across the border of Ivory Coast and into Liberia. His aim was to overthrow the government of President Doe. Reminders of our first departure back in 1985 was brought to the forefront. Since that initial coup d'etat four years before, tensions had been swirling and rising all around us, but never had we seen as deadly a movement as this rebel army storming the upcountry area of Liberia. We, by the way, also lived upcountry, so we realized that we might be facing some dire consequences.

However, I don't think we could have imagined what we would experience in the following ten weeks. God was merciful to not allow us to see the future. How effective could we really be and how would we ever see the amazing power of God if we knew what was coming and chose to squirm and dodge every hardship? Where then would grace abide? His strength above measure? How would we experience His all-sufficient and amazing peace and provision?

If I had the choice to know the future which would give license to change my future or to simply know the all-consuming Jehovah God in the midst of the hardest storm, I would like to think that I would ultimately and solely choose God. He has convinced me of His goodness and matchlessness! Would I be strong enough to choose Him every time?

A Little Different This Time

As the small single-engine Cessna zoomed around the small town of Tappita announcing our arrival to any that might be waiting, my heart swelled with joy and peace at being back there. It was right. It was time. I had missed my African home. Even Michelle and Stefanie peered eagerly out the plane's window looking for familiar landmarks and wondering if their friends would be waiting for them at the hangar. Briefly, I remembered back to the first time we touched down on that grass runway and how afraid and anxious I had felt. Not knowing what to expect and cringing at the native ruggedness around me, I caved and hid in my fears.

This time, I was practically dancing as I got out of the plane with my two girls. Greeting the missionaries and then our African Bible school friends who were there to meet us, I felt so at home. Then my dear African friend Mary Kwiah came and gave me a really long hug. Mischievously, she touched my stomach and felt the "baby bump." That precipitated a huge outcry of joy and I was quickly lifted by the strong arms of my African woman friends who felt so excited that I had indeed brought "belly" back and would again experience the birth of another baby with them. I don't imagine that there is any drug that could ever take me as high as I felt at that moment!

Our house was so clean and welcoming! The girls ran to find forgotten toys, Jeff to check the tool shed and to turn on the generator so that we could have some electricity while we unpacked. I just walked around the house that just a little over four years ago had been so strange to me. Now, my own special touches were everywhere. I touched the curtains, the knickknacks, my dishes, and just smiled. I was home.

Tensions Rise

The weeks clipped along as we found a routine that worked for our growing family. We had brought back a school curriculum that would help us teach Michelle first, second, and third grade, as well as have Stefanie dabble a little in preschool activities. Thankfully, there were a couple of other missionary families that had children near the same ages as ours, so we pooled our resources and energies and opened a little "schoolhouse"–using an abandoned building at the back of the property. We scrubbed, cleaned, and brought some necessary equipment down and really made it seem like our little red schoolhouse. The kids enjoyed going to school every morning, and we usually were able to finish up by noon leaving us the afternoon for other things.

News of the rebel uprising accelerated throughout our county and people were beginning to feel a little uneasy at the direction it looked like the rebels were taking. In the wake of the rebels' advance, many young Gio and Mano men dropped their shovels and garden tools and picked up machetes and guns, joining Charles Taylor's quickly growing army. What seemed, at one time, as an insurgence that would eventually peter out, became a dynamic with unknown results for the country's future.

President Doe's military brawn attempted to reach into the upcountry, but were not nearly as effective to stop the spreading interest growing about this new "savior" of Liberia—Charles Taylor. The promises that Taylor made were daunting, and we realized that they were, most likely, too good to be true. But, for the oppressed tribes that had suffered under the mutinous present administration (who also came into power by force), Taylor's promises seemed like a breath of fresh air. He had planned well and knew what he was doing by maneuvering his way through the region where the majority of the Mano and Gio people lived. His calculated entrance through the economically and physically oppressed north part of Liberia fed the "itch" those forgotten citizens of Liberia had for retribution. A political avalanche had begun, and it did not look as if anything could stop it.

Too Hot To Stop

As my baby belly grew larger and the political uprising gained momentum, we tried to maintain a semblance of normalcy on the compound. The Bible Institute was to begin a new school year by the middle of March, and I was set to teach an English class in the 7:00 a.m. slot. Three weeks later, we heard that the rebels were only about fifty miles from our compound. We felt that, most likely, if Taylor and his men knew about our compound, it would be on their "to take" list since we had heard that he was sucking up all available resources in his path much like a tornado would do.

The men had been in contact with a missionary couple, Tom and June Jackson, who lived about 30 miles from us. He was the "white Gio man" whom I made reference to in chapter two. As we attempted to keep in close contact with Tom and June by shortwave radio, we often heard gunfire in the background as we talked with them. We were extremely concerned with their safety, but they chose to stay in their home, ministering as they could.

During that momentous week, at a scheduled station meeting with all the missionaries, we formulated a serious evacuation plan considering the strong possibility that we might have to step out of the way of this ensuing revolution. The Cherokee 6 airplane was operational by that time and could fly six people with very little extra load. Because I was pregnant and had small children, I was placed on the first flight. It was strongly advised that everyone pack a small "evacuation" bag and have it ready–just in case. That whole meeting seemed so surreal because none of us wanting to fully embrace what was slowly but surely happening.

Not wanting to acknowledge the fact that our second term in Liberia was not going as I had envisioned it, I went home and packed two small bags for Michelle and Stefanie with play clothes and pajamas. Part of me thought the whole situation was too bizarre and that we were probably overreacting; the other part of me embodied a fear that I refused to speak out loud. Somehow in my mind and probably in the mind of others on our compound, we chose to believe that the war would go on around us, that we would be used to encourage and evangelize during that uncertain time, but that life for us would not need to change much at all. Naïve? Yes, but not an unusual mindset from those who had never experienced war, hatred, and animosity on that larger level!

On March 28, 1990, during my 7:00 a.m. English class, Jeff came into the Bible institute classroom to tell me that I would need to dismiss my class as there was a mandatory station meeting to be held at 8:30 a.m. Some very serious news had come across the radio airwaves—serious enough that it precipitated a meeting of all missionary personnel on the compound. While talking with Tom Jackson that morning, he seemed quieter than usual, telling the men that it was over for us all. Then the last words we ever heard him say was, "Pray for Liberia like you have never prayed before." He then signed off the radio. The men brought this information to us all, and after praying and talking, it was unanimously decided that we would stay. It was not time to run. We would continue our ministries there in Tappita until God made it crystal clear that we should step out of the way.

CHAPTER TWENTY-FOUR

O Lord, I know that the way of man is not in himself; It is not in man that walketh to direct his own steps. Jeremiah 10:23

Handwriting on the Wall

In difficult and uncertain situations, don't we often wish that God would write the answer on a wall somewhere? Make it abundantly clear? Nearly five hours after our first impromptu station meeting where we had decided to stay put for the time being, God did that. Because of the volatile situation around us, the men had decided it was best to keep the shortwave station radio on throughout the day and night. While Chick and Joan Watkins were eating lunch, a fervent call came from the American Embassy.

Earlier that day, Tom and June Jackson had been used as hostages by government soldiers who were caught behind enemy lines. Thinking that perhaps the rebels would not want to do harm to white missionaries, the soldiers forced Tom and June to drive them through enemy lines. Caught in a hostile crossfire, the vehicle was riddled with bullets and everyone inside killed. War was war. Whether the rebel soldiers who fired on the missionary vehicle had known that there were missionaries inside the vehicle is still a mystery to us. I found it surreal that the rebels (most of them of the Gio dialect) would even purposely consider killing the very man who had been translating God's Word into their dialect. But war does not take time to consider those things of love.

The American Embassy told us in that afternoon communique that they had reason to believe Taylor's rebel force was in our area and would soon attempt to secure our mission compound. In light of the Jackson tragedy, they were mandating that we all leave immediately! If we chose not to adhere to the strong suggestion of the American Embassy, they reiterated that they could absolutely not guarantee our safety from that day forward. The situation was too inflammatory for anyone to know what would happen next.

As we finished up a lunch of spaghetti, Jeff was called to another meeting at the home of Richard and Millie Dodson to hear this news from the American Embassy. I had just put Stefanie and Michelle in the bathtub to wash off the spaghetti sauce residue when Chick Watkins drove up outside our dining room. "Hey, Kim," he said as he sat alert on his motorcycle. "Evacuation plans are being put into effect, and since you are on the first flight out, I need you and the girls at the airplane hangar in 45 minutes. Don't know when we'll be able to come back, so pack accordingly. Jeff will explain what has triggered this." I stood as an effigy, lifeless and stunned, trying to fathom the fruition of all the fears that we had envisioned in the recent days. War had been all around us and now it had come pounding on our door.

I knew deep down that this war was not ours to fight, but the love and acute responsibility we felt for the Bible school families on our compound was almost emotionally debilitating. We had the airplane and vehicles. We could fly off into the sunset and find safety. My precious African friends could not. As I turned toward the noise my two girls were making as they splashed in the bathtub, my prayer was not long, elaborate, or eloquent. "FATHER, WIPE THE FEAR AND ANXIETY OFF MY FACE AS I LIVE THROUGH THESE NEXT FEW MINUTES. HELP ME TO SAY THE RIGHT THING TO MY CHILDREN. I NEED TO LIVE ABOVE MY FEARS." Children are more astute than we give them credit for, and I knew that my almost seven-year old Michelle was even more so. My face had always been an open book–any emotion I might be feeling was clearly written there!

"Girls, guess what?" I attempted to sound eager and excited as I walked into the bathroom. "We get to ride on the airplane today, in a few minutes so we need to hurry and get ready!" As you can imagine, there were the tirades of "Why's" and I did my best to give them an answer. Honestly, I do not remember what I told them, but I must have shared a semblance of the truth because after they were dressed, Michelle started packing a paper bag full of toys to take. Stefanie ran to do the same.

I will never forget this moment. It is as clear today as it was then. I looked deeply into the eyes of my daughters as they came out carrying their toy bags and said, "YOU CAN ONLY TAKE ONE

SMALL TOY EACH. JUST ONE. The airplane will have other people to carry, too. I'm sorry, sweeties, but we must just leave the rest of your things here." It wrenched my heart to watch their perplexed looks as they tried to process what I was saying. The clock was ticking and by that time, we only had about twenty minutes left before we needed to be at the airplane hangar. It is significant that both girls chose to take with them a little musical lamb that Dr. and Mrs. Jack Hudson had given them when they were both babies. When wound, the lambs played the song *Jesus Loves Me*. What a great reminder for them and for me!

Jeff came back to the house while I was getting the girls ready, but he went straight to the office, pulling files, and trying to think of what needed to go with us. He then told me that he and a couple other missionary men had decided to drive their pickup trucks out later that day. The plane would only make three trips. Feeling extremely uneasy about being separated from him, I did try to be brave. We hugged briefly, but both of us were dealing with emotions and thoughts that could not be spoken, could not be explained, so we did not even try. He did ask me if there was anything in particular from the house that I would like for him to bring in the truck. I do not remember if I told him anything or not, but it did prompt me to get the red and cream king-sized quilt that my grandmother Horrell had made for us before we left the States. I quickly folded it and placed it beside my small bag of clothes.

My nerves were jingling, and my now seven-month pregnant belly was tight and aching to the point I thought I was going to pass out. I asked one of our Bible school workers to please take the girls in the wheelbarrow to the airplane hangar and watch them. Their questions were too much for me at the time.

It was then that I saw my best Liberian friend, Mary Kwiah, coming onto my porch. I ran to meet her and we just hugged–tightly. As I told her of my fears for her, she reminded me that because she was a Gio, she was not in any danger from the arrival of the rebel army. Handing her a couple of large bags, I told her to go in our pantry and refrigerator and take any food that she wanted. Other women and men from our Bible school town flooded our yard and porch. Most of those were not of the Gio tribe, and because this war was founded on tribal animosities already, I knew they could be in great danger. They, too, were scared and uncertain, and my heart almost exploded at the thought of leaving them. A couple of the Bible school wives were very pregnant and I knew that it would be extremely difficult for them to run into the bush with their loads and children. I felt again like a pampered American and had to fight the impulse to flee with them into the bush just to prove that I was one of them!

My journal of March 28, 1990, read:

> *For our Liberian Christians it is not as simple as crawling in an airplane and being whisked off to safety. They had to prepare for a long trek through the jungle with little food for their families. My heart wrenched to have to leave them in this way. They fear for their lives and we know their fears are viable. Many of them do not know where to go. Some of their home towns have long been burned or taken control by rebels.*

For those reasons I pleaded with Jeff to take a couple of those wives and several smaller children in our Isuzu Trooper when he left later that day. He promised to do his best. He had already been asked to take household goods for some of those families. While our houses were large and filled with many things, an average Liberian who lived in the bush could carry their belongings wrapped tightly in a couple of large table clothes. It was, however, all they had and replacing them would be extremely hard.

Truthfully, though, other than my grandmother's quilt, I thought nothing of my "things" that I was leaving behind. Not at that moment. The people milling around us, scared, anxious, and needy were overwhelming my senses. I realized at that moment how much I had fallen in love with them. At the forty-five minute mark, Jeff and I left the house and headed towards the airplane hangar. Tension, uncertainty, and something else unnamed filled the air around us. Some of the Bible school women walked with me, carrying my load, holding my hand, and talking quietly of their fears and wanted to hear my promise that we would return after this passed over. It was one of those moments that pulsated with pure joy and sorrow all at the same time!

Jeff and I had talked often during the previous four years of how we believed we could easily walk away from all the material things in our wonderful home in Tappita. After all, they were just "things" and things can easily be replaced. We failed to discuss or even consider the awful impact of walking away from our Christian friends and the many ministries which had embedded themselves into our very souls. But, God was still sovereign. We had to trust in His providence, knowing that He was holding our hands as well as the hands of our beloved African sisters and brothers.

Besides my two girls and me, Millie Dodson, Joan Cuthbertson and her brand new little baby girl, Ruth Marie, who was born the night before, were passengers in the first evacuation flight. Chick Watkins was the pilot for this flight, and he exuded a calmness that was a balm to my soul that day. Though I know he was heavily concerned about the turn of events around us, he remained planted in the promises of God. It really helped me to try to do the same.

The Cherokee 6 was weighted down more than it should have been, but those were not ordinary circumstances, so Chick said a quick prayer and we started off. My heart jolted painfully as I looked, one last time, at the many Liberians standing around watching us. Trying to smile and wave at them, with tears streaming down my face, I finally had to look away. I silently cried out for the peace He promised that was way beyond my understanding. Folded underneath me on the airplane seat, was the quilt that my grandmother had made me. I used it as a cushion, determined that it would not be left behind. I painfully wished the same for my dear African friends looking longingly after the moving airplane–that I could have brought them with me.

As Chick pushed full throttle and the airplane plunged ahead, it soon became evident that it was struggling to lift off because of the extra weight. As we passed the point of where the plane usually made its liftoff, Chick turned to us and say, "Ladies, we must pray and ask God to get this plane off the ground NOW!" With absolutely not an inch to spare before we would surely come into violent contact with the tall rubber trees at the end of the runway, the airplane hit a bump which levitated it into the air. Breathing as one, we could almost imagine the wheels of the plane brushing the tops of the trees as we lifted into the sky. On the ground, Jeff and the other pilots were also catching their breath. They had known that the plane was struggling and it had looked less and less likely that it would take off and gain proper altitude.

In the fifty-five minutes it took to fly to Monrovia, there were times when we talked of the situation we were living out, but there were also profound moments of silence, each person slipping into their own world of deliberation. None of us knew exactly what would be the next step. I determined that I must try to take care of myself as much as possible in the next days because of those two little girls sitting behind me clinging to their one toy and their many unspoken questions, but also for the little one growing inside me. Reality was setting in and my mind reacted by making me feel numb. I remembered a statement that Elisabeth Elliott had said when asked how she survived the days after her husband, Jim, was killed. She said, "I just did the next thing." And that is exactly what I did. No more, no less. Just what needed to be done.

Meanwhile Back In Tappi

It will be necessary for me to revert back and forth between Monrovia where the girls and I were and to Tappi where Jeff was still frantically packing and preparing to leave our African home for an undetermined amount of time. I hated to leave him to handle the many household decisions, but we both knew that I had my own huge responsibility; our children–born and unborn. He moved around the house, going from room to room, as several Bible school students followed him, pleading for him to take their families and some of their things. Pressed for time and needing to be able to concentrate, he told a couple of the men to go ahead and get their wives, small children, and their load over to the Trooper, tying their load on the top of the car.

Jeff went back to packing important papers and shutting off the kerosene refrigerator and freezer. He recalls that an eerie quiet filled the house as he took a quick minute to pray. Packing a small bag with some clothes, he sadly locked up the house, handed the keys to James Kwia, who was a professor in the Bible schools whom we were leaving in charge of the entire compound while we were gone.

So intent on the work he was doing inside the house, Jeff had not noticed exactly what was going on with the Isuzu Trooper outside. More than two dozen women and children stood around the truck as a couple of the Bible school students were tying load after load on top of the vehicle.

When Jeff opened the driver's door to look inside, to his amazement, the roof had caved in three separate places because of the weight of the load! Owing to the fact that this unexpected and abrupt departure was stressing everyone, he reacted more harshly than he would have liked as he saw the damage being done to his car. He did realize that unless he got the weight off the roof and onto the roof supports, he would be unable to sit in the driver's seat. Tense and overwhelmed by the events of the day, he lashed out at the men around him as he demanded they take everything off the top of the car and help him repack it.

Forty-five minutes later, he had redistributed the weight of the load onto the roof supports and put the rest of the load in the very back of the Trooper. Taking time, he pushed the roof back into its proper place, and packed thirteen women and children in the vehicle with him. As impossible as that may seem, that was a fairly average number for a vehicle in Liberia. Already behind schedule because of the repacking, he drove away from Tappita with similar feelings of sadness and apprehension about our future ministry there. He headed south towards the town of Buchanan which was believed to be away from rebel activity.

God's Timing

The girls and I arrived in Monrovia by 2:30 p.m., and tried to settle in. For the kids, it was an unexpected holiday. As each flight arrived adding more people to our small BMM compound in Monrovia, we knew that we would have to cram in and share apartment space with other families. Each family was given one bedroom, and the kitchen space was shared. I remember that it was comforting to be with other families during those uncertain times. They all helped me so much with the girls that afternoon, so that I was able to rest and try to relax my belly which was trying to prematurely contract.

Later that evening, all the Tappi missionaries who had arrived in Monrovia that day went out to eat together at a Chinese restaurant. As we were sitting around the very long table, a couple of Peace Corp guys came in and recognized someone in our group. One of the Peace Corp guys started talking to the missionary men at the other end of the table, and I became curious when I saw them looking my way a couple of times. Stepping outside with the Peace Corp guys for a few minutes, one of the missionaries eventually came back in, walking slowly to my end of the table. Do you know that feeling when your body puts up its defenses as if to fend off a physical blow? That's what I felt as he asked me to walk outside for a minute.

Once the Peace Corp workers were introduced to me, I was told the story that has superseded any other in my life since I have been married to Jeff. The news moved me to literally clutch my chest and believe that my heart would surely stop. The Peace Corp guys had also traveled the road from Tappi to the town of Buchanan earlier that day and had suddenly come across a beige Isuzu Trooper, identical to our car, sitting cockeyed on the side of the road riddled with bullets, everyone inside and outside dead.

Though there was no time to search extensively because of possible danger, they did not remember seeing a white man in the driver's seat. He most likely was on the other side of the vehicle facing the bush. I just remember being held as I cried, trying to not fall completely apart. Thankfully, someone had the foresight to keep my children inside the restaurant, so that this news would not affect them. Not yet.

I was encouraged to take hold of faith and compose myself for the sake of my children and my unborn baby. Perhaps there was another Isuzu Trooper just like ours. Perhaps Jeff had gone for help and was on his way to us now. Perhaps. How I hated those words at that moment! I cried, yes, for the acute possibility that I would never see my husband again, but also for my precious Liberian friends and their children who were inside the car with Jeff.

My heart felt like it would explode. But grace ensued. Amazing, all-consuming grace held me tightly as we drove back to the mission compound. Calling on every possible resource that God could give me, I begged Him for my children to be spared of this news. Of this possibility. And He did. God's resources, I realized that night, were LIMITLESS. The evening wore on and Jeff did not arrive. The things that I later said to God that, the things I asked of Him that night, the way I leaned heavily into Him would have certainly felled the strongest human counselor. But He is not a God created by human hands!

Making a phone call to Jeff's and my family, I chose my words carefully as I talked to them and updated them on our evacuation from Tappi, but withholding the possibility of the dreaded news. I asked them to pray for Jeff's safety without giving any more of what I knew. It grieved my heart not to tell Jeff's parents everything, but I wanted to spare them–just in case it was not true. After that call, I went back into the room that I was sharing with my girls that night. Beth Wittenberger had bathed them for me and put them to bed. How she blessed me in those crucial hours!

I can still see myself as that scared young pregnant woman sitting in the rocking chair by the window in the small, quiet bedroom. So afraid, so burdened, but trying to hold on. Faith faltering but not completely gone, I tried to keep hoping and claiming God's promises. Fears assailing, I tried to allow God to dispel them. I rocked all night long. I sang quietly to the little one growing inside me who stayed up with me most of that night. Looking at my two little girls sleeping peacefully, I thought again of their father: sweet man with a heart like none other. I almost crumbled under the stark reality of what I might need to face the next morning. But for that night, I told myself, I would dream and pretend that none of it was true.

God's grace was real, as real as human arms holding me tightly, pouring into me peace and strength that had no limit. I remember that above all else. And as the early morning sun peeped over the horizon, I slept for a little while. Exhausted beyond measure and knowing that I had to be careful not to overtax my body anymore than it already was, I lay down for a little while. When I woke up, I heard noise all around me and noticed that the girls were not in their beds. I lay still and listened in the muted sounds of the morning. Scraping of chairs being moved, whisperings of conversations, children screeching in play, and then...what? What was that sound that made my heart start beating again? A toot of the horn and the sound of a vehicle with a diesel engine pausing at our gate! Could it be? Impossible as my heart closed in to protect itself!! Sounds, clapping, exclamations, shouting.....yes! It was possible!

I ran as quickly as my belly would allow me, ran towards the gate and saw my husband driving through the gate in his beige Isuzu Trooper. Where were the bullet holes? I lunged at the vehicle, screaming in release, barely containing myself. I remember being held back until the vehicle stopped, but as soon as Jeff stepped out of the car, I tackled him–baby belly and all. He hit the ground hard and I fell on top of him, crying, blubbering, talking almost incoherently. All the pent up fears and anguish of the past few hours released in an array of overpowering emotions.

Jeff, always the one to care more for propriety and protocol than I, looked up sheepishly at everyone standing around. He admitted to me later that he worried I had gone off the edge and was heading towards insanity. That's how intense the reunion was. Chick explained with five words, "SHE THOUGHT YOU WERE DEAD." With that reality, he just held me, soothing me, and I calmed at the sound of his voice. Chick continued to explain to Jeff what we had heard as we both sat on the ground in each other's arms.

There were sniffles and impassioned sounds of relief all around. Right there we prayed. We thanked God for protecting Jeff and the others on the trip. We also prayed for the families involved with the killings in the other Trooper, the one just like ours, and for the families of those that would struggle with real loss that day and in the future of a country on the brink of civil war.

Over breakfast, Jeff told his side of the story. God's timing was all over it. After leaving Tappi some forty-five minutes late, he had headed out on the Buchanan two-track road. When they had been traveling for about an hour, they came across a disturbing sight. Sitting on the side of the road, riddled with bullet holes, was a cream color Isuzu Trooper exactly like ours. The most disturbing thing was that absolutely no one was moving. Inside the car, outside the car, death was apparent. With women and children screaming inside our car, Jeff decided that it was probably not safe to stop,

238

so they sped on down the road. They prayed, they sang, they were diligent in watching the roads. He had no idea that the scene of that horrible sight would precede him and bring concern for his life. His heart hurt with all I had experienced because of that.

After leaving Tappi, he had reflected on the unexpected delay in leaving and had become increasingly embarrassed by how angry he had gotten about his car. In his own words, "What a growing spiritual moment that was. I was so concerned with the vehicle (a material thing) that I completely lost sight of what God was doing. He caused a delay that probably saved my life."

Even while attempting to drive after coming across that ambush site, he could hardly hold back the tears of rejoicing. Jeff was humbled that God had used Liberian friends who had crushed in his roof with heavy loads to delay them, ultimately keeping them from harm. God was all over that story and he was humbled. As the weary travelers entered the coastal town of Buchanan, he dropped off all of his passengers and their load, then headed out of town. At a checkpoint on the outskirts of town, he was told that there was a government-mandated curfew for anyone traveling after dark. So, having no choice, he slept in the vehicle until the sun came up the next morning.

Though there are circumstances that might try our patience and ruin OUR plans, He still compels us to trust Him. Every delay, every hindrance, every frustrating "monkey wrench" thrown into our tightly woven plans, could very well be our Heavenly Father answering our prayers of safety, protection, and provision. We are such self-centered creatures to assume that God should always provide for us, protect us, and care for us in the way we think is best! He is the Master Engineer! Day by day, trial by trial, he is teaching me to trust His timing in every part of my life!

CHAPTER TWENTY-FIVE

For He shall give His angels charge over thee, to keep thee in all thy ways.
Psalm 91:11

Angels All Around

My head was spinning with all the lessons God used to continue showing me who He was. I am convinced that we will never stop struggling with the doubts and cares of our flesh until it is thrown off for the incorruptible; however, as we grow stronger in Him and strive to become more like Him, the sinful wiggling shouldn't be quite as pronounced! (Romans 6)

It is hard to recall whether it was the first or second morning after our Tappita evacuation when some of us were able to hear from James Kwiah, a foundational Christian leader in Tappita to whom we had handed all the keys of every building before we left (as of March 2010 he has gone to be with the Lord). During the regular morning radio time, we hailed the Tappi station hoping to hear from James Kwiah. Instead a rebel soldier spoke to us.

During the conversation with the unknown rebel soldier and later being able to talk with James Kwiah, we learned that there had been a large division of rebels waiting in the edge of the bush around our compound as we were evacuating everyone. Not wanting to involve American citizens nor desiring to create panic, they were told to wait until all Americans had left the compound before seizing it. This takeover happened very soon after Jeff pulled away with his Trooper. Charles Taylor's rebels had taken control of our mission compound, and we could not even imagine what that meant.

As the news settled in, all of us that had been evacuated less than twenty-four hours prior felt very strange indeed. We had actually been watched by keen rebel eyes while we packed up. We were being watched by soldiers with guns. We were being watched with the understanding that if we had not willingly left when we did, most likely we would have been forced to leave by gunpoint. It was unnerving. But, again, that was not a surprise to God. He knew where the rebel soldiers were. It was He that kept them away from us. It was He who had shielded us at the time from the horrible knowledge that the rebels were closer than we had imagined.

Angels Unaware

It did not take us long to realize that the war was only going to heat up drastically and would eventually make its way to the capital city before it was finished. For me, time was not on my side since airlines did not often permit pregnant women who were beyond their seventh month to fly, especially on international flights. Also, because of the trauma we had faced over the last few days, my body was exhibiting symptoms that could have potentially meant trouble for the baby.

Weighing all these things, Jeff decided that the girls and I would leave for the States before the end of the week. Several other missionary families also decided that it would not be beneficial to remain in Liberia. Jeff promised that he would soon follow, but he and several other men had chosen to stay for a while and settle some things for our mission and perhaps encourage the churches in the Monrovia area.

A couple of missionary families were on the flight from Monrovia to Amsterdam. Before boarding the plane, the girls and I clung tightly to Jeff and begged him to hurry home to us. During the night flight, the girls slept soundly, but I had never been able to sleep sitting up no matter how tired I was. So, again, I was left alone with my thoughts while it seemed everyone around me snoozed. The traumatic events of the past few days were catching up with me and I did not know where to turn. Arriving in Amsterdam, the girls and I said our goodbyes to the other families as we all went to check the status of our various flights that would take us to different cities in the States.

Michelle was almost seven and helped me as much as she could. Stefanie was four and was flittering around with more energy than I could imagine anyone could have that early in the morning. While carrying the bulk of the carry-ons, I walked purposely with the

242

girls, doing my best to read signs, answering their questions, and trying not to feel despondent and alone. It was difficult to remember exactly how it happened, but as we were winding our way through the very clean and spacious Schipol Airport, Michelle and I realized that Stefanie was gone! She had just disappeared! As we stopped and set down the bags we were carrying, I swallowed the panic that was building up. The baby inside me was awakened with the adrenaline that no doubt was coursing strongly through every vein in my body.

It was early morning and the airport was not crowded at all, but I knew that I could not leave Michelle and the bags to go searching for Stefanie. Whatever I did, we would need to haul everything with us! Frantically I searched the terminal with my eyes still not seeing my sweet little Stefanie. Biting back the accusations that again raised questions about me being a fit mother, I bent down in an urgent conversation with Michelle because she had started crying.

I saw her suddenly gaze beyond me with a strange look on her face, and standing up quickly, I turned, praying that it would be Stefanie. It was Stefanie holding the hand of a man who had such a memorable face that I can still see it in my mind's eye today. My little girl seemed perfectly at ease with this man and even my heart ceased its pounding as I looked at him. "You lose something special?" he asked kindly. I took Stefanie into my arms and held her tightly. She squirmed until I put her down, and remembering that I needed to thank the wonderful man who had brought my little girl back to me, I looked up to where he had just been standing.

I am not kidding. He had disappeared. We were standing in a very large, open area and would have seen him walking away. Turning 360 degrees, I simply did not see him. Stefanie said, "That man was so nice, mommy." As I stood there perplexed but yet somehow feeling succored, it hit me with a touch to my heart. Was that an angel? Surely not said the part of me that limited God to my own safe box. But who was I to say what God could and could not do? "STEFANIE, SWEETHEART, I THINK THAT WAS AN ANGEL SENT FROM GOD TO HELP US FEEL NOT SO ALONE," I said with resolve. Michelle nodded and said that she felt very comforted by him and was thankful that he had brought back her little sister.

Whether you believe in angels or even that God uses angels in that way, I am here to tell you that I felt touched with an unexplainable love and peace. Here I was, a young mother with two little children and a babe in the womb, standing in the middle of a strange airport, having had recently experienced traumatic situations beyond anything I had ever known. Why would my Heavenly Father not come down and touch me with His love by sending one of His very own messengers? That experience remains one of the most poignant ones in my life when I need to dwell on His astoundingly personal and powerful love!

The Normal During the Abnormal

When the girls and I arrived back in the United States, our family and friends rallied around us in an unbelievable way. For the life of me, I cannot remember where we lived during the first two months before Jeff joined us. Most likely, we just lived with either my parents or Jeff's parents during that time. One of my first responsibilities was to enroll Michelle in school. Though it was late in the year (first of April), I knew that it was important to help reestablish Michelle in her academics no matter what else was happening in our lives. School was just one of the ways we could find our "normal" in the midst of being displaced.

The first grade teachers and the elementary staff at Northside Christian Academy were priceless in their help and advice to me. It was evident early on that Michelle had indeed been more affected by being uprooted than she knew how to express. In our little red schoolhouse there in Liberia, Michelle was reading rather well for a first grader. However, when tested by the Northside teachers, we were taken back to realize that she could hardly get through the alphabet past A-B-C-D-E-F-G...... While this is not an uncommon thing when a major upheaval happens in a child's life, it was the first for me; so, of course, I took it very seriously and very personally! Parenting is often like walking in murky waters, never knowing what is underneath the surface until you have walked it a couple of times.

Anticipating the birth of a baby had a way of making the world around us seem that it would be okay no matter what else was going on. Soon after arriving in the States, I made an appointment to see my obstetrician. Admittedly, he was surprised to see me as we had said our goodbyes some three months before that, and after hearing all that had been going on in my life, he requested that I have an ultrasound to check on the health of the baby. Thankfully, although there were some signs of stress, our third little girl was in good shape. When we had left for Liberia a few months before, we did not know the sex of the baby. However, during this ultrasound, Lauren showed us that she was a girl in bold, living color! There was no mistaking it! I began to cry as I said softly, "Hey girl, hey Lauren. Ah, I'm sorry for all this confusion and such lately. Just hang in there. A few more weeks and we'll see you! My Lauren Denae." My third little girl had traveled with me to Africa and all the way back to the States. Oh, what a story we would tell her one day!

A Baby Angel

Concurrently, Jeff and a couple of the other missionaries were encouraging the Liberian Christians in several of the Baptist churches located in Monrovia. Never had the churches been so packed! Never had people been so willing to make things right with God. It was indeed a time of sowing and reaping. Jeff and I would try to talk about once a week, and every time I would ask him when he was planning to leave. He could never give me an answer except that he would know when it was time, but he did promise to be home before our little Lauren was due.

By the end of May, my baby belly was growing rapidly; I was tired, sluggish, and overwhelmed with the instability in our lives and can remember distinctly asking God to put it on Jeff's heart to come home. The very next morning, Jeff said that he had woken up and was asking God to use him for His glory that day. He also asked that God show him when it was time to leave. Within minutes of that prayer, he heard gunfire off in the distance. Rapid, unfaltering, unceasing gunfire, enhanced by the faint sounds of yelling and screaming. He had never heard the fighting so close and it seized his heart with an unexplained feeling. Not really fear because it was expected, but a compelling reality that it was indeed time for him to leave. Any day the city could be shut down with the fighting. God had made it clear that the time was fast approaching when the window of escape would be little to none.

On July 3rd, 1990, Charles Taylor's rebel forces stormed the capital city of Monrovia with devastating blows. Hospitals, restaurants, places of business, banks, churches, and hotels were ravaged and looted. Nothing was sacred. All was fair game for these blood-thirsty rebels who would change the dynamics of this precious country for many years to come. It was also on that day that our little Lauren Denae decided to make her debut into the world, reminding us of what a different kind of experience it would have been if we had stayed in Monrovia to have her. Our hearts were heavy with concern for our Liberian Christians all over that country, but at the same time we felt so blessed. Our third beautiful daughter had arrived! Life and death are the only two opposites that seem to be able to live together in harmony in a person's heart.

In Another Place

The devastating Civil War in Liberia, fracturing our amicable dreams of working in that country for the remainder of our lives, also compelled us to turn our eyes toward Heaven and rethink our commitment to being God's missionaries. It was not the place that needed to be the focus nor was it necessarily the people though we had naively assumed so. There are those who have the privilege of spending decades in one place with one people. That would not be the case for us. Why God chooses stability for some and unsettledness for others is beyond me. But ultimately, in either place, it is for His glory that we must choose to serve Him in total obedience.

In the aftermath of the Liberian Civil War, we had no template to add to the blank piece of paper we had been handed, but that is when God delights in showing us what He has in His mind! Again, if I could have seen the future days and years that God had designed for us, it would have stopped me in my tracks. But I do like to believe that after all God had shown me in those previous five years in Liberia, I would still have walked forward – in His strength and by His grace.

246

Those sweet, memorable days as missionaries in the rainforest of Liberia would serve as the catalyst to future ministries in which God would invite us to participate. As He had shown Himself so faithful, so amazingly precise in His timing, and so utterly wonderful in all His workings in that place, we had to believe that He would continue to do the same wherever He led us. In Every Place.

Now thanks be unto God, which always causeth us to triumph in Christ, and maketh manifest the savour of His knowledge by us in every place.

II Corinthians 2:14

EPILOGUE

Wherever you are, be all there. —Jim Elliot

My journals stretch far beyond the years we worked in Liberia. They chronicle the uncertain and often dark days of refugee relief work in western Ivory Coast, a two-year interim ministry in Jamaica, a long year of French language training in Canada before heading back to Ivory Coast, and then finally a crescendo of change in 2002.

As I said before, if I could have seen the future standing on the jagged precipice of 1990, I would have fallen to my knees in disbelief, begging God to change it all. But we could not know and so we headed straight into the heart of days that refined me in impermeable ways! Disillusionment, spiritual warfare in chilly vividness, unfortunate rifts between Jeff and I as we both struggled to make sense of it all, the death of my brother three weeks before we were to return to West Africa, the rebellion of two of our children, and finally the culmination of our African ministry in a dramatic and notable incident! In it that, you will find emotions that most everyone recognizes. The places and faces may be different, but we are all human. We all reel when tragedy happens and stumble when uncertainty takes a swipe at us.

My next book, *In Every Place,* chronicles the second part of our African ministry from 1991 - 2002. If God wills, it should be published in the fall of 2011. In the meantime, please write and ask any questions, let me know how the book touched you. Pray for our CBF campus ministry so that the nations (who are at our doorsteps here in America) may be invited to know Christ. Visit my blog located at http://ineveryplace.blogspot.com.

And above all, my friend, continue to ask God to make you more like Him – wherever you are. IN THIS PLACE. That's where it all starts, my friend. Right where you are.